Night Riders

Night Riders

Defending Community

in the Black Patch,

1890–1915

Christopher Waldrep

Duke University Press

Durham and London 1993

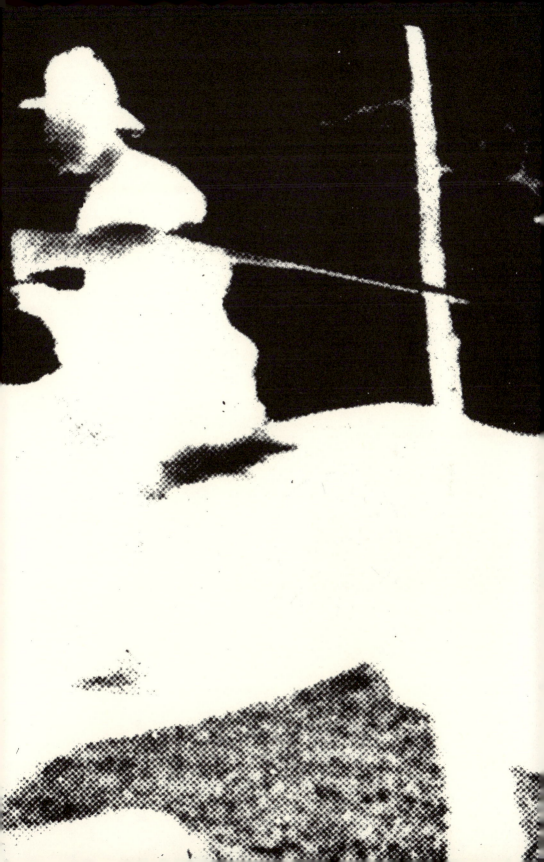

© 1993 Duke University Press

All rights reserved

Printed in the United States of

America on acid-free paper ∞

Typeset in Cheltenham

by Keystone Typesetting, Inc.

Library of Congress Cataloging-in-

Publication Data appear on the

last printed page of this book.

For Pam, Janelle,
and Andrea

Contents

Illustrations

Acknowledgments

ℂ

I have been researching and writing this book for fourteen years. Along the way I fear I have accumulated more debts than I will be ever able to acknowledge. But I must begin with my mentor at Ohio State University, Les Benedict. His sharp, certain analysis is apparent on every page. Jim Klotter and Joe Cartwright read this book before it became a dissertation; Bert Wyatt-Brown and David Thomas Konig read it after it stopped being one. All offered helpful criticisms and comments. Tom Appleton generously offered to read the final draft and saved me from more embarrassments than I care to remember. But whatever faults remain are mine.

The Filson Club deserves special appreciation. Without their careful cataloging of Augustus Willson's papers I would never have thought this project possible. Jim Holmburg was always helpful. Bill Marshall and Claire McCann of the Special Collections Department at the University of Kentucky's King Library have graciously helped in countless ways. Jim Prichard of the Kentucky Department for Libraries and Archives Public Records Division responded promptly to my urgent cries for help and microfilm by telephone.

Numerous elderly Black Patchers took me into their homes and patiently explained who the Night Riders were and what the Black Patch war was all about. Their names appear in the bibliography and I thank them now. Their participation made this project exciting and rewarding.

I began writing this book as a series of journal articles. Many editors and anonymous readers provided necessary direction, guidance, and criticism. Some of chapter 1 appeared first in an article I wrote for the *Journal of Social History* 23 (Spring 1990), " 'So Much Sin': The Decline of Religious Discipline and the 'Tidal Wave of Crime.' " Much of chapter 2 originally appeared as "The Reorganization of the Tobacco Industry and Its Impact on Tobacco Growers in Kentucky and Tennessee, 1900–1911," in *Mid-America* 73 (January 1991). Some of chapter 3 originally appeared in a different form as "Planters and the Planters' Protective Association in Kentucky and Tennessee," in the *Journal of Southern History* 52 (November 1986). Chapter 4 appeared in a much different form as "Tobacco Farmers, the Tobacco 'Trust,' and the Federal Government," in the *Journal of Kentucky Studies* 1 (July 1984). Some of the information in chapters 6, 10, and 11 originally appeared in the *Register of the Kentucky Historical Society* (vols. 81, 82, and 83). Some of chapter 8 appeared as "Augustus E. Willson and the Night Riders," in the *Filson Club History Quarterly* 58 (April 1984). Portions of chapters 9,

10, and 11 appeared in "Federalism and Community Justice: Kentucky and Tennessee Night Riders and the Law," in the *Georgia Journal of Southern Legal History* 1 (Fall/Winter 1991).

My parents awakened a love of history and the Black Patch in me that proved enduring and made this book not just possible but imperative. I completed much of the research for this book while teaching in Washington Court House, Ohio. Don Moore, Tom Gauldin, Pam Feick, and all my colleagues there helped ease my burdens at work so I could complete my research. Dave Stone never doubted this book would be published even when I did. My aunt, Corinne Wadlington, never left the Black Patch and always welcomes me back. I finished writing this book at Eastern Illinois University. By being the professional historians they are, my colleagues at Eastern motivated me to bring this project to completion.

My wife, Pamela, accompanied me on many trips from Washington Court House, Ohio, into the Black Patch during our summer vacations, weekends, and holidays. We spent many hours talking about the Black Patch war and what it meant. She patiently pored over thousands of papers in filthy court house attics and basements and traveled the backroads of the Black Patch. It was an adventure. She also showed me the advantages of being married to a librarian. Without Pam I would never have completed the research necessary for this book. My daughters, Janelle and Andrea, joined the project late, but by learning to read books as I learned to write one, they made the whole project worthwhile.

After the Civil War, urban-based national and international business organizations expanded into rural America. By extending their
reach into the countryside, capitalists found they could control
raw material costs. The price a farmer could command for his produce declined for no apparent reason other than the hunger of
huge "trusts" for bigger profits.

By the end of the nineteenth century dismay had turned to violence. Early in the twentieth century one such spasm of violence
erupted in an agricultural region of Kentucky and Tennessee called
the Black Patch for the dark variety of tobacco grown there. Tobacco farmers fought a "war" with the "Tobacco Trust." They were
led by an elite segment of society descended from slave-holding
aristocrats.[1] Some of these men reasoned that twentieth-century
farmers could compete only if unified like business into a trust-like
organization. They wanted to use modern tactics to preserve a
traditional, hierarchical society. In some ways, their thinking resembled that of those southern Whigs who opposed secession in
hopes that remaining in the Union would preserve slavery. Like
their twentieth-century counterparts, Whigs had supported economic development—modernization. They were not much bothered by the fact that the programs they advocated to foster development also fostered inequality. Elitists, they expected deference
and practiced paternalism.[2] Forty years after the Civil War some
Black Patch planters theorized that participating in the national
economy was the best way to preserve peonage. They expected
their black workers to remain forever in the tobacco patch laboring
in the same fields as had their enslaved parents and grandparents.
But they understood that to maintain this structure, they had to
adapt modern, businesslike methods.

They also understood that to use such methods they would have
to discipline independent-minded small farmers. To do so, they
turned to "politics-out-of-doors," mob action designed to enforce
a community's will. This kind of mobbing had a history dating
back at least to the first stages of the English industrial revolution.
During that earlier period of turbulent transition workers rioted
to enforce their popular code or moral economy over business-
oriented law. Citizens regarded riots as just, and their leaders as
heroes. Rioters seized markets, forcing prices down to reasonable
levels. Women raided bakeries, setting prices and appropriating
goods. In some cases rioters confiscated grain on roads or docks.[3]
This tradition of resistance transferred to colonial America, and in

the Revolutionary era British officers competed with an indigenous legal structure, enforced by riots. Against this community justice outsiders could have little impact. After the Revolution, communities—and community leaders—sometimes continued to rely on extralegal mobs to enforce local justice in the absence of effective legal authority.[4] As late as the 1840s urban gangs and fire companies still fought turf wars on behalf of their neighborhoods. This kind of violence pitted rival ethnic and racial groups against each other, but only because ethnic groups settled in the same neighborhoods. Geography mattered more than ethnicity. Local leaders sanctioned the violence as it defended community interests from outsiders. People got hurt, even killed, but not very many—especially compared with "modern" rioting.[5]

But for this kind of "traditional" (not strictly ethnic) mobbing to work, geographically defined communities must unite around a shared system of values, forcing lawmen to acquiesce. In primitive cultures, where citizens share the same work and develop similar outlooks on life, this can happen fairly easily. In such communities little tolerance exists for dissent from the neighborhood's consensus. Everyone was expected to think in more or less the same way. In the South such a consensus could be achieved, in part, only by discounting the presence of African-Americans. Blacks had to become virtually invisible to allow whites to think they had organized the whole of society around a collective ideal. But improvements in communications and transportation introduced foreign ideas and offered new loyalties. As one historian has written, "individuals in a community may all be caught up in different webs of connection to the outside."[6] Once communities shatter to be reconstituted along nongeographic political, class, racial, or ethnic lines, disciplined, united action cannot be sustained. Rather than protecting their neighborhood and the values it stands for, rioters from many different neighborhoods coalesce to rally interests perhaps antithetical to their neighbors. They see themselves as representatives of a racial or ethnic group rather than a geographically defined community. When this happens, they have become "modern." In the nineteenth century American rioting everywhere made this transition. By 1812 Baltimore rioters no longer defended geographically defined communities. Rather, rioters from scattered points in Baltimore united just because they were white. New York rioters protesting Civil War conscription crossed community lines to attack blacks, seeking to unite whites of all neighborhoods against blacks.

They wanted to control not only their neighborhood but the entire city. Similarly, rioters in 1866 Memphis combined racial hatred with aggression across community boundaries.[7] By 1900 Black Patchers too had begun to divide along economic and racial lines rather than by neighborhoods, as had Baltimore, New York, and Memphis rioters many years earlier. The Night Riders tried an antique style of mob action that required a unified community in a society that had already begun to divide along class and racial lines.

The Black Patch war was first traditional and then modern. Black Patch vigilante leaders sought to define their region as a community of shared interests. This first wave of Black Patch violence victimized few blacks. Moreover, the original Night Riders targeted property in their big raids far more than they did people. In their restraint they closely resembled the republican crowds in the Anglo-American mob tradition. Only after 1908 did the Night Riders become truly "modern." Then they turned on the blacks in their midst. This so-called modern style of violence forced many Kentuckians and Tennesseans to rethink their traditional allegiance to vigilantism. Anarchic racial violence convinced them that mob violence was less a tool to protect their communities than a menace to their traditional way of life.

Thus, the Black Patch war presents a more complex and nuanced reaction to industrialization than that usually pictured by historians. Scholars typically depict isolated communities clinging to their autonomy, resisting capitalists' incursions.[8] The Black Patch was never so simple. Planter-leaders of the Planters' Protective Association and the Night Riders did lead their followers in a war against a capitalized power. But they shunned neither progress nor modernization; they hoped to harness both to their own purposes. They formed something unprecedented in the Black Patch: a regional organization that centralized control of tobacco and forced farmers to surrender the autonomy of their communities. This modern organization defended a traditional racial hierarchy with ancient roots. To enforce discipline in this tobacco organization they formed a community-based vigilante force. But the community they based it on was more abstract than the Black Patch's farming neighborhoods. This community united men from many neighborhoods. Eventually, Black Patchers saw it too as "modern."

To complicate matters further, the violence these traditionalist/ modernizers unleashed empowered white iron workers in the area called Between the Rivers. These working-class whites did not want to preserve a racial structure that pitted them in competition with blacks for jobs. Their willingness to turn on their own neighbors makes them "modern." But these vigilantes also tried to impose moral unity on incipient communities, directing their violence against moonshiners and malcontents who disrupted their neighborhoods. In some ways their moral policing resembled the actions of colonial and antebellum mobs. But these Night Riders threatened to overturn established authority and plunge their region into chaos. In the Black Patch war vigilante leaders transformed mob violence into something modern. When they did so, Black Patchers would reject vigilantism.

At the turn of the twentieth century, rapid industrialization and advances in transportation confused and frightened many Americans as changes threatened their rural way of life. But in only a few places did they turn to violence to resist outside encroachment; one of those places was the Black Patch of western Kentucky and Tennessee. There columns of horsemen stormed through the night, terrorizing the servants of the great tobacco trusts and the farmers who had betrayed their neighbors by surrendering to them.

Robert Penn Warren recalled these terrible times in his novel of the Black Patch, *Night Rider*. In it he chronicled the tragedy of the vigilante leader Percy Munn. Warren makes Munn a modern man with few ties to any geographically defined community. Belonging nowhere and longing for a sense of community, Munn turned to vigilantism and violence. He and his fellow vigilantes formed a new kind of community, one based not on neighborliness but on an idea, an abstract notion of justice. They challenged the traditional Black Patch community consisting of a few farms scattered around a church or a crossroads store.[1] At least by 1900 the Black Patch was clearly not a republican community populated by like-minded citizens. Many realized they lived in a modern world, facing new, more powerful evils. Railroad promoters promised connections to a wider world. Mail order catalogs linked the most rural farmer to distant cities. Local merchants told their customers that higher prices were the inevitable consequence of monopolized industry.

But many clung to the old order. The real story of the Black Patch is one of tension and diversity. These divisions are mirrored in the landscape. Travelers going from Nashville, Tennessee, to Paducah, Kentucky, pass rolling farmland, columned mansions, and then broken hills dotted with rude frame dwellings. The economy and politics of the area are equally diverse.

But despite these differences, the Night Riders hoped to forge a regional community united by an idea. Such thinking was not preposterous, in that inhabitants considered the Black Patch a distinct region. Its farmers grew a dark, olive-colored variety of tobacco, cured in barns over smokey fires. In the growing season, the dark leaves stood out from the green of Kentucky and Tennessee's other regions, so they called it the Black Patch. Spread over two states, the Black Patch of the Night Riders era offered a variety of vistas. There was the quasi-plantation landscape around Hopkinsville, Kentucky, and Clarksville, Tennessee, known as the Pennyroyal or

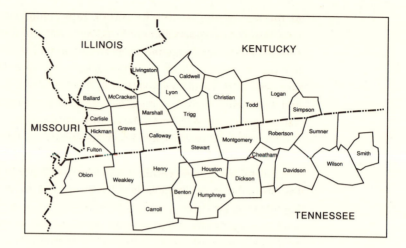

Pennyrile. Due west is rougher, hilly terrain, where farmers tilled hardscrabble farms. When farmers with a little plot of ground on a Trigg County ridge met the owner of a Christian County estate, they spoke the common language of tobacco. But both were aware of the vast gulf dividing them.

Standing on one side of the gulf were planters, meaning cultivators who relied on tenant labor. For example, C. M. Bourne, of St. Bethlehem, Tennessee, told an interviewer that he owned 475 acres and grew 50 acres of tobacco with four tenant families. "The tenants raise the tobacco," he said. It is clear from his answers to various questions that Bourne made all the decisions regarding the crop, including when and to whom it should be sold. It was Bourne's crop, though he did not till his soil himself; he reaped the labor expended by his tenants.[2]

Planters ruled the Pennyroyal Plain, known as the Clarksville and Hopkinsville District or, more formally, as the Eastern Dark Fired District.[3] Planters here enjoyed a prosperity unknown in surrounding counties. Slavery had been more extensively established here than in the rest of the Black Patch. In the three counties at the center of the Pennyroyal, nearly 22,000 slaves and about 600 free blacks lived with 34,000 whites in 1850.[4] In 1860 fewer than 1 percent of farmers in most of the Black Patch owned farms five hundred acres or larger. But between 2 and 5 percent owned farms of that size in the Pennyroyal. The farms in the Pennyroyal averaged $5,000 to $7,500 in value, compared to under $5,000 in surrounding counties. Planters even wealthier than Bourne built white-pillared mansions; even in the twentieth century their tenants often still lived in old slaves' quarters or something similar. Most of these planters voted Whig. A geographer visiting the central Pennyroyal in the 1920s found the area "reminiscent of the traditional south." He noted that although farms averaged only about eighty acres, some were much larger. He occasionally found the remains of plantation-style mansions in parks with clusters of slave cabins. Tennessean Felix Grundy Ewing built a 2,500-acre plantation with 19 tenant families, 101 buildings, and over 14 miles of fencing. Visitors to the "Big House" enter through a 24 × 40 entrance hall paneled in solid oak and decorated with brocaded tapestry. The house contained 27 rooms and 10 baths, but even that was not enough. After visiting neighboring planters' new homes, Ewing added a back porch to ensure that his house remained the grandest in the community.[5]

Tobacco buyers claimed the tobacco produced in the central Pennyroyal, heavy and gummy with nicotine, was of a higher grade than that grown elsewhere in the Black Patch.[6] In 1905 one tobacco handler attributed the high quality to the heavy clay soil and deep subsoil as well as to the care farmers took in housing and curing their crops. In the first years of the twentieth century, this district produced between sixty and sixty-five million pounds of tobacco annually.[7]

Outside the Pennyroyal, in what tobacco men called the Paducah District or the Western Dark Fired District, the terrain grew hillier.[8] Tobacco men in Hopkinsville and Clarksville scorned the Paducah District's coarse, common tobacco. At the turn of the century, Paducah District growers produced about fifty-five to sixty million pounds of tobacco. Here yeomen, growing their tobacco with little or no help from tenants, predominated. Yet this is hard to demonstrate through the 1900 census, which counted tenants but not plantations. In that census the difference between the two districts is best indicated by the numbers of black farmers. In the Eastern District, about 16 percent of the farming population was black. In the Paducah District, blacks constituted only 7 percent of farmers. Whites here voted Democratic, and their party established a stronghold in western Kentucky that endures to the present.[9]

But these economic differences between the Pennyroyal and the Paducah districts underlay a more crucial division within the Black Patch. All Black Patchers had some connection to the world market, but they developed dramatically different attitudes toward it.

Many enjoyed their rural isolation. Living among kin and doing business with friends created a stable, predictable social environment. But while many residents viewed theirs as a way of life worth preserving, others resented their isolation. Some feared permanent segregation from the world at large. They shared the frustrations of the Texas farmer who complained that he was "250 miles to the nearest post office; 100 miles to wood; twenty miles to water; 6 inches to hell."[10] Other Black Patchers enjoyed connections with the outside world and confidently anticipated even closer connections. One Tennessee planter marveled over the technological wonders of the new century. "We begin this century," he exulted in his diary, "with a telephone in our house and can converse 200 miles easily. We all wonder what invention of this century can be more wonderful than this one."[11]

But even farmers preferring isolation could not completely ignore the outside world. Black Patch farmers grew their tobacco chiefly for export, and therefore they all had some connection to the world market, however remote. Truly global, the market for tobacco linked Kentuckians and Tennesseans with the exotic reaches of the planet. One tobacco salesman, born in rural North Carolina, saw his first cigarette—manufactured in Egypt—at the Philadelphia Centennial in 1876. Later he boasted of introducing cigarettes in such exotic markets as Japan, Java, Borneo, Malay, Tibet, Korea, and Russia. He journeyed with his American cigarettes to almost every European country as well as to Mexico and Tasmania. North Carolina tobacco magnate James B. Duke established tobacco factories in China. As a result Chinese could buy five good smokes for a copper coin worth half an American cent. The Chinese consumed so much Carolina tobacco that Duke and his men wondered if American farmers could keep China's 450,000,000 people supplied. Duke became so well known in China that schoolchildren there studied his life; at least one wrote an essay on the great man.[12]

But some farmers maintained closer and more regular relations with this world market than others. Even before the Civil War, merchants had established a permanent tobacco market in Clarksville. But elsewhere merchants speculated in tobacco at their peril, frequently going bankrupt. Even in Hopkinsville—a tobacco market center by 1900—merchants with permanently established warehouses did not begin regularly buying and selling tobacco until 1869.[13]

Until then, how fully Black Patch tobacco growers could participate in the world market depended on where they lived. Proximity to rail transportation helped determine a farmer's relationship to the international trade in tobacco. Railroads had served the economy of the Tennessee Black Patch long before they entered Kentucky's Paducah District. An 1883 railroad map of Tennessee and Kentucky showed only a single line passing through the western edge of the Clarksville and Hopkinsville District. In contrast, railroads crisscrossed the center of the Pennyroyal, connecting towns there with larger tobacco markets.[14]

There are other measures of isolation. The uneven distribution of banking facilities and population in the Black Patch demonstrates variations in cosmopolitanism in the region. Pennyroyal counties had more banks than Paducah District counties. In the Pennyroyal Plain, banks carried out their business in villages as small as Cedar Hill and Adams as well as in county seats. The only bank in the Paducah District county of Caldwell operated out of Princeton. Moreover, the Pennyroyal, with towns like Hopkinsville and Clarksville, was more densely populated than counties farther to the west. In the Pennyroyal farmers had years of experience as a part of a wider community, while residents of the Paducah District may well have felt isolated, cut off from the modern world.

But divisions in the Black Patch were even more complex than those between the planter-dominated Pennyroyal and the Paducah District. The residents of Caldwell and Trigg counties, for example, lived in the yeoman Paducah District but occupied distinctive and antagonistic communities within their counties. They differed in politics, commitments to commercial agriculture, railroad development, reputations for violence, and access and use of credit. Southern Caldwell County differed from northern Caldwell County in a variety of ways. The differences went back to the original settlement at the end of the eighteenth century. The northern part of Caldwell County had been settled in 1797 when Presbyterian minister Terah Templin led his Washington County, Kentucky, congregation to the Fredonia Valley. There he established the Livingston Presbyterian Church. A church historian later described Templin as profoundly influential on the morals and habits of area residents. One repercussion of Templin's moral teachings may well have been an ambivalence toward slavery. In 1850 more than 60 percent of Caldwell County's total population of "free persons of color" lived in Fredonia. A historian of Caldwell County, noting that freed slaves usually lived in the same neighborhood as their former masters, concluded that Fredonia residents freed their bondsmen more readily than did slaveowners elsewhere in the county.[15]

In northern Caldwell County, ex-Whigs had established a more commercial culture early on. They created the town of Fredonia—a minor commercial center and the largest town in Caldwell County outside of the county seat of Princeton. Perhaps because they had longer enjoyed the fruits of a commercial culture—however local— they seemed more satisfied than Democrats with the commercial connections already in place. They were unwilling to extend themselves and risk their property for deeper involvement in international markets.

Residents of southern Caldwell County lived in an entirely different economic landscape. Rather than building a town comparable to Fredonia, they fashioned an economy characterized by crossroads stores. In this landscape, so bereft of commercial development, a hunger for change grew. Dissatisfied with their access to markets, Harmony farmers eagerly sought a railroad for their neighborhood, voting to tax themselves to build one in 1868.[16] In the nineteenth century the railroad symbolized progress, advancing technology, and connections with the wider world. Some Black Patchers feared the railroad and what it represented. Others resembled the man who felt himself six inches from hell; they craved transportation. This split became evident in Caldwell County when residents voted on the question of "Shall the County Court subscribe for 4000 shares in the Elizabethtown and Paducah Railroad?" Supporters claimed a "yes" vote beckoned progress and prosperity for their county. Farmers in Caldwell County's tobacco-producing Harmony precinct eagerly supported the railroad and the connections to markets it promised. They voted seventy-one to four for it. But in northern Caldwell County voters overwhelmingly rejected the Elizabethtown and Paducah Railroad, fearing the loss of their independent, subsistence-farming lifestyle. The railroad boosters won this election, but even so railroads did not cross Caldwell County for four more years (table 1).[17]

After the Civil War farmers in southern Caldwell County, especially in the Harmony district, greatly increased their production of tobacco. In 1860 the average farmer in Harmony produced just over five thousand pounds of tobacco. By 1892 he produced nearly eight thousand pounds. Production of wheat also increased, but Harmony farmers sacrificed production of subsistence staples, such as

Table 1 **Caldwell County's 1868 Railroad Election**

Precinct	For the Railroad	Against the Railroad
Princeton	402	31
Precincts in northern Caldwell County		
Donaldson	1	86
Fredonia	34	133
Farmersville	23	65
Precincts in southern Caldwell County		
Bucksnort	59	13
Harmony	71	4
Tennessee	79	27

Source: Caldwell County poll books, May 30, 1868 (Caldwell County Circuit Court Clerk's Office).

corn and hogs, for cash crops. Despite the many divisions pitting Black Patchers against each other, tobacco united its cultivators. The crop that bound the Black Patch together and made it a distinctive culture was a dark, brooding plant with huge, drooping dark leaves. Tobacco was the traditional cash crop, but more important, the procedures used to produce it were unique to the Black Patch. Rich or poor, black or white, Black Patch farmers spoke a common language, exchanging remedies for pests and blights, discussing marketing problems or curing techniques.[18]

At the turn of the century, before Black Patch farmers diversified into lighter tobaccoes, this unique tobacco culture was a legacy from the earliest tobacco production in America. The procedures they used closely resembled those used by their forebears at Jamestown. A farmer first nurtured his tiny tobacco plants in a plant bed. Children helped, cutting timber and piling it on the selected site. Workers burned the plot to sterilize the soil and then worked it with hoes. A farmer "fixed [his plant bed] better than you fixed your garden," one of them remembered proudly decades later. When the farmer had finished working on it, the ground was as smooth as a floor. He planted the tiny seeds by scattering one heaping tablespoon per hundred square yards.[19]

While the seeds grew in the beds, workers plowed and replowed the land where they would transplant the seedlings. The men laid the field off in a grid. Using hoes, young boys worked up the tobacco hills at the corners of the checks. Workers—often including children—drew the plants from the seedbed, setting them in the

Black laborers transplanting young tobacco plants in the fields. White planters wanted to keep such labor cheap and in the Black Patch. Author's photograph, courtesy of Mack Linebaugh.

field. Sometimes they used a tobacco peg to make the hole for the plant, but often they just used two fingers. Laborers then bent over hoes to clear out weeds. Whereas with cotton there came a time when even the meanest laborer found "there was nothing to do but lean on the fence and watch it grow," with tobacco the work never ended.[20] Schoolboy James S. Street recorded in his diary in 1871 that he started hoeing tobacco in mid-June. With monotonous repetition he devoted day after day to hacking at the orange ground. "Hoed tobacco," he wrote; he "hoed tobacco" again and again, each day, all day, until mid-July. Then he began worming, stooping over each plant to pluck and squash the scores of worms that could riddle the leaves. Worming took every day except Sundays from mid-July through August.[21]

Tobacco growers topped their plants—broke the top of each plant off as it was buttoning (budding) to strengthen the plant's leaves. Growers disagreed as to when to top their plants. Some let the plants grow twelve or more leaves before topping; others topped as soon as the plants developed eight or ten leaves. Fewer leaves meant fewer suckers (or shoots), a smaller expenditure of labor, and, some said, heavier and better quality leaves.

Just a few days after topping, suckers grew out from each leaf, to be pulled off during the hottest time of year. The plants left the growers covered with sticky tobacco gum, which some of them removed with green tomatoes. Some workers reported that suckering left their hands blistered, and many found the odor of green tobacco sickening. Cultivators had to bend lower and lower over the plants, first removing the highest suckers and then the lower ones. Children complained to U.S. Labor Department investigators in the 1920s that their backs ached from constantly bending over the plants.[22]

Rich planters let their tenants do the work. Tenant farmer Herbert Carney remembers that planter Henry Rosson's nine tenants lived in former slave cabins, grouped together in what the laborers called "Rosson Town." The tenants worked as a gang until topping time. Then Rosson drove stakes into his field, allotting six to eight acres of his 600-acre plantation to each family, depending on how many workers each tenant had available.[23]

As early as mid-August growers began cutting the tobacco, though not all the plants matured at the same time. Once a farmer decided a plant was fully ripe, he split the stalk almost to the ground, cut it off at the base, and turned the plant upside down over its stump. After the plants wilted, laborers gathered them by the armload and hung the split plants on sticks. They then suspended the sticks in tobacco barns. There, they propped the doors shut and built a smoldering fire under the tobacco. Although modern tobacco growers use sawdust to make a smokey fire, in the first years of the twentieth century tobacco men burned hickory logs, which they chopped and hauled themselves. Robert Holt remembered the barns got so hot one could not stand to be in them. A smokey haze hung around barn roofs, filling the air with the musky and pungent smell of hickory and dark tobacco.[24] In not much more than a day, the hot fire cured the tobacco. Farmers pulled the leaves from the stalks and sorted them by grades. By that time the farmer had already started burning a bed for his next crop. Only a planter with a reliable supply of labor could lean on a fence.[25]

These tobacco farmers developed unusually close ties with their neighbors. Even a small crop of tobacco required so much effort that family farmers swapped off working on each other's farms.[26] Women frequently joined their husbands and fathers in the fields, especially when worms began eating the plants.[27] Neighborhood women worked so closely together to clothe their families, sharing patterns and sewing techniques, that communities developed distinctive styles of dress and residents could immediately identify outsiders by their clothes. Only rarely did neighborhood girls marry out of the community. Local boys drove off outside suitors by hurling rocks at them, or worse.[28] Black Patchers often relied on esoteric nicknames and spoke in a cryptic language incomprehensible to outsiders. One young resident baffled a visitor by telling an outsider his father had "gone across the river to wash rats." The befuddled stranger later learned that the man he wanted was visiting Washington "Rat" Cunningham.[29]

A shared tradition of anecdotes reinforced Black Patchers' sense of community and made it difficult for outsiders to gain access. A similar phenomenon occurred in isolated Cades Cove, Tennessee, where residents remembered an astonishingly wide variety of human behavior or misbehavior. Observers were staggered by the ability of Cades Cove residents to recall large numbers of such anecdotes in detail. This folklore functioned as metaphors for emotions insiders wished to communicate among themselves. By recalling a key incident or detail from a larger story, folk could invoke the whole story without actually recounting it. Thus insiders communicated in a kind of code bewildering to outsiders.[30]

Black Patch residents inherited a similar tradition of anecdotes. They taught these stories to their children, repeating them over and over until the youngsters could recite every detail. In 1973 one former Black Patcher recalled a story her mother told about a tenant couple. "The way they had of signaling to each other when not to say anything to the other one when the other one was mad. She said that when he was mad he had a signal to turn his hat brim up and she knew not to say anything; when she was mad she would pin up the corner of her apron and he knew not to say anything. One day he came home and he had his brim turned up and she had the corner of her apron turned up and boy how the feathers did fly." The story had a moral, the necessity of mutual toleration, which knowledgeable insiders could invoke with a kind of shorthand. The mere mention of a hat brim or a pinned apron could, in the right company, suggest the whole incident, complete with community-agreed-upon meanings.[31]

Just as Black Patch folklore documented a stubbornly persisting community spirit, burial customs offered local folk opportunities to reinforce traditional clannishness. In the American North, death lost its communal significance by the middle of the nineteenth century, the most important measure of this being the professionalization of funeral preparations.[32] But Black Patchers circumvented this professionalization, which came late to Kentucky anyway. Af-

ter 1910 they understood that technological advances in embalm-
ing required the work of an outside professional, but they reasoned
that the body had to be first "prepared" by the community. So,
before the undertaker arrived, the neighborhood women gathered
and ritually washed the body. This rite, which continued well into
the 1950s, allowed—really required—the community to comfort
surviving family members. Even in an increasingly complex society,
the death of an individual retained its communal significance in the
Kentucky Black Patch.[33]

But the most distinctive feature of Black Patch provincialism may
have been residents' propensity for violence. Lawmen entered
Black Patch communities warily. An 1890s Christian County deputy
sheriff recalled that "people who lived in the country were . . .
inclined to consider the law a private matter, to be administered
among themselves." He had seen three officers killed trying to arrest a man for a trivial offense.[34] Some of this clannishness may be
attributed to the rigors of tobacco growing. Tobacco production
required art as well as labor, and growers developed instincts and
skills that promoted a pride that corn and wheat producers never
understood. Tobacco men could identify which hogsheads of tobacco in the warehouse were the produce of a particular grower,
and they judged that grower's skills accordingly. The pride this
fostered fired a resentment toward tobacco buyers. Such resent-
ments had been common even in colonial times. The tensions between tobacco buyers and tobacco growers on the colonial Chesapeake would have been familiar to farmers and marketers in the
twentieth-century Black Patch. In colonial times Chesapeake tobacco growers had organized themselves to combat monopolistic
buying practices. When their crop brought too low a price, they
rioted. Such outbreaks of violence occurred consistently enough to
suggest they were a characteristic of the relations between tobacco
growers and the outside world.[35]

The Black Patch tradition of vigilantism has led some historians
to describe the Black Patch as extremely violent. But despite a
consistent record of vigilantism, the Black Patch was not unusually
violent until the later nineteenth century. Antebellum Trigg County,
Kentucky, had lower rates of violence than parts of the Deep South
(table 2). It was only after the Civil War that the Black Patch compiled uncommonly high murder and assault rates. In 1870 grand
jurors in Trigg County returned twice as many indictments for violent actions per 1,000 population as they had in 1860. The propen-

Table 2   **Violent Crime in Antebellum Trigg County, Kentucky, and Chatham County, Georgia**

	Trigg County		Chatham County	
	No. indictments	Per 1000 Population	No. indictments	Per 1000 Population
1854	7	.66	40	1.67
1855	5	.47	19	.79
1856	5	.46	47	1.51
1857	4	.37	41	1.32
1858	9	.82	10	.32
1859	7	.63	32	1.03
1860	11	.99	22	.70

Source: Trigg County Grand Jury indictments, Commonwealth Order Books (Trigg County Circuit Court Clerk's Office, Cadiz, Ky.); Edward L. Ayers, *Vengeance and Justice: Crime and Punishment in the 19th Century American South* (New York, 1984), 298.

pensity to violent behavior in Trigg County increased through the 1880s and 1890s.

One reason for this upswing in violence may be that Black Patch society lost an important check on violence as the influence of churches diminished. Throughout the nineteenth century, churches had served to discipline the disorderly and to peacefully settle disputes and quarrels. Faithful church members expected their fellow worshipers to take disagreements to church rather than court. In fact, the faithful thought "going to law" a sin. Church committees visited neighborhood miscreants to inform them of their transgressions. Most quickly humbled themselves in church, begging the forgiveness of their kin and friends. Although not every resident of the Black Patch belonged to a church, many did, and religion served as an important restraint on their emotions.[36]

Church discipline broke down in the Black Patch at the end of the nineteenth century. Extant church records reveal a steady increase in the numbers of church prosecutions from 1800 into the 1850s.[37] Thereafter the numbers decline sharply albeit with a brief upswing after the Civil War. By 1900 some Black Patch churches no longer coerced good behavior from their members. Fifty years earlier, or even twenty years earlier, the Harmony Baptist Church in Robertson County, Tennessee, had excluded members for nonattendance. But in 1903, when two prominent and influential citizens stopped going to church, the rest of the congregation resolved to apologize to the two members, "and earnestly crave their forgiveness and beg that they will take their place in all services of the church."[38] While few churches had to beg their members to attend, most no longer enforced community standards as they had in the past. A Kentucky minister told his congregation in 1898 that, in a final message to her fellow worshipers, a dying member had pleaded for "the church to be more faithful, especially the male members."[39]

Contemporary southern church leaders recognized that discipline had collapsed. In 1900 the leadership of one Baptist association of churches complained of members' indifference toward drinking members.[40] The leaders suggested that Baptists wondering why their fellow worshipers seemed less spiritual had only to watch the back door of any saloon and see who went in. Intemperance, Baptists recognized, had "entered the church of Jesus Christ, and many, yea far more than we suspect, professing Christians are under its influence." In 1907 an evangelist told a Black Patch audience that "if God were to lift the lid off of Hopkinsville it would be seen to be as foul and rotten as hell." The preacher accused Christians of smiling at sin. Although the Black Patch's Little River Association of Baptist churches had called for temperance at least since the 1850s, some member churches gave up enforcing temperance in the 1890s. Many Baptists not only drank but danced as well, and by 1901, some Baptists openly supported liquor interests.[41]

Industrialization created villains no church could humble. Power congealed in huge corporations that seemed for a time more powerful than government. Whether the heads of these organizations were robber barons or not, Black Patchers thought they were. At the same time local lawbreakers rampaged apparently unchecked. With the collapse of church discipline, local courts were left to regulate neighborhoods. Courts proved less effective than churches, more bound by procedural constraints. There seemed no force capable of disciplining the lawless. In the absence of effective institutional policing, extralegal violence increased.

However, church discipline broke down elsewhere without similar increases in violent behavior. We may simply not understand the relationship between Black Patch residents and their churches well enough to appreciate fully the special significance of the breakdown in church-enforced morality in the Black Patch. But without question church discipline declined and the number of crimes prosecuted in Black Patch circuit courts soared.[42] Robert Penn Warren remembered his native Black Patch as "a world of violence" where "you accepted violence as a component of life."[43]

Black Patchers greeted the twentieth century with a confused mélange of attitudes about industrialization, with some welcoming change and others fearing it. Many Black Patchers worked their crops and lived their lives in much the same way their parents and grandparents had. They forged powerful bonds with their neighbors that united them against outsiders and, in their minds at least, even legitimated violence against outsiders. But even they had to know that their fellow tobacco growers in other counties, other parts of their own county, and even within their own neighborhood had developed ties to the outside world incompatible with their own. Meanwhile, in New York the commercial buyers of their tobacco made plans that would change the lives of tobacco growers in rural Kentucky and Tennessee forever. The tobacco companies were about to combine into a gigantic trust, a behemoth of modern commercial and industrial power. Similar combinations would alter the lives of people throughout the United States. In that by the end of the nineteenth century the collapse of church discipline had made the Black Patch a more violent place, almost certainly some level of violence would greet twentieth-century industrialization. No one knew what form this violence would take. Most Black Patchers harbored romantic notions of resistance where neighbors would unite across class and even racial lines to defend their communities. But ominous divisions had already appeared, dividing neighbor from neighbor. Should Black Patchers unite by neighborhoods to resist the tobacco companies, the result would be highly disciplined mass action. But should the divisions already apparent divide Black Patchers against themselves, splitting communities, that violence would careen bloodily out of control.

The dramatic economic and social changes that America experienced after 1870, as businesses grew in scale and markets were systematized, promoted an organizational society disorienting to denizens of a face-to-face culture. By the 1920s so many Americans had been alienated by the new depersonalized culture that advertisers learned to capitalize on their disaffection by offering products designed to boost the morale of consumers "lost in the crowd."[1] But in the South more was at stake than morale. Only later would many learn to make racism work in a "lonely crowd" society; in 1900 those economically dependent on the fruits of racism thought the new, competitive, bureaucratic culture threatened their way of life. It was the antithesis of the racial paternalism and patronage traditionally practiced in the South. In a bureaucratic culture all the traits southerners use to evaluate each other—family, race, reputation—matter less than they do in a face-to-face culture. In the South, integration into the national economy threatened the existing delicate structure of race relations. In Black Patch "island communities" whites jealously guarded their local prerogatives, especially with regard to race. They did not want national organizations headquartered in Chicago or New York upsetting the Black Patch's racial hierarchy.

In the early twentieth century tobacco buyers would epitomize the ambiguous relationship Black Patchers maintained with the outside world. Tobacco companies recruited their buyers from the local population, and in that they tried to hire those tobacco men whom locals regarded as the most expert, those chosen often had broad local connections. But as employees of distant corporations they developed loyalties other Black Patchers could not really understand. They found themselves explaining policies formulated in New York or Virginia or even Italy to farmers who had known them when they were children. In the rural Black Patch, these local men personified the world market. But Black Patchers could not simply be divided into opponents and proponents of change. Undoubtedly, these buyers felt conflicted, just like the farmers. Many felt confused and frightened but also regarded modernization as somehow inevitable. Both buyers and farmers could see the future, but felt the past.

Black Patch connections with the international tobacco trade developed slowly through the nineteenth century. For most of the nineteenth century growers of dark fired tobacco in Kentucky and Tennessee looked to New Orleans as the primary market for their crop.[2] Some cultivators traded directly with New Orleans merchants while others sold to local businessmen with ties to the Crescent City. These speculators usually dabbled in tobacco only as a sideline to their regular business. They risked their capital to buy the crops of a few farmers, shipped them to a port city, and hoped the price went up rather than down after their original purchase. The trade of J. H. Rackerly and Company of New Orleans with two Caldwell County farmers illustrates the link between farmers and the port. In 1840, a young farmer, Cyrus Beavers, shipped Rackerly and Company two hogsheads of tobacco valued at $81.56. Beavers had to pay $21.04 for freight, drayage, inspection fees, insurance, and commission charges. Rackerly advanced Beavers $20 and also sent him sugar and Rio coffee that cost another $50. Therefore, in August 1841, the Kentucky farmer wound up owing $16.18. He paid Rackerly and Company with a promissory note; thus he was already in debt for $16.18 when he began plowing his fields for a new crop.

Not all planters ended their season in debt. Ira Bellsford also shipped two hogsheads of tobacco to Rackerly and Company in New Orleans, but inspectors judged his tobacco to be of higher quality than Beavers's crop. While Beavers's crop brought only a little over four cents a pound, one of Bellsford's hogsheads sold for about seven cents a pound and the other for over five cents a pound. In all, Bellsford's crop sold for $127.69. After the sale Rackerly and Company deducted various sums that Bellsford owed, subtracting $22.20 for shipping costs, $10 for coffee Bellsford had ordered, and $50 to pay back a previous loan, leaving the farmer with a profit of $54.69.[3]

Black Patch businessmen also played a role in the tobacco trade. Although Beavers and Bellsford sold their tobacco in New Orleans, directly to a Crescent City businessman, they might ship to J. H. Rackerly and Company through a local merchant on the Cumberland River. But sometimes these local merchants served as more than merely a conduit for farmers' connections with the New Orleans market. Like Rackerly, Black Patch merchants occasionally advanced money in expectation of their crop. Local merchants advertised themselves as "Commission Merchants, & Dealers in Groceries," promising "Cash Advances on Tobacco Delivered to us for Shipment." They promised "liberal advances in Cash on Tobacco or other produce which may be delivered to us for shipment to New Orleans or other markets." Some of these advances came in the form of merchandise rather than cash. As early as 1788 a merchant had advertised "a likely Negroe wench" in exchange for tobacco.[4]

Black Patch merchants sometimes speculated in tobacco on their own accounts. Most of the extant bills of lading from the files of Kentucky merchant R. R. O'Hara and Son list merchants as owners of the tobacco O'Hara shipped to New Orleans.[5] The records of R. G. Dun and Company, which rated the credit-worthiness of firms throughout the nation, show that a few Black Patch merchants tried to speculate on tobacco, but still fewer made a profit at it. Those who traded in tobacco successfully had considerable resources, allowing them to sustain the occasional serious loss. In 1855 the Dun correspondent in Caldwell County described William D. Tinsley as a "trader in tobacco & any & everything else." As president of the Farmers' Bank of Kentucky, he could afford to speculate boldly. In 1856, Dun estimated his debts at $50,000. But he owned a hundred slaves, a thousand acres, twenty or twenty-five lots in Princeton, and $30,000 in bank stock. Tinsley had the financial wherewithal to gamble on the price of tobacco.[6]

Speculators less well-equipped than Tinsley could not long survive in the tobacco trade. The Caldwell County Dun correspondent described a Fredonia merchant as honest and of good character. He would "be called a safe man if he did not deal in tobacco," the Dun man wrote. When less skeptical Dun correspondents expressed confidence in the prospects of tobacco traders of modest means, they usually blundered. A Tennessee Dun agent wrote an enthusiastic report on a Springfield merchant, even though he had no property of his own and speculated in tobacco: "He trades in tobacco in Nashville and has made some money at it." But Dun followed that optimistic report with a terse notation just a year later that the Springfield trader was "out of business & bankrupt."[7]

Milton Dudley and Company was a typical example of a merchant financially ill-equipped for the tobacco trade. In 1850 Dun and Company's Princeton reporter noted that Dudley had stopped dealing in dry goods and had begun to trade in tobacco. The reporter worried that Dudley might not be able to survive the periodic losses attendant on tobacco speculation, but he relayed rumors that Dudley had a rich patron. In 1851 the correspondent estimated Dudley's losses at no more than three or four thousand dollars; in 1852 he lost another $2,000; and by 1856 Dudley appeared on Dun ledgers as "hopelessly insolvent."[8]

For much of the nineteenth century, tobacco speculation remained a rich man's game. Those who miscalculated, thinking themselves richer than they were, suffered. Walter Wilson graduated from Bethel College, inherited his grandmother's money, and thought he was "the richest man in ten states." When he lost his "fortune" speculating on tobacco, a friend reassured him that every speculator lost money on tobacco that year. Ruefully, Wilson replied, "They could afford it. I couldn't."[9]

Whether they sold to speculators like Wilson or traded directly with New Orleans merchants, tobacco farmers viewed the price assigned to their crop not primarily as the result of market forces but as a judgment on their skills. Farmers took a low price not as the result of some abstract market but as a personal insult, a comment on their farming. The reputations of a farmer and his buyer both depended on the price the farmer's crop fetched. A farmer's standing with his neighbors and his self-image depended largely on the quality of his tobacco, as measured by the price it brought. The reputation of a businessman buying tobacco rested on a more complex interplay of forces. A speculator known for undervaluing farmers' tobacco had a poor reputation, slight respect, and little business, but Black Patchers also praised keen traders. The community expected the best traders to buy at the lowest honest price and sell at the highest price possible.

The negotiations between Black Patch buyers and farmers were affected by personal understandings built on years of face-to-face negotiations. Scholars have found that buyers and sellers in rural areas often reached agreement not only because they settled on a compatible price but because they found each other compatible.[10] Buyers wielded a terrible power. By the price they paid, they declared farmers' tobacco "trash," "prime leaf," or something in between, determining not only the farmer's income but his status and honor. But this power was limited by the competition of other buyers. As early as the 1820s some Kentucky businessmen guaranteed this competition by setting up public auctions for tobacco.[11] If one buyer slandered a farmer's crop, other buyers would right the wrong by offering a fair price. Successful buyers carefully avoided affronting the sensibilities of cultivators.

By the end of the nineteenth century, industrialization threatened this system. Technological changes in transportation and communication precipitated the growth of national bureaucracies. As railroads reached into nearly every corner of the country, they forced a transition from neighborhood to regional and national markets. In 1850 Kentucky railroads operated only 233 miles of track—about the same as Alabama, but a hundred miles less than Tennessee and one-fifth the mileage of Indiana. Between 1870 and 1880 Kentucky railroads increased their mileage by 50 percent, building 513 miles of new track. In 1884 and 1885 they laid an additional 190 miles, surpassing that total in 1887 with 244 more miles. By 1889 2,835 miles of rail crossed the Commonwealth.[12] Improvements in communications were just as important. The ability to transmit up-to-date prices into the interior empowered local speculators. Armed with current price information, they could compete directly with port-city merchants. With closer connections to growers, they quickly—if temporarily—gained the upper hand over more distant competitors.[13] Better communications opened commercial opportunities for businessmen. Merchants in Cincinnati, Louisville, and Paducah found they had access to new markets in rural areas of the Commonwealth. Competition made participation in these new markets mandatory. Businesses that hesitated often failed.

During this period, the federal government also allowed, and even fostered, business concentration. The United States Supreme Court stopped state prosecutions of trusts.[14] Congress moved to regulate corporations, but, ironically, the new legislation actually encouraged business combinations. The authors and promoters of the Sherman Anti-Trust Act intended to incorporate the common law's prohibition of unreasonable restraints of trade into the federal code.[15] But in 1897, the Supreme Court construed the Sherman Act to make any contract designed to restrain trade illegal, whether the restraint was reasonable or not. This rendered unlawful any agreement among competing companies and any association, alliance, or confederation to rationalize prices, markets, or other elements of competition.[16] The only alternative to such agreements was for an aggressive company to buy competing companies.

Congress found other ways to promote the centralization of economic power, awarding money and land to businesses and ignoring corporate misdeeds. Senators and congressmen received retainers from the corporate recipients of millions of dollars of public monies and millions of acres of public land. Not surprisingly, Congress failed to oversee or regulate corporate use of the public largess. "Once Congress had acted," historian Robert Wiebe wrote, "power effectively dispersed to the recipients. Even where broad government management seemed imperative, people simply muddled along without it."[17]

The result of an expanded transportation network and such federal policies was an environment conducive to the growth of larger business organizations. In this milieu, the tobacco industry, like other sectors of the economy, consolidated at the end of the nineteenth century. In 1889 and 1890, in a series of meetings in New York, James B. Duke established the American Tobacco Company, a trust made up of five formerly competing cigarette manufacturers. The American Tobacco Company—incorporated in New Jersey—controlled 90 percent of the cigarette business and monopolized the machinery necessary for large-scale cigarette production.

American Tobacco next overwhelmed competitors in the chewing-tobacco market. Duke crushed rivals with tactics borrowed from other predatory trusts. He offered rebates to jobbers willing to sell only ATC products; he priced his well-advertised "Battle Ax" chewing tobacco below manufacturing costs. His strategy succeeded, and in 1898 the American Tobacco Company bought out its now-weakened rivals in the chewing-tobacco market. Duke next attacked the snuff market. Once he had control of that trade, he tried to gain control of the cigar market, though the many small independent manufacturers confounded his efforts. Nevertheless, by 1900 Duke controlled the sale of every tobacco product sold to American consumers except cigars.[18]

Duke also applied strategy to his company's acquisition of raw materials. As early as the 1880s tobacco companies had created their own purchasing departments to reduce the cost of raw materials by eliminating middlemen. Companies began buying directly from auction warehouses. Almost certainly to avoid competing with one another, companies deployed their buyers in different auction areas. W. S. Kimball and Company, for example, bought only in Oxford, North Carolina; Duke's company bought in Durham, North Carolina, and Danville, Virginia.[19]

Foreign companies copied and elaborated upon Duke's system of dividing territory and using professional buyers. Black Patch farmers were more affected by these actions than by Duke's because foreign countries bought 80 percent of Black Patch tobacco.[20] Foremost among these foreign consumers of Black Patch tobacco stood the Italian "Regie," as it was called by American farmers, who called any company operated by a government or regime a "regie." This monopoly, which manufactured cigarettes, cut tobacco, cigars, and snuff, predated the Italian government itself. The small independent states of Italy had long recognized the value of tobacco as an important source of governmental revenue. To exploit it, they formed state-controlled monopolies. For most of the nineteenth century the Italians depended on the smokers and chewers of American-grown tobacco to finance the operations of the governments of their small states and kingdoms, and the new Kingdom of Italy nationalized these provincial tobacco monopolies in 1862. Italian government officials mismanaged and only loosely supervised the operations of the monopoly, usually leasing it to private firms, but in 1884 the regime took direct control. In 1893 a department of the Finance Ministry known as the Direzione Generale delle Privative managed the Tobacco Department, along with the salt and lottery monopolies.[21]

Tobacco Department officials forged the tobacco monopoly into a money-making machine, setting the price Italian smokers had to pay for tobacco products. Critics complained that government officials showed little interest in the weight, dimensions, or quality of what they sold. Officials closely monitored production costs and immediately passed increases on to consumers, but when costs declined the state alone reaped the benefits. Tobacco Department officials kept the wages of their factory workers low and working conditions abysmal, precipitating bitter labor disputes. At the same time the government set the percentage of the price kept by private retailers selling government manufactured tobacco. Between 1893 and 1914 government officials repeatedly lowered these commissions and demanded higher and higher rebates. As a result, Italy's Tobacco Department achieved remarkable success in generating money for the government. Between 1902 and 1912 the profits increased more than twofold.[22]

The Italian monopoly stationed a government official in the United States to contract with American firms for the purchase of raw materials. This agent, Joseph Ferigo, purchased twenty-five million to forty million pounds of dark fired tobacco for his government per year. In Hopkinsville, Kentucky, and Clarksville, Tennessee, Ferigo, by buying most of the crop, virtually set the price. Contractors whom Ferigo hired to buy for Italy bought about 30 percent more than what the Italian government wanted, reselling the surplus to companies such as the American Snuff Company, the British Imperial Company, and the Spanish Regie. Other buyers bought tobacco in the Black Patch, but in certain regions nearly all the crop went to Italy. In other areas dark tobacco went to England or to the American Tobacco Company-owned American Snuff Company.[23]

Ferigo bought tobacco for his government through a New York-based syndicate of three tobacconists, George Reusens, E. G. Toel, and M. Abenheim. Reusens, Toel, and Abenheim created competition by buying through various tobacco dealers who bid against each other. In 1896 the Italian government decided it could acquire tobacco cheaper outside this syndicate and contracted with a single dealer in the Black Patch, E. C. Morrow and Company of Springfield, Tennessee. Initially the Italians' efforts to centralize their buying boosted prices. Hoping to persuade the Italians to go back to buying through their syndicate, Reusens, Toel, and Abenheim bid against Morrow. Temporarily, this forced the price up and farmers' profits soared. The syndicate, however, finally bowed out, and E. C. Morrow controlled the Italian export tobacco market in the Black Patch from 1897 through 1900.

Through the nineteenth century, the warehouse operators and speculators in each Black Patch town had formed a board of trade. These boards of trade elected knowledgeable men to inspect and grade farmers' tobacco. Since the grade assigned to a crop of tobacco determined its value, grading tobacco represented considerable power. Buyers called the poorest tobacco "trash" and paid little for it. The president of the Clarksville Board of Trade regarded this prerogative as a "treasure" to be jealously guarded from outside encroachment.[24] Once they had control of the tobacco market, the cartel insisted on grading their own tobacco. Soon farmers began accusing inspectors of deliberately grading their tobacco low so as to pay a lower price. Tobacco companies vigorously denied such charges.[25]

Sometimes the Italians' grading schemes ran into resistance. Some American buyers regarded grading as a function of their professional expertise and refused to grade low to maximize profits.[26] When Morrow balked, Ferigo replaced him with J. R. Cunningham and Company, a firm composed of Cunningham and W. G. Dunnington. In 1903 Cunningham dissolved his company and Dunnington became the Regie agent for all of western Kentucky and Tennessee. Unlike Morrow, Dunnington had no compunction about grading farmers' tobacco low enough to guarantee better profits for the Italians.[27]

Walter Gray Dunnington centralized Italian tobacco buying. His efforts sparked the Black Patch war. Photo courtesy of Dolly Dunnington Orgain.

Walter Gray Dunnington, born in 1849, was a nineteenth-century entrepreneur, albeit one equipped with the technology and organizational advantages of the twentieth century. Dunnington controlled the dark fired tobacco market in Kentucky and Tennessee from his offices in Farmville, Virginia, over seven hundred miles away in Virginia's dark-tobacco district. In 1898, W. E. B. Du Bois called Farmville "easy-going, gossipy, and conservative," but it had served as a tobacco market almost as long as New Orleans. In 1819 four tobacco dealers had operated in the town, processing 1,090 hogsheads of tobacco. As early as 1856 Dunnington's father had manufactured tobacco products in Farmville. Joining his father in business in 1876, the younger Dunnington rapidly made his company the leader of Farmville's tobacco trade, representing Norway, Italy, and Austria. In Farmville's large, wooden barnlike tobacco factories, women, young men, and children untied farmer-created "hands" of tobacco leaves, cutting out the stems and steaming the leaves. In 1898 Dunnington paid his workers fifty cents per hundred pounds of tobacco; a hard worker could make $9 a week—for five to seven months a year. Dunnington sold the tobacco these laborers packed around the world.[28] In 1899 the Farmville *Herald* described Dunnington as the "prince of the tobacco buyers." Residents of Farmville recalled with pride a day in 1902 when Dunnington loaded a train of thirty cars with tobacco he had bought for Norway.[29]

Although he would later claim to have no political inclinations, Dunnington campaigned in the 1890s for the "gold bugs" or hard-money candidates, opposing farmers' demands for an inflated currency. This proved a singularly unpopular position in overwhelmingly agricultural Farmville, and may well account for his later claims to have been uninterested in politics. Active in civic matters, he served as town trustee, helped found a bank, incorporated the Farmville water company, served as a trustee of Hampden-Sydney College, and lobbied for a railroad to Farmville.[30] A short, wiry man, Dunnington impressed some acquaintances with his forcefulness. Others described him as quiet. He "keeps his own counsel," the Farmville *Herald* reported in 1902, "and scarcely lets his right hand know of the movements of the left." Dunnington could certainly be secretive. Shortly before he contracted with the Italians, the Richmond *Dispatch* reported that Dunnington had positively denied rumors that he had or would ever have any connection with Italy.[31]

Although Dunnington later claimed to have been a friend of farmers, championing a fair price for their tobacco, farmers saw things differently. They avowed that the "most gigantic and ruthless corporation that ever oppressed mankind" set the price artificially low.[32] Dunnington's response was best stated in 1896 by his partner. Farmers drove the price down by flooding the market with low-grade tobacco, he insisted. To improve the price, growers had only to improve quality.[33] Such arguments infuriated farmers, challenging their tobacco-growing skill and, by extension, their honor and pride.

When Dunnington took over the western market for the Italians, he found the arrangements he inherited from his predecessors unsatisfactory. He had to furnish his own money to buy tobacco for resale to the Italians, so his profits depended on which way the price of tobacco went in a given year. After the first year, when Dunnington lost eleven thousand dollars, he determined to change procedures. He prevailed on Ferigo to get the Italian government itself to supply most of the money, thereby reducing his own risk. He also wanted to change the way he bought tobacco. Morrow had purchased tobacco both from the warehouse auctions and directly from farmers. Dunnington wanted to buy all his tobacco directly from farmers, skipping the local auctions. He divided the Black Patch into districts, maintaining a single warehouse and buyer in each, and instructed the buyers to visit farmers' barns instead of bidding at public auctions. Without competition, Dunnington's buyers could dictate the price Black Patchers received for their tobacco crop.[34]

Dunnington relied on supervisors to enforce boundary lines between his districts. He was unyielding on this rule. In eastern Montgomery County, Tennessee, he drew the boundary between two districts down the middle of Rosson Road. Polk Prince, whose barn was on the west side of the road, had his tobacco examined by the Regie agent from the district on the east side of the road. This agent offered six cents a pound, far more than the Regie agent controlling the district on the west side of the road would offer. Prince appealed to the Regie supervisor, who told him the Adams agent could not buy out of his district even if it was only across the road. Prince eventually sold his tobacco to the American Snuff Company for four and a half cents a pound for the leaf and three and a half cents for the lugs.[35]

These practices enabled Dunnington to set the price of tobacco in the Black Patch. He communicated with his subordinates each week, and some later admitted that Dunnington periodically directed them to lower the prices they paid farmers. J. D. Ryan of Jenkins, Ryan, and Company explained that his company received instructions from Dunnington weekly on how much to buy and at what price. "My territory was prescribed and I could not buy any tobacco outside of this territory," Ryan recalled. He made weekly reports to Dunnington. "Regie buyers had no competition and continually depressed prices, till the farmer could not make a living."[36]

Farmers suspected that Dunnington had worked out at least three agreements with rival companies. First, buyers refused to bid against each other. If a buyer visited a farmer and made a bid on his crop, other buyers considered that grower off limits. Besides testimony from men like Ryan, farmers believed they had other evidence that the Regie had worked out secret buying agreements with rival tobacco buyers. A farmer in Oak Grove in Christian County, Kentucky, described a visit in October 1904 by a buyer for the American Snuff Company. When he learned that a Regie buyer had already been there and made an offer, he refused to bid and left. Another farmer stated that a buyer for the American Snuff Company came to his farm, stayed the night, but refused to go into the barn and examine his tobacco when he learned that a Regie buyer had already made a bid.[37]

Second, farmers claimed that to keep opposing buyers from entering his territory, Dunnington bought tobacco "in the round." That is, he bought a farmer's whole crop, even grades not suitable for the Italian market. These he would transfer to his competitors.

A Montgomery County farmer recalled that in 1903 he saw hogsheads of tobacco marked "W. G. Dunnington and Company" in an American Snuff Company warehouse. Imperial and American Snuff Company buyers, instead of bidding for tobacco in districts where the Regie maintained buyers, simply picked up what they needed from the Regie itself.[38]

To maintain his good relations with the Italians, Duke performed a most useful service. Independent tobacco buyers, shut out of the Italian market, had only a single outlet for their tobacco purchases: Bremen, Germany. In 1903, the American Tobacco Company apparently deliberately sabotaged this market by dumping many hogsheads of dark fired tobacco at absurdly low prices in the Bremen market. Independent speculators lost heavily as the Germans purchased the underpriced tobacco, leaving other tobacco to rot on the docks. Many independents did not survive this experience. Those who did hesitated to buy dark tobacco for the Bremen market, for fear they would again be undersold by American Tobacco.

The Italian Regie emerged as a prime beneficiary from this affair, freed from competition from independent buyers selling to the German market. Tobacco men familiar with the Bremen incident cited it as proof that the American Tobacco Company had allied with the Italian Regie. No one knew what the Italians offered the Americans in exchange for this service, but observers reasoned that there must have been a quid pro quo.[39]

Growers also had the testimony of disgruntled cartel employees. They confirmed farmers' suspicions that the Americans, the British, and the Italians had formed a cartel. A. O. Dority, a tobacco buyer based in Pembroke, Kentucky, worked for the Italians in 1902 and for the American Tobacco Company's American Snuff Company in 1903. Changing jobs from one supposedly rival company to the other involved no transition at all, he found. He bought in the same territory both years and shipped the tobacco he bought to the same companies. He said later, "The very day that the Italian people decided not to put a buyer in that territory the A[merican] T[obacco] C[ompany] contracted with me to buy in that territory for them."[40]

After losing his inheritance in tobacco speculation, Walter Wilson also bought tobacco for the cartel. He first worked for the Hopkinsville Board of Trade, the tobacco buyers' organization, as a tobacco inspector, sampling farmers' crops and judging the quality of the leaves. "The tobacco men got behind me," Wilson said, and they "made me Tobacco-Inspector." Later a tobacco company hired Wilson as a buyer for $100 a month. He became a quintessential twentieth-century organization man; he worked for a boss, lived in a mortgaged house, and drew a salary.[41]

The emergence of a cadre of hierarchically organized salaried professional buyers like Dority and Wilson marked a sharp departure from the past. Until well after the Civil War, general merchants had continued to purchase tobacco from growers much as they had in antebellum times. But tobacco buying gradually became a distinct occupation. What most distinguished twentieth-century buyers from their predecessors was their position within hierarchical organizations. Men like Dority and Wilson were at the bottom of a vast organization, supervised by middle-level managers. Like Dority and Wilson, these middle-level men surrendered their economic independence in return for the security of a salaried position. Most had managed independent warehouses before joining the cartel. Ed Tandy may represent a typical example. He worked in Hopkinsville, Kentucky, tobacco offices and factories for ten years before being admitted as a partner in a leaf tobacco brokerage firm in 1894. He later became a Regie supervisor.

Two characteristics marked the careers of these new tobacco professionals. First, unlike antebellum speculators, Dority, Wilson, and Tandy were not farmers or general merchants who bought tobacco on the side. Tobacco was their sole endeavor. Second, they lacked the independence speculators had enjoyed in the nineteenth century. They took orders and carried out instructions from their bosses.[42]

The activities of men like Tandy alarmed Black Patch farmers. The employees of supposedly rival tobacco companies seemed on most intimate terms. When the American Tobacco Company entered the English market in 1901, it hired Edwin Hodge to supervise the purchase of tobacco suitable for the British trade. The British traditionally preferred dark fired tobacco from a five-county area around Henderson, Kentucky, known as the Henderson stemming district. From 1901 until 1903 Hodge operated out of the American Tobacco Company's office in Henderson on the corner of Third and Water streets. He shared an office with American Tobacco's buyer of unfired tobacco for the domestic market, Bland Beverly. When Duke withdrew from the British market, Hodge became the Imperial Tobacco Company's general manager for Kentucky and surrounding states. But he continued to share the same offices on Third and

Water streets with Beverly. Observing these arrangements, farmers concluded that Hodge and Beverly must have informally agreed on a price for tobacco each season.[43]

Despite the importance of impersonal market forces, individual character played a crucial role in relations between buyers and farmers. The cartel's tobacco men claimed to be mere creatures of the market. Walter Wilson told farmers that the low prices he offered were "the best I could do. . . . I'm just hired out, you know." Even his superiors "have no more to do with setting the price than I do," he added. But sometimes buyers tried to impress farmers with their importance. J. D. Ryan described the attitude of his fellow Regie buyers as "dictatorial." One of his colleagues would lower the price even more if a farmer complained, sneering, "Well, damn you, you will take less." Another buyer said, "Who in the hell are you going to sell it to, no one else can come in my territory."[44]

These buyers represented a powerful new force. Tobacco growers quickly understood that the buyers owed their chief loyalty to their company, not to the community. Never before in the Black Patch had a significant portion of the population been so independent of community control. Many planters feared these younger organization men. In the past planters discouraged buyers from dealing directly with their tenants. By controlling and dominating their communities, planters could influence local markets, and in a purely local market, tenants could not escape the power of their landlords even when they took their crop off the plantation and into town. But now planters faced something new. Men not beholden to the local economy, men beyond their control, destroyed the local market—literally driving many auction houses out of business. Planters did not know if these buyers would respect local racial etiquette or not.[45] They understood that simply by purchasing black-grown tobacco directly from tenants at the same price they offered landlords, buyers could revolutionize Black Patch race relations. And the community—which had always governed race relations—could do very little about it if buyers chose such a radical course.

Black farmers produced a significant portion of the Black Patch tobacco crop. In 1900 they constituted about 16 percent of the total number of Eastern Dark Fired District farmers (6,787 of 42,737).[46] From the beginnings of Kentucky's tobacco trade race was a touchy issue. The Commonwealth's earliest compilation of laws included a statute forbidding warehousemen from employing blacks. Warehousemen judged farmers' tobacco, and white planters might resent having their crop judged by a black, or even in the presence of blacks.[47]

Many white landowners maintained a patron-client relationship with their black laborers, often exploiting their employees with less regard for their well-being than they had exhibited for their slaves.[48] However, patronage probably best characterized the relationship between white employers and the floating pool of black labor. Many Black Patch planters regarded their long-time hands not as patrons but as childlike wards. Moreover, they often viewed even transient workers as their responsibility.[49] As one tenant explained, "You get groceries, dry goods on credit, you know, but they's charged to you, but the landowner, the man you's working for, he had to stand for it. He was the man responsible for your bills."[50] When laborers spent more than they had, landowners made gifts or loans to carry them over. One planter noted in his diary a gift of $5.00 to "my man Frank" after Frank squandered his wages.[51]

Gifts to favorites sometimes went beyond money. In 1982 an elderly black tenant farmer still proudly displayed a chipped shaving mug a white doctor had given his father seventy years before, when the doctor had approved his proposal to operate a barbershop. The doctor's patronage had protected the barber when he angered lower-class whites. As his son observed, "Dr. Amoss was a mighty good man to us colored folks."[52] In 1904 a white planter offered a candid description of paternalism: "We white people teach [blacks] all they know and take care of them." He added that blacks feared "they will be sent away off out of the country where there are no white people to help them."[53] This planter indulged in fantasy; he had little or no understanding of the black laborers he exploited. But his feelings of paternalism were real enough. It was a kind of racism, more subtle than some varieties, but brutal in its own way. Paternalists destroyed character, or tried to, demanding childlike docility from the victims of their largess.[54]

Dunnington's tobacco buyers did not generally challenge this system. If tobacco buyers had judged the tobacco grown by black labor superior or equal to that produced by whites, they would have challenged white pride and honor. One Black Patch resident remembered a threat to the established order involving "an old colored fellow that had a nice farm." When a tobacco buyer paid more for his tobacco than he did for that of a white neighbor, the angry white farmer set fire to the buyer's warehouse, destroying the tobacco.[55]

Buyers almost never so crudely challenged local racial etiquette. William Faulkner's words come to mind: "You simply cannot go against a community. . . . you cannot stand against the cold inflexible abstraction of a long-suffering community's moral point of view."[56] More often, buyers followed the less risky path of accepting the white community's traditional discriminations against black cultivators. Henry Dinwiddie represents a typical case. He reported that buyers tried to purchase his tobacco for $4.75 per hundred pounds. He refused, asking a white man to sell it for him. The white farmer sold the same tobacco for $6.75 per hundred pounds.[57] White landlords noticed that tobacco buyers "made it a point to try to get the colored man's tobacco cheaper" than that of whites.[58] For example, Washington Anderson complained that warehousemen lent black farmers money to buy fall clothing as a device to get control of their tobacco. Shortly after they made the loan, the warehousemen demanded repayment. They warned that a buyer would soon appear and the farmer "had better" sell when he did. Warehousemen sometimes held farmers' mortgages and foreclosed when they balked at the prices proffered.[59]

Black agriculturalists complained bitterly about the new class of tobacco men. One recalled cultivating six acres of tobacco in 1901, producing about four thousand pounds. Half went to the landlord, leaving the tenant free to negotiate the sale of two thousand pounds. He hoped his tobacco would cover his indebtedness of $49, spent for clothing and other necessities, but the first buyer he approached offered only $1.50 per hundred pounds for his leaf and 75 cents for his lugs—not enough to cover his debt. He complained later that when he sought competitive bids from other buyers, they offered even less than the first. To pay his debt, the tenant went to Evansville, Indiana, to work in a glass factory at $2 a day. He sent back enough money to cover his debt and then returned to raise tobacco once again. Conditions had not improved. His interviewer noted that he wore a borrowed coat and that his family could only attend church one at a time, because they had to share clothes. Other blacks agreed with the tenant, adding that few of their number could clothe their children sufficiently to go to school.[60]

But while tobacco professionals accepted and exploited traditional racism, by the beginning of the twentieth century they had emerged as a distinct class in Black Patch towns. The 1900 manuscript United States census for Christian County includes seventy-eight men variously identified as tobacconists, tobacco dealers, tobacco brokers, and tobacco merchants. This does not include tobacco packers and other laborers in Hopkinsville's many tobacco warehouses and factories. In her memoir of life in Hopkinsville, Emma Wilson recalls tobacco men as wearing "brown clothes just the color of tobacco." Often profit alone guided these professionals; they lacked the paternalism characteristic of landlords.[61]

By the end of the nineteenth century and the beginning of the twentieth, the tobacco business had changed dramatically. Fewer and fewer individual speculators operated, increasingly falling victim to large tobacco companies. Instead, an international cartel fielded a cadre of salaried professionals, functioning in tightly controlled, hierarchical organizations. The cartel's employees dictated the price farmers received for their tobacco, claiming that low prices simply reflected the market. But the low prices reflected more than the market; they reflected the ability of the company buyers to manipulate the market. Unconstrained by the paternalism characteristic of southern planters, buyers often bullied farmers, especially black farmers. Tobacco growers now confronted arrogant, domineering tobacco buyers. They perceived this as a challenge to their position and status. Even if the new tobacco bureaucrats did not immediately challenge the existing racial etiquette, allowing outsiders influence in areas of race relations posed an intolerable potential threat. Impersonal market forces could not be counted on to maintain the existing racial hierarchy. In the face of such a powerful enemy, Black Patch communities began to fight back. Experiences with the tobacco trust convinced farmers that the only way to resist organized economic power was to organize themselves.

By 1900 professional tobacco men were in a position to challenge the power of the Black Patch planter elite. Professional buyers judged planters' crops, evaluating their art and skill. This was nothing new, of course, but now they did so without competition as power shifted from grower to buyer. Some buyers enjoyed a wealth that allowed them to challenge the planters' position as the sole community resource for those seeking capital. But buyers threatened planters most directly by lowering the price of tobacco and cutting profits. Emancipation had forced planters to use money rather than force to control their laborers, and without it, or with less of it, they faced a crisis. One effect of lower prices would be a migration of blacks out of the Black Patch in search of higher wages. Traditionally, planters measured their status by the labor they controlled. As labor became scarcer, some saw their own position slipping. And less abundant labor meant higher wages, cutting further into planters' own profits. To resist, some Black Patch planters would urge their fellow growers to organize a tobacco cooperative designed to give them control of their own crop. Planters would fashion a modern organization to preserve a traditional structure.

Farmers had been losing status compared to professionals and even to African-Americans since the end of the Civil War. The loss of their enslaved black labor led many planters to the depressing conclusion that they no longer controlled their own lives. While planters dirtied their hands with work once performed by blacks, postbellum professionals suffered the loss of slavery less directly, and after the Civil War many surpassed agriculturalists in social standing.[1] One planter wrote bitterly, "If a doctor, or lawyer, or editor, or carpenter, or bricklayer, or a kinky-headed little negro has a right to put a price on his labor, a man who owns a farm has a right to put a price on the product that represents his labor."[2]

Victims of industrialization had several options. The first was to fight the future, clinging to a bygone time. Granger literature, for example, coming out of the nineteenth-century movement to promote the interest of agriculture, indulged in rural nostalgia, romanticizing farm life and waxing eloquent about the husking-bees and other frolics country people enjoyed.[3] In Missouri traditionalists resisted an expanding corporate-based economy by drawing on folk memories to keep alive imperiled values and traditions. Another option lay in adopting the tactics of the enemy. This meant seeking to participate in the new industrialized order on the same terms as their adversaries. Farmers had to "act like captains of industry, restrict production, withhold surpluses, control markets," and make farming a business. Farming became just a way to make money, no longer a communal way of life.[4]

But farmers recognized that they could adopt some of the tactics of their enemies and still protect their traditional way of life. Farmers advocating agricultural cooperatives participated in the new economic order without surrendering the most positive aspects of their culture. In the Black Patch, some tobacco farmers hoped to follow this path—to be a part of the new economic order and still enjoy their autonomy and community life.[5] The Patrons of Husbandry, or Grange, sponsored the first nationwide drive for agricultural cooperation. The Grange urged cooperation both to combat exploitation by business and to preserve the traditional culture of agriculture.[6]

All Americans feared losing their independence in the new economic world. But farmers were especially concerned that big business would reduce them to mere laboring status. Granger orators articulated this fear explicitly, defining a laborer as one without the power to put a price on the fruits of his toil. Farming, they declared, was "not raising crops to sell at such price as the buyer may arbitrarily choose to offer." Grangers warned that if farmers did not assert themselves more boldly than they had in the past, they would lose status, becoming hirelings. "There must now be no step backward. If the farmers of the country now fail in asserting and maintaining their just rights, they will cease to be free agents, and become fitting subjects for the virtual slavery into which they will then surely drift."[7]

Grangers and other promoters of cooperation also warned that in a modern world organization constituted a key element of success. Urban dwellers united themselves into communities and organizations, Grangers reminded farmers: "Financiers have their Boards where they meet to lay plans. . . . Railroad companies have their societies. . . . Why should there not be organized effort among farmers?"[8] An Indiana proponent of cooperation told farmers that "organization is the law of the industrial and commercial world."[9] He predicted that "isolation will yield . . . to combination."[10]

Advocates of cooperation claimed that agricultural society was naturally conducive to the kind of organized effort necessary for survival in an industrial world. The Grangers defined farm life as "that counsel and assistance between neighbor and neighbor that draws close the bond of brotherhood, and by co-operation renders each one in the community helpful to the other."[11] Others claimed that farming was a business, "quite as truly as manufacturing." Thus, if businessmen could organize successfully, so should agriculturalists.[12]

The mutuality and neighborly help the Grangers urged on their members closely resembled the traditional communal structure Steven Hahn and others have found in the southern backcountry.[13] But Grangers did not retreat from the world. They challenged local merchants' control of the market by engineering boycotts and opening up new channels of trade. Grangers pooled their produce for sale outside the local market; likewise, they pooled orders for goods to bypass local merchants. Montgomery Ward got its start chiefly by filling Grange orders.[14] In the Black Patch, Grangers launched a war on local business in the 1870s. In 1874 nineteen Granges operated in Christian County alone. There farmers pooled their tobacco and appointed a committee to negotiate with Hopkinsville warehousemen. Grangers hoped the warehouses would compete to offer the tobacco growers the best rebate for the privilege of handling the Grangers' crop. In the early 1880s, Hopkinsville tobaccomen broke the Grange scheme, destroying any "collusion" among farmers by boycotting Grange tobacco.[15]

The next push for cooperation among tobacco growers came shortly after. Arkansas farmers formed an organization they called the Agricultural Wheel in 1882. The Wheel spread to other states and coexisted with another farmers' organization, the Farmers' Alliance. In 1888 the Wheel merged with the southern wing of the Alliance. From 1887 to 1891 Farmers' Alliance lecturers toured rural America preaching cooperation. Like Grangers, they argued both for traditional values and for more effective participation in the market.[16] In 1888 Alliancemen, Wheelers, and Grangers met in Clarksville, Tennessee, to organize an agricultural trust. Farmers would store their tobacco in communal warehouses or sheds in districts throughout the Black Patch and would get cash advances when they deposited their crop. But when farmers asked where the money would come from, organizers had no answer. Banks were the enemy; the Alliance could not borrow money from them. "Advise with the brethren and make other arrangements for money and after one year every farmer will be able to make a crop without advances," the Nashville *Weekly Toiler* suggested. Alliancemen assured skeptics that "arrangements will be made within the organization to supply the necessities of those who are compelled to have money before prizing their crops." The Alliance would hold farmers' tobacco "until buyers come to the farmers' demands."[17]

Alliancemen devised a warehouse stratagem which they hoped would do better than simply holding farmers' crops while awaiting a better price. They wanted to promote competitive bidding. In Texas the Alliance opened a central exchange for the display of cotton samples drawn from cotton stored in Alliance warehouses scattered around the state. Historian Lawrence Goodwyn credits the Alliance with bringing competition into hitherto monopolized local markets.[18] The Alliance and the Wheel operated a tobacco warehouse, sometimes called the Exchange, in Clarksville, Tennessee. Farmers talked of organizing a Wheel warehouse in Springfield, Tennessee, and did open one in Fulton, Kentucky, in 1888. According to the *Weekly Toiler,* the Alliance's warehouse in Clarksville saw "lively bidding by the home and foreign buyers." In 1890 the *Toiler* told its readers that the Alliance would shortly send a man to Europe "to contract direct with the buyers there so as to get the very highest European prices."[19] However, only a minority of Black Patch farmers ever participated in the exchange program. It soon failed.

As early as 1890 Black Patch planters talked of organizing in reaction to their "oppressed commercial condition." Apparently several wealthy Robertson County, Tennessee, planters conceived of the idea more or less simultaneously. John M. Foster, a Nashville lawyer who moved to Robertson County for his health, approached Felix Ewing and Joseph E. Washington with his idea that planters should form some sort of association. Both Ewing and Washington told Foster they had already toyed with the idea. At some point he discussed his ideas with another wealthy Robertson County planter, Charles Fort.[20]

Fort, Ewing, and Washington emerged as the chief proponents for a farmers' organization in the Black Patch, inasmuch as they stood at the top of the social hierarchy in Robertson County. Ewing was one of the county's foremost planters, having married the daughter of George Augustine Washington, who, with property valued in 1860 at over half a million dollars, believed himself to be the largest dark tobacco grower in the world.[21] George's son, Joseph E. Washington, operated his father's plantation, named Wessyington. In 1904 he owned almost three thousand acres valued at just under $30,000. Fort's ancestors came to Tennessee in 1789, traveling from

Edgecombe County, North Carolina, with their slaves, horses, and cattle. They became a leading planter family in Tennessee, but the Civil War and emancipation threatened the Forts' wealth even more than it did cotton barons.[22] For tobacco growers, access to labor rather than land determines wealth. But the Forts survived the end of slavery with their fortune intact. By 1904 Charles Fort owned 633 acres valued at $5,800 in a county where the average landowner had just under 85 acres.[23]

But these wealthy planters recognized that their poorer neighbors were not yet "ripe" for organization. They had to be educated. Planters had to work with their neighbors, persuading them to pool their crops. In the beginning the planters' pools were quite small. In Robertson County one 1900 pool consisted of just three planters who made a pact not to sell separately, forcing buyers to take all three crops or none at all. Their efforts served as a model for their neighbors.[24]

Pooling efforts received a boost in 1901, when word spread among farmers that the Regie planned to divide the Black Patch into districts with a single buyer assigned to each. The Regie's intentions to buy tobacco directly—and privately—from farmers rather than at public auction frightened tobacco farmers. Some farmers doubted that their crop would sell at a fair price outside the auction system.

Plans for cooperation shifted dramatically by the end of the century. While early organizers had seen local mercantile interests as the enemy, advocates of cooperation now forged an alliance with local businessmen against the greater danger—the tobacco trust. In one way, this effort resembled earlier attempts at agricultural cooperation. The Grange, the Alliance, and other postbellum farmer organizations always had the Black Patch's wealthy elite in leadership positions. In 1901, this elite stepped forward again. But now they were joined by local independent tobacco buyers and warehousemen. By buying directly from farmers, the Regie had put many middlemen out of business. Recognizing that their enemy was no longer the local furnishing merchant or even warehousemen in Hopkinsville and Clarksville, farmers thought it natural to join with townsmen against a common enemy. Unlike Grangers and Populists, twentieth-century advocates of cooperation now formed an alliance between town and country. This alliance became a characteristic of farmers' twentieth-century organizing efforts.[25]

In October 1901 merchants, planters, and farmers met in the

Clarksville, Tennessee, courthouse to organize against the Italian Regie. The assemblage elected Charles Fort chairman and C. N. Meriwether secretary. The assembled planters placed Fort at the head of a committee to draw up plans for a permanent organization. Some urged Fort's committee to propose a boycott of tobacco buyers. On October 17, the Clarksville *Daily Leaf-Chronicle* advised farmers to hold their crop off the market: "The price can not be worse, unless all competition is driven out and this is what farmers have got to look to."[26]

In this atmosphere, Fort's organizational committee met on October 21, 1901, to draw up plans for a permanent organization. Himself a planter descended from planters, Fort had been radicalized by the growth of corporate power. He regularly contributed fiction to the antibusiness magazine published by Georgia Populist Tom Watson. Most of his short stories described the comic antics of urban slum-dwellers. But one story, "A Radical Corpuscle," makes the bloodstream a metaphor for the society. In the story, a corpuscle asks, "Why are we placed here in this Man?" A greedy financier-corpuscle answers, "To get all we can out of it!" The financier has little patience with the question: "Already there is too much murmuring against my invested rights!" To save the doubting corpuscle from a gathering mob, his disciples have to hustle him into hiding.[27] In 1901, Fort had no more success than the radical corpuscle in persuading his fellows to join him in a campaign against business. When farmers met again, two days after the October 21 meeting, Fort's committee reported its members could not settle on a plan. They could agree only on a name for the new organization, the "Clarksville District Tobacco Growers' Association." With that limited action, the farmers decided to meet again in December.[28] By then, their interest in organizing had ebbed even more. Tobacco companies decided to squelch the new farmers' organization by offering higher prices. The ploy worked. Eager to settle with croppers and get ready for Christmas, farmers accepted the higher prices. Fort's committee held a hasty meeting on a Saturday afternoon. Distracted and anxious to return to their farms, the members decided to take no further action, agreeing to wait for a more favorable time in the new year.[29] More than two years passed before that time came.

Lower prices inflamed farmers' passions. In 1903, farmers flooded the market with a huge crop, driving the price down. Tobacco buyers claimed that the crop had been too big to care for properly and the quality had suffered. Such criticism always rankled growers, but the low prices bothered them even more. Farmers and local warehousemen again tried to organize in 1904. In January 1904, tobacco businessmen, or "jobbers," and farmers first tried to form a "Growers and Jobbers" organization. Farmers and jobbers from Todd, Logan, and Christian counties in Kentucky and Montgomery, Robertson, and Cheatham counties, Tennessee, met in the opera house in Guthrie, Kentucky. In February, they met again in Mayfield to work out a "policy of protection."[30] But once again the efforts withered.

Nevertheless, in the summer of 1904 Tennessee planter Felix Grundy Ewing urged farmers to organize. Signing himself "Cactus," Ewing addressed a series of newspaper articles to Black Patch farmers. Cactus told farmers they must overcome their "great conservatism." Noting the growth of business power, he argued that "concentration is the watchword of the hour."[31] People might consider concentration a disease in the economic body, he wrote, but "if we are not trying to catch it, we should be, for it is the essence of success today."[32] Tobacco growers must be organized into a streamlined, modern force, modeled on business trusts, he wrote. Such a farmers' trust would have to represent every class and category of tobacco grower to succeed. As representative of all tobacco growers, the head of the association would be a tobacco tycoon, negotiating on an equal footing with business tycoons.[33]

The organ of Clarksville business, the Clarksville *Leaf-Chronicle,* endorsed Ewing's plans and urged local businessmen to join with wealthy farmers, organizing a stock company. The newspaper advised farmers to sell shares in the association and advance the proceeds against the crops of poorer farmers. Three days later the *Leaf-Chronicle* reported that a prominent businessman in Clarksville had embraced the idea, adding that it was "good business to help farmers keep trade in Clarksville." He thought Clarksville's banks would be "glad to advance on tobacco."

Uniting town and country to fight outsiders appealed to small town boosters. A reporter for the *Leaf-Chronicle* rhapsodized about a time before trusts when "the streets [were] so packed and jammed with country wagons, delivering tobacco and carrying groceries and all kinds of goods, that it was almost impossible to pass along the streets on horseback[;] we hope to live to see this case again." To recapture this bygone time, the newspaper advocated a "defensive alliance" between farmers and warehousemen.[34]

In the wake of Ewing's "Cactus" articles, farm leaders scheduled a mass meeting for September in Guthrie, Kentucky. Ewing hoped that thousands of farmers would attend to "concentrate" themselves for their battle with the trust. As the date of the September mass meeting approached, other writers joined "Cactus" in urging the formation of a new association. John M. Foster warned that if planters did not attend "you will deserve the name of cowards, and the very women and children will crook the finger of scorn at you."[35]

The organization Ewing encouraged farmers to join would largely be the vehicle of elite planters trying to maintain their status as the leaders of their communities. Planter life rested on a hierarchical social-economic structure where planters farmed their land with dependent laborers. Since the end of slavery, those laborers share-cropped, staying on the land because landlords "stood" for their store bills. Low tobacco prices, combined with higher cotton prices, threatened this structure, in that cotton growers came to Tennessee and Kentucky to recruit black labor, enticing workers away from tobacco fields with promises of higher wages. In 1904 the Nashville *Banner* described "a stampede" of blacks leaving Kentucky for Mississippi.[36] The Hopkinsville *Kentuckian* commented the following year that "the trust has about starved out the farm labor of this section."[37] Martin Van Buren Ingram, a retired newspaperman who in his younger days reviled carpetbaggers and then promoted the Alliance, complained that sharecropping was a curse. Though he added that "there are still some good crops where labor is tied down and can't get away," Ingram was right.[38] Labor was getting away in the Black Patch. In March 1904, Trenton farmers reported the loss of twenty-five blacks to Mississippi in one week and twenty the previous week.[39] "NEGRO EXODUS," the *Kentuckian* headlined.[40] Planters complained about the scarcity of labor and the high price it commanded. "Many of the laborers have left this region and there is a scarcity. There have been twenty-three laborers left my neighborhood on account of not getting anything for the tobacco they produce. Wages were formerly about $10.00 or 12.00 per month. Now is [*sic*] 14.00 or 16.00 per month."[41]

Census statistics confirm the bleak picture newspapers and planters painted. In 1900 Christian County had 846 black tenants; ten years later only 571 remained. In Montgomery County, Tennessee, blacks declined from 40.5 percent of the tenant farming population in 1900 to 35.79 percent in 1910. Robertson County showed a similar decline, from 38.3 to 32.2 percent. The counties most dependent on black workers lost the largest number. The number of black farmers actually increased in some mostly white, yeomen-oriented counties.[42]

The loss of black labor hurt planters. Some measured their status in much the same way as the old slaveowners had—by the labor they controlled. But even those who kept their eye on the bottom line understood that a smaller labor force meant a smaller crop, and a smaller income. But this does not mean that all planters would join Ewing's Association or that all those joining did so to keep their black laborers. Montgomery County planter Joe Gerhart was one who refused to join, though he agreed with Association propagandists that tobacco buyers were in collusion. "From observation," he said, "it would seem that the buyers got together and agreed on a price." Gerhart expected the Association to have a positive effect on the price of tobacco, but he refused to join because he did "not think it would be [good] business to surrender all control of this property [tobacco] to the organization." He wanted to be able to reject a price that the Association might accept.[43]

Not every planter welcomed the formation of an Association. John B. Ferguson of Montgomery County, who told an interviewer, "I raise no tobacco myself—all with tenants," opposed the Association outright. It was "quixotic, visionary, revolutionary and impracticable," he expostulated. Ferguson refused to believe tobacco buyers conspired to fix prices.[44] Despite such dissidents, planters and larger farmers joined the Association in higher proportions than smaller growers. The heart of the Black Patch, where planters predominated, was the center of strength for the Association.

Planters employed the traditional rhetoric of southern virility to appeal to yeomen farmers. Black Patch men fighting the trust did so on behalf of their women. Again and again advocates of a unified front evoked the image of women and children to claim a moral imperative for organization. Charles Fort's brother, Joel, did so poetically:

> Oh! God, hear the cry of the needy
>   And poor;
> The rich man has comforts and
>   Lags;
> In the bounties that control the labor-
>   ers door;
> Oh! Remember the woman in rags.[45]

Association organizers like Fort would later observe that Black Patch women played a key role in the formation of the new organization. Such women "purified, ennobled, and elevated" the fight with the trust. More than that, they put "into the heart of southern men the sentiment that irresistibly forces them to defend the purity of woman even with his life." In a poem entitled "Stand by Your Guns," Joel Fort told farmers that "Fair women urge you to fight." Association propagandists likened Black Patch women to Spartan women, requiring that their men emerge victorious in battle or die in the attempt:

> Then said the mother to her son,
> And handed him his shield,
> Come with it when the battle's done,
> Or on it from the field.[46]

Such appeals were not only effective with men but made necessary by women. Women expected to find recognition of their role when they read Association publications. By publishing tributes to Black Patch womanhood, Association propagandists not only shrewdly appealed to the virility of Black Patch men, they also acknowledged that they dared not offend the wives, mothers, and sisters of those men by neglecting them.

Black Patch women wielded a power similar to that exercised by southern women in the Civil War. Notoriously touchy about their manliness, southern men were especially vulnerable to the criticisms of their women.[47] Advocates of organization presented farmers with a stark choice between honor and dishonor. Will farmers "submit," they asked. Will they humiliate themselves before their women, or "rise up . . . and assert their manhood and independence."[48]

Many rose up. The Louisville and Nashville Railroad carried thousands on special trains to the meeting in Guthrie, overwhelming the village with a crowd five times its normal population of about a thousand. Local restaurants, hotels, and liveries could not begin to handle the throng. Man and beast went hungry. Farmers filled every seat at the amphitheater at the fairgrounds. Onlookers lined the rafters, their legs dangling over the heads of the crowd. Worn and impoverished tenant farmers mixed with well-dressed planters and businessmen. Tobacco buyers circulated through the crowds, arguing that tobacco sold for what it was worth, but farmers paid no heed. Anger and resentment at the tobacco companies had

A rally of Association farmers in Princeton, Kentucky. Photo from *Hampton's Magazine* 22 (March 1909): 344.

reached a fever pitch: "They are mad with the trust, and they are going to down it," the Nashville *Banner* reported. "They feel . . . that their rights are being trampled upon." A variety of politicians made fiery speeches and "Cactus" himself appeared to propose a plan for organization that the audience promptly adopted.[49]

Ewing envisioned a "strike" by farmers against the tobacco companies. Although farmers would continue to work, those agreeing to join the Planters' Protective Association (PPA) pledged to deliver their tobacco crop to the organization rather than to tobacco buyers. The Association would hold the tobacco off the market until tobacco companies had no choice but to buy at the price the farmers established. For such a plan to be successful, farmers had to unite. Recruits promised not to sell their tobacco themselves, signing a contract making the PPA their sole bargaining agent. Handing their tobacco over to the Association, farmers surrendered all control. Association members in each county would elect county chairmen and district chairmen. Ewing, though, intended for these local representatives to be mere functionaries, without real power or influence. He proposed to focus power at the top of the Association, in an "Executive Committee" under his own control. "Each member realizes that without a united front and willing obedience

Association organizers (1) Felix Ewing, (2) Joel Fort, and (3) Congressman
Ollie James called on farmers to organize. Photo from *Hampton's Magazine*
22 (March 1909): 345.

to the actions of the Executive Committee no good can be accomplished," the *Leaf-Chronicle* reported.[50]

Despite the enthusiasm, farmers would find it difficult to unite as Ewing envisioned. Joining the Association meant a grower could not sell his crop until the tobacco companies agreed to pay the price set by the PPA. No one knew how long that would be. Almost all the income of poorer growers and their families, like Fort's "women in rags," came from the sale of tobacco. How could they join an organization that would delay their income for an extended time? Somehow, they had to get paid for their crop. "Money," the Clarksville *Leaf-Chronicle* decided, "is the thing wanted to make this movement a great success."[51]

Black Patch businesses supplied the necessary money, joining farmers in their crusade against the tobacco trust. Aside from solving the money problem, this amounted to an unprecedented union of town and farm against a common enemy. It shows that support for Ewing's Planters' Protective Association reached into every corner of the Black Patch.

Thirty-seven banks agreed to furnish money to sharecroppers and renters when they stored their tobacco in Association warehouses as collateral. Newspapers published the names of cooperating banks and bank officers providing cash to Association members.[52] Charles Fort noted in his diary that the Bank of Adams had agreed to advance three to four dollars per hundred pounds of tobacco to farmers with crops in Association warehouses. This was not surplus money. Bank directors borrowed $10,000 for loans to Association farmers. Banks in other towns supported the Association in the same way.[53]

This arrangement between farmers and bankers was the essence of Ewing's organization. Without the bank loans there would have been no organization. There were too many small tobacco growers for Ewing and other larger planters to ignore if they were to effect anything like a successful blockade of tobacco going to buyers. Since the small growers were in no position to give up their tobacco income even briefly, the advances were crucial in persuading them to join the Association. Banks lent money almost exclusively to smaller planters. In Todd County growers who received money from the Elkton bank grew an average of 1,440 pounds of tobacco, the production of less than two acres.[54]

Tobacco handlers also provided financial support for the Association. Lewis Ladd of the Clarksville tobacco firm of Warfield and Ladd claimed later that the firm enthusiastically "took up its cause, staked everything they had and every dollar they could raise and worked night and day for sixteen months, advancing nearly $400,000" to Association growers.[55]

The banks' requirement that the tobacco be centrally stored before they would advance money to growers served Ewing's interests perfectly.[56] By requiring that farmers physically hand over their tobacco to Association warehouses, where it was tightly pressed into hogsheads, Ewing gained a more secure grip on Black Patch tobacco than if he had depended on mere promises and pledges. Moreover, by packing its own tobacco, the Association gained control over grading and pricing. Farmer Robert Holt's neighborhood outside Port Royal in eastern Montgomery County was typical of the Association's operation. Association farmers delivered their loose tobacco to H. W. Bennett. Bennett prized it into hogsheads in a long barn just below his house before shipping it to the Association warehouse in Clarksville. The Association advanced money to farmers, "settling up" when the Association salesmen sold the hogsheads.[57]

As its founders hoped, the PPA attracted all sorts of farmers, from planters to sharecroppers. But not all farmers joined.[58] The organization held a special allure for farmers who considered themselves enlightened. One Association supporter signed his letters to the *Farmers' Home Journal,* "An Up to Date Farmer."[59] Farmers knew Christian County Association leader and PPA general counsel William T. Fowler as a progressive farmer who promoted pure-bred Jerseys in the area. He encouraged farmers' organizations so enthusiastically that the local newspaper called him "The Father of Farmers' Clubs," and he secured the first county agricultural agent in Christian County. President of the Christian County Crop Improvement Association, Fowler is still remembered as favoring "anything he thought would improve the community or the nation."[60]

These enlightened men were convinced that curtailing tobacco production would solve many of the problems faced by the growers. They also knew that tobacco growers were reluctant to reduce their crops. When the Association produced a scale urging farmers to limit their tobacco acreage according to their total acreage, the idea proved so unpopular that Ewing dropped it. Instead, Ewing learned that he could always win applause from audiences by ridiculing those who blamed the low price of tobacco on overproduction. Farmers preferred to blame low prices on price fixing by the tobacco trust.

While the Association merged businessmen, planters, and small growers, the planters predominated. Ewing reserved leadership roles in the Association to a few large planters and kept most authority in his own hands. Called "Pa" by his followers, Ewing served as general manager while Charles Fort acted as president.[61] Together they dominated the executive committee that controlled the PPA.

Lesser elites dominated the leadership of the Planters' Protective Association in counties and districts. The two most important leaders in Christian County, Kentucky, were sons of antebellum planters. William Whitfield Radford was a large tobacco producer himself and the son and grandson of leading tobacco producers. His grandfather produced 31,000 pounds of tobacco in 1850 on his 570-acre farm; in 1860 his father held thirteen slaves. The other leading Association man in Christian County, John Clardy, was also descended from Christian County's slaveowning aristocracy. His father held eighteen slaves at his death in 1855. Clardy, owner of large tracts of land, had been a candidate for governor, a member of the Constitutional Convention in 1890, and a Grand Master in the Grange. Planters made up the top leadership of the Christian County PPA.[62] This pattern is also clear in the other Pennyroyal counties. In Robertson County, Tennessee, John W. Dunn, a doctor and former Alliance activist, served as chairman. In 1904 he owned 577 acres valued at $4,700. J. B. Jackson, Sr., Logan County chairman and one of the largest tobacco growers in his county, produced 25,000 pounds of tobacco in 1892. Only eleven men in Logan County grew more tobacco than Jackson did that year. The Montgomery County chairman, Polk Prince, was also a large planter. Prince told an interviewer in 1905 that he owned 500 acres and produced 40,000 pounds of tobacco a year.[63]

A diverse group filled the lower ranks. A survey of the Association chairmen in outlying counties reveals that most held acreage larger than their county averages. Some of these district chairmen, like J. D. Guier in Trigg County, J. W. Long in Robertson County, K. E. Speight in Henry County, and R. E. Thomas in Stewart County, owned farms of planter proportions.[64] A notable exception was Edward P. Martin, chairman of Stewart County, Tennessee. But Martin was hardly a pauper. Perhaps the only merchant serving as chairman, he sold off at least five different tracts in the years before 1900.[65] Despite the planter leadership, a list of one hundred rank-and-file Association members in Trigg County, compiled in 1905, reveals PPA members to have been a diverse group. In addition to the eighty-three farmers on the list, there were five merchants, a lawyer, a surveyor, two men who described themselves as "landlords," and a carpenter. An alliance had been forged between farm and town.[66]

This planter-led alliance between farm and town challenged an enemy more powerful than that confronted by previous farm organizers. While the cotton farmers in the old Farmers' Alliance had battled scattered furnishing merchants and bankers, Ewing led farmers into a war with powerful monopolies. Cotton was sold in many international markets; the dark tobacco grown in the Black Patch had only a handful of customers.

Such a fight required the Association to call out every resource, including the region's strong religious tradition reaching back to the 1800 Great Revival, which began in the Black Patch before spreading across the South.[67] Previous farmer organizations had used the trappings of religion to promote their own cause, and the Farmers' Alliance was thought by some to have been a "quasi-religious organization." Protectors of the status quo, Alliance and

Wheel organizations had investigated the conduct of their members in much the same way churches did. The Planters' Protective Association also took on many of the trappings of a religious order in keeping with the mood of the times, wherein throughout the South people organized to defend conservative values. The Masons enjoyed a revival. Cult-like men's Bible classes and prohibition clubs sprang up. Like these organizations that wanted every last member of their communities to join, Ewing's tobacco association exerted compelling forms of pressure. In an area where religious values were so deeply felt, Ewing had to tap the traditional social processes of Protestantism to unify town and country. Newspapers hailed Ewing as the "Moses of the Black Patch." He was leading "the children of toil out of the wilderness." Association meetings sometimes took on the appearance of religious services, complete with "sermons" and the penitent begging forgiveness.[68]

The use of such traditional religious forms suggests a deeply conservative, even reactionary organization filled with farmers rejecting progress. Actually, most of the farmers joining the Planters' Protective Association had two goals. They wanted to participate in the modern tobacco market fairly and effectively, and to retain the traditional community values they associated with farming. But the leader of the Planters' Protective Association had little interest in preserving the traditional virtues of rural life. Ewing's plan to centralize control of the Black Patch tobacco crop in his own hands was alien to traditional Black Patch society. Ewing spoke the language of modern industry. He saw himself as a modern man, leading backward farmers into the twentieth century. His use of traditional forms of community life, like church ritual, was merely a cloak for his true design.

By 1905 Ewing had taken great strides toward his goal. Ten thousand farmers pledged their crops to the Association.[69] At Association rallies, farmers celebrated their solidarity and pledged their undying loyalty to the organization. But Ewing feared it would not be enough. He knew the trust was a behemoth with power beyond their imagination. To challenge such an enemy, they needed help from the federal government.

For Black Patchers, the Civil War had generated a special aversion to the federal government. Thus their decision to ask federal authorities for help is especially striking. It shows that they were not as determined to resist centralized authority at all costs as historians often find when they study the reaction of rural communities to industrialization. At least by 1900 many in the Black Patch understood that tobacco companies had to be controlled by the federal government. They needed federal intervention in their lives. Black Patchers' rationale for violence begins with the federal government's rejection of their appeals for help, forcing them to turn to their own resources.

Planters' decision to seek federal help flew in the face of the Black Patch's long history of hostility to the federal government—a hostility intensified by a Civil War experience with centralized power Black Patchers regarded as hellish. In fact, at the beginning of the twentieth century most Americans still had the traditionally restrictive view of federal power.[1] Like most other Americans, residents of the Black Patch had little experience with the federal government before the Civil War. For most antebellum Americans, government meant the local constable or sheriff, and even the constable and the sheriff exercised authority only very lightly. Individuals enjoyed considerable autonomy. Few could even conceive of the federal government's exercising power in their daily lives. But the Civil War changed all that.[2] The Black Patch, where slavery was firmly entrenched and the Confederacy popular, was one of the first areas in the United States where ordinary citizens directly felt the awesome power of the federal government.[3] The Black Patch's Tennessee and Cumberland rivers formed a natural avenue for armies bent on invading the Deep South, a fact not lost on Ulysses S. Grant. He mounted a joint naval-land expedition that pushed deep into the Black Patch, attacking Confederate forts Henry and Donelson early in 1862.[4]

The occupying force Grant left behind expected to regulate the lives of local residents, supplanting the authority of state and local government. But the Union army never subdued the Black Patch. Residents waged a savage guerrilla war. Marauding rebels infested the countryside, harassing loyalists.[5] Although Union officials stationed deputy provost marshals in every major town, most did not dare remain at their posts—guerrillas murdered at least one who did.[6] In 1864 a Union officer reported that it was unsafe to station army recruiters in any part of the Black Patch except at Paducah,[7] and even at that strongpoint, Unionists feared they might not be able to hold their position in a district "swarming" with guerrillas.[8] Local gangs of rebels skirmished with Union troops throughout the war. As late as April 1865, a Union naval officer battled a band of 150 to 200 armed Confederates in Lyon County.[9]

For their part, local residents accused federal officials of instituting a "reign of terror." Federal occupiers trampled on the Black Patch's tradition of dispersed authority by imposing harsh taxes by fiat and seizing the property of rebellious residents. Local residents charged that Northern troops arrested and shot local residents without trial. In one such incident U.S. soldiers angered residents of Mayfield when they executed a seventeen-year-old schoolboy for espionage. His family erected a monument over his grave inscribed "shot by order of the Federal tyrant."[10]

For many, the most egregious exercise of centralized power came when Union officials deliberately challenged local white supremacy. Black Patchers reacted with extraordinary anger when federal authorities stationed black troops in the Black Patch and set up recruiting stations to raise "colored" troops. In Mayfield, Union officials impressed local whites into labor battalions supervised by black troops. This last really rankled. In 1948 a Mayfield historian considered this incident to have been worse than the execution of the schoolboy.[11]

A de facto civil war continued in the Black Patch for at least three years after 1865. In many parts of the Black Patch, the Confederate flag waved proudly at public gatherings well after the end of the war. Returning Confederate soldiers retained their arms and traveled around the Black Patch in bands, intimidating returned federal soldiers. Some Unionists feared for their lives and hid in the woods.[12] Elsewhere in the South planters formed alliances with Freedmen's Bureau officers, but in the Black Patch former slave owners continued to treat freed blacks as chattel, resisting the authority of the Freedmen's Bureau. Black Patch courts emerged as a tool wielded by ex-Confederates against their enemies and against emancipation. Local lawmen hunted down and indicted Union men in local courts.[13] Blacks fared even worse in Black Patch courts as white juries were "ever ready to 'damn a nigger.'"[14]

Whites openly stated that their purpose was to make blacks "know their places."[15] Blacks who knew their places did not go to school or worship in separate churches. In Princeton, local whites refused to sell land for a black school or church. The only school was run by an old, crippled black man in his own house, described by Freedmen's Bureau agents as a "miserable delapidated [sic] old shanty." In many parts of the Black Patch, whites prevented blacks from starting a school at all,[16] forcing them to hold religious services in open fields. Armed and masked bands cowed freed blacks from one end of the Black Patch to the other.[17] This violence was racial, but not just racial. By abusing blacks, Black Patchers paraded their disdain for the federal government as well.

But even as local elites disdained federal authority, they petitioned state and federal government for favors. Taxes imposed by Union forces quickly taught Black Patch residents to appeal to government for relief. In 1868 one Black Patcher wrote his state senator, "I think the Legislator could Shureley do Something for the people which would be greatly appreciated by the people any action for the benefit of the people while in distress would never be forgot."[18]

The Civil War also shook—at least for a time—Black Patchers' faith that their local traditions took precedence over national concerns. In 1880 the Kentucky Court of Appeals declared unconstitutional Kentucky's law disqualifying blacks from service on juries. The Kentucky justices explained that they had little choice, because the United States Supreme Court had struck down West Virginia's exclusion of blacks from jury service.[19] Although the Kentucky legislature did not strike the word "white" from statutory qualifications for jurymen for two more years, one Black Patch court immediately ordered the sheriff to dismiss the jurors already selected and empanel new jurors including both blacks and whites. This change proved temporary, but a Black Patch court had recorded an unprecedented recognition of its subordinate position in the federal system.[20]

The outrage, anger, and hatred the "federal tyrant" unleashed in the Civil War had abated by the last years of the nineteenth century. Residents of the Black Patch changed their attitude toward the federal government enough to call on Washington for help in fighting the tobacco trust. All across the South thoughtful ex-Confederates recognized that emancipation had created a new nation-state which subsumed regional elites. Planter elites may have retained their land and local influence, but they recognized that they now had to operate in a new order.[21] Black Patchers called on federal authorities first to eliminate the onerous tax on tobacco, which Congress had first levied in 1872. The tax law benefited big business by keeping small operators out of the market in two ways. First, it required the sellers of tobacco to buy a dealer's license and put up a $5,000 bond. Large corporations could easily post such a bond whereas growers could not, so the effect of the law was to make illegal any direct trade between farmers and consumers. Few farmers dared violate the law, as Congress had empowered any revenue officer to seize the "horse or mule, wagon, and contents, or pack, bundle, or basket" of any peddler refusing to display a certificate proving he had paid the bond.[22] Second, the law required any manufacturer of tobacco, no matter how small, to pay taxes on products sold. So a farmer who twisted a tobacco leaf for sale to his neighbor had to pay the same tax demanded of the American Tobacco Company. The tax not only kept farmers out of the market; it also prevented regional warehousemen from turning to manufacturing and challenging the American Tobacco Company. Black Patchers petitioned Congress to no avail. The bond and tax remained in force.[23]

Farmers next sought to persuade government prosecutors to prosecute the tobacco trust as an unlawful restraint of trade. From the farmers' perspective, the tobacco trust brazenly oppressed tobacco growers; it scarcely hid its corruption. It violated traditional principles of free enterprise enshrined in both Kentucky's antitrust act and the federal Sherman Anti-Trust Act.

Many states had successfully regulated big business in the nineteenth century, but in the Black Patch Tennessee and Kentucky could do little against corporate power. Kentucky's highest court ruled against corporations for price fixing and illegal pooling—but only against those businesses foolish enough to carry out their nefarious activities by written contract.[24] Moreover, the South's characteristic localism was unusually well entrenched in the Black Patch. In Kentucky citizens actually legislated localism into the structure of the government. As Robert Ireland has shown, Kentucky fashioned a county-centered government of "little kingdoms" and created more counties per capita than any other state in the union.[25] Kentuckians expected their counties—not the state—to enforce their laws and enact their reforms. In the 1890–91 Constitutional Convention delegates hoping to make it easier for every county attorney to sue or indict trusts considered requiring all corporations doing business in Kentucky to maintain an office in every county where they did business. This measure failed to make it into Kentucky's constitution, so lawmakers made it a statute.[26]

But they neglected state authority at the expense of local power. While every county had two prosecutors, the county attorney and the district commonwealth attorney, the governor of Kentucky could not employ a single lawyer to prosecute any offense against the Commonwealth. The attorney general and his assistants could not interfere with or initiate any such prosecutions. Kentuckians ordered themselves through 152 elected prosecutors serving in 119 counties and 33 judicial districts. To win a prosecution against a business combination, these prosecutors had to prove an illegal action within their jurisdiction. A price fixing scheme hatched in New York lay beyond the reach of Kentucky prosecutors. These many scattered lawyers were ill-equipped to deal with powerful corporations.[27]

Thus, Black Patchers had little choice but to turn to the federal government. There is no evidence they even considered asking for state help. The federal government's reaction would be a test of the legitimacy of federal authority and indeed the new industrial order. If the federal authorities would not regulate such a conspiracy, then big business had hopelessly corrupted the federal government. If the government could not, Black Patchers could fall back on a long tradition of vigilantism and community violence to enforce local norms.

In 1904, they demanded a federal investigation of Black Patch tobacco buying, calling on Black Patch congressman John Wesley Gaines for help. Gaines, a Democrat, pressed the Justice Department to investigate the tobacco trust but found he could not budge Attorney General Philander Knox. So, the leadership of the Planters' Protective Association went to Washington. On December 5, 1904, Felix Ewing visited Knox.[28] In contrast to Gaines, Ewing succeeded in persuading Knox to act, and the attorney general ordered the United States attorney for Middle Tennessee, Abraham Tillman, to investigate. Tillman toured the Black Patch and issued a report about three months later verifying Gaines and Ewing's allegations that tobacco companies had eliminated competition. But he made it clear that he did not want to engage in an onerous struggle with the trust in court. "I understand that it is not expected or desired that I should give this matter attention to the neglect of regular official duties," he wrote Knox.[29]

But if Tillman and Knox remained unimpressed by the evidence against the tobacco trust, another Justice Department lawyer took the situation more seriously. Tennessean and future conservative

Supreme Court justice James C. McReynolds agreed with Tillman that the problems in the Black Patch resulted from tobacco-trust lawbreaking. But unlike Knox he wanted to take action against the trust and emerged as the chief advocate of legal action against the American Tobacco Company within the administration.[30] Despite his efforts, the Justice Department chose to ignore farmers' grievances.

The government's decision to disregard farmers' complaints against the tobacco buyers convinced farmers that they stood alone against a powerful enemy. "There is no hope from law or Congress," a Clarksville *Leaf-Chronicle* correspondent wailed. In the absence of government action, "farmers must rise in their own might." The newspaper editorialized, "The Black Patch is the only trust buster . . . in the world. Trusts may buy up Congress and men in power."[31]

Even without direct federal intervention on their behalf, tobacco farmers could resist the tobacco trust only through their own protective association. Like business, they had organized, concentrating their power. The success or failure of the Planters' Protective Association in forcing the Regie and other buyers to improve their prices would be another test of the legitimacy of the postbellum economic system and federal law.

In the fall of 1905 it seemed that there would be no provocation by the Regie and tensions would subside. Joseph Ferigo approached the Association through Ed Tandy, W. G. Dunnington and Company's supervisor for the Black Patch. Association leaders told Tandy that the farmers wanted six dollars per hundred pounds for the cheapest grades of tobacco and eleven dollars per hundred for the best grades. The Association had already sold 7,500 hogsheads of tobacco to France and Bremen for the prices given to Tandy; 15,500 hogsheads remained unsold.[32] Early in September, top officials of the Italian Regie checked into the Hotel Latham in Hopkinsville. As Joseph Ferigo, W. G. Dunnington, E. R. Tandy of Clarksville, William McMurray of Springfield, and W. C. White of Cadiz strode across the Latham's lobby, Felix Ewing and Association salesmen also arrived in town. Rumors of a deal raced through both Hopkinsville and Clarksville.[33]

The first news coming out of the negotiations was quite good: Ferigo had agreed to the Association's schedule of prices. But after looking at a lot of tobacco samples and throwing out those that did not seem suitable for the Italian markets, Ferigo graded all the remainder second and third class. The Italian told Ewing the Association farmers had grown no first-quality tobacco at all! Naturally Ferigo and Ewing arrived at radically different prices, even though both computed their average prices from the same scale, six dollars for the lowest and eleven dollars for the best quality tobacco. The difference was in the grading. Ferigo classed the tobacco lower than Association inspectors. "I cannot class the tobacco in a different way from which I have been instructed to do by my Government," Ferigo told Ewing. "The classification does not change to please the seller, but is made according to general rules." The difference between the two prices was so great that Ferigo decided to advance his price immediately to the maximum. He offered the Association an average of eight dollars per hundred pounds, but the Association wanted an average price of $9.50.

Unable to reach agreement on the 1904 crop, Ferigo suggested that they negotiate the price for the 1905 crop. "It seems to me," Ferigo said, "that as we are willing to pay decent prices to the farmer, why not let the Association sell the tobacco in a loose state to our buyers, provided we can agree on the price?" Ferigo hoped to bypass Association inspectors entirely. By buying tobacco loose, not packed in hogsheads, Ferigo meant that the buyers would visit farmers' barns and buy directly from growers. The buyers would determine the grades, not Association inspectors. This would, in effect, maintain the trust-dominated system. Instead of negotiating prices, the buyer and the farmer would negotiate the grade, with the buyer still in the dominant position. The grades would determine the price.

Of course, Ewing rejected Ferigo's offer, which challenged the most fundamental tenet of cooperative marketing. Black Patch farmers had banded together to maximize their power at the market place; they knew they exerted much more power together than separately. Ewing told Ferigo that he would not sell Association tobacco loose to anyone and the Italians would have to buy their Black Patch tobacco in one large lot, not from individual farmers.

Ferigo responded by demanding the right to choose the tobacco he wanted from what Association farmers produced. "I do not see how you can compel the Italian Government to buy all the Italian tobacco handled by your Association, when you allow all the other buyers, including the French and Bremen buyers to buy only what they require. It looks to me that simply is a discrimination of your Association against the Italian Government," he said. Ewing re-

torted that the Planters' Protective Association did not discrimi-
nate. "We want to raise just as much tobacco as is required to
supply the demand and not any more, and in order to do that we
have to follow this course. Of course, we agreed to let the French
buyer have what he wanted but that was only a matter purely of
convenience."

With that, the negotiations broke off. Ferigo told his men to instruct their buyers to seek out tobacco not pledged to the Association, offering prices higher than he had just offered Ewing. This was
not an attempt to break the Association, Ferigo insisted. "We were
compelled to consider the Association tobacco out of the market,"
he explained later, "and having less tobacco by which to supply our
demand we were compelled to pay higher prices for the tobacco
that was held by the independents in order to make ourselves independent." But everyone understood what the consequences would
be if he were successful. To the farmers in the Association it was
clear that Ferigo planned to destroy the organization.

The newspapers portrayed the situation in the best light possible. The Clarksville *Leaf-Chronicle* headlined, "Selling Tobacco! Selling Tobacco! And the Boys Are All Jolly, Scrambling for Who Shall
be First Served." It described Association exchange rooms as busy
despite Ferigo's rejection of Association tobacco in favor of "hill
billy" tobacco. "This [Association] tobacco is going to be sold," the
Leaf-Chronicle assured its readers, "because the market is short
and the demand is calling for every pound of it. Farmers will just
have to be patient."[34]

Ferigo left the negotiations determined to destroy the Association. Approaching other tobacco buyers after he left Hopkinsville,
the Italian proposed that they agree not to buy tobacco from the
PPA for two months. That would be long enough, Ferigo believed, to
put the Association out of business. Word of Ferigo's proposal got
back to the Association. Infuriated, they contacted the newly created federal Bureau of Corporations.[35]

Congress had created the Bureau of Corporations, headed by a
commissioner of corporations, in 1903 in an amendment to the bill
establishing the Department of Commerce and Labor. Although it
was authorized to make a "diligent investigation into the organization, conduct, and management of the business of any corporation," many businessmen looked favorably upon their new watch-
dog.[36] The Bureau had no police powers, operating merely as a
publicity office, punishing "bad" corporations with negative pub-

licity. Moreover, it favored the same looser, common-law interpretation of the Sherman Anti-Trust Act that business favored. This interpretation banned only "unreasonable" restraints of trade. From 1897 until 1911 the Supreme Court prohibited *any* restraint of trade.[37]

Corporations also came to see the Bureau as helpful in their occasional fights with the Justice Department. Corporate executives usually did not hesitate to supply the Bureau with whatever information it wanted, in that they knew it was unlikely the information would ever be used against them in court, because defendants cannot be forced to incriminate themselves. If the Bureau did hand the results of its investigations over to the Justice Department, the effect would be to give the company under indictment an "immunity bath"—that is, immunity from prosecution.[38]

The Bureau had already begun an investigation of the tobacco trust. But, like the Justice Department, at first the Bureau of Corporations had little understanding of or interest in farmers' problems with tobacco buyers. In August 1905, Albert C. Muhse, Bureau special agent and chief investigator of the tobacco trust, indicated that the Bureau intended to send agents to the Black Patch.[39] Herbert Knox Smith, the commissioner of corporations, discouraged Muhse from directing his agents to speak to the farmers themselves about their grievances. Smith instructed that the investigation should instead be directed at determining the cost of production of the manufactured product and the methods used by the trust to buy tobacco.[40] Muhse agreed with Smith. "What information we will obtain there [in Kentucky and Tennessee] must come from the packers and manufacturers rather than the farmers," he told the commissioner.[41]

The Association's protest following the collapse of negotiations with the Italians changed the Bureau's investigative strategy. The Bureau dispatched Special Agent Thomas P. Littlepage to Tennessee to interview farmers. Thirty-two years old, Littlepage was a native of Indiana who had worked as a schoolteacher until 1900, and then as an employee of the Census Bureau. He joined the Bureau of Corporations after receiving his master's degree from Columbia University. When Littlepage arrived in Clarksville over one hundred farmers and businessmen came to his hotel offering to help with his investigation. In the weeks that followed, Littlepage continued each day to receive ten to twenty-five visitors, each offering information and cooperation. The Clarksville Chamber of Commerce supplied him with an office, and his presence at a Planters' Protective Association meeting prompted a resolution thanking President Theodore Roosevelt and Commissioner Herbert Knox Smith for looking into the tobacco controversy.[42]

Charged with discovering proof of an illegal combination by the American Tobacco Company and Regie buyers, Littlepage traveled the dirt roads of Montgomery, Robertson, and Todd counties, interviewing farmers and other tobacco men. "You have no idea in work of this kind," he wrote, "how much sifting and work it takes to get real information and statistics of any value. If I could begin at 8 AM and would work until 6:30 PM each day I could only interview two farmers and ask them all the required questions."[43]

Littlepage's evidence substantiated claims of wrongdoing by the tobacco companies. In fact, the special agent discovered more illegal activities than farmers knew about—kickbacks and discrimination against black tobacco growers. W. H. Simmons of the tobacco firm of Couts, Simmons, and Company alleged a price-fixing agreement existed between the British Imperial representative in the Black Patch and the Italian Regie. Former buyers admitted buying millions of pounds of tobacco below the cost of production because the Regie had eliminated competition. One guilt-ridden buyer confessed that his company's policies deprived farmers' children of enough clothing to wear to school.[44] Luther Graham of Z. C. Graham and Company told Littlepage that he had been forced to pay a 20 percent kickback on tobacco delivered during the two years he worked for the Regie. Black farmers had proof they received a lower price than that received by white farmers.[45]

Littlepage warned his superiors that tobacco growers might turn to violence if their grievances were not addressed. On his arrival in Clarksville in October 1905, Littlepage found the sentiment against the Regie and the tobacco trust to be "almost revolutionary."[46] At the end of the month, Littlepage wrote that the attitude of farmers was still "very dangerous." He had heard of a "vigilance committee" being formed in each district to burn Regie warehouses and that some farmers openly threatened to shoot Regie buyers on their property.[47] On November 12, Littlepage reported that feeling against tobacco buyers was becoming more intense every day. "It is predicted that unless the Regie and the Association come to some agreement very soon that a reign of lawlessness will envelope eight or ten counties and result in great destruction of property."[48]

Clerks in the Bureau filed Littlepage's warnings. Determined not to interfere in matters they felt belonged in the provenance of the states, Bureau officials did nothing. Littlepage was ordered to drop his inquiry. Black Patchers had learned to swallow their hatred for federal power to ask for help. In doing so they learned a new and bitter lesson. The powerful federal government, apparently so eager to regulate their lives in detail during the Civil War and after, would not insure basic economic fairness in the Black Patch—even though Washington's own agents warned of violence if the government remained idle. Planters still faced the enormous power of the tobacco trust; now they knew they had to face it without the help of the national government.

In formulating a strategy to make their organization work, Association leaders demonstrated again the ambiguity of the Black Patch's relationship with nationalizing forces. To engineer a new regional organization and centralize control of Black Patch tobacco, Ewing would rely on community rhetoric—language designed to isolate his enemies. He would use traditional means to accomplish a progressive end. But in a divided landscape like the Black Patch, he ran the risk of inciting bloodshed.

In 1906 Ewing and his fellow planters had good reason to believe such a strategy would work. Despite their failure to enlist the aid of the federal government, Black Patch planters could take some satisfaction in the success of the PPA. At the start of 1906 the Association boasted nearly seventeen thousand members and holdings of thirty-five thousand hogsheads or 55 million pounds of tobacco. Association leaders claimed to be masters of the Black Patch tobacco crop. At least half the crop remained outside the Association, but the trend lines were all moving in the right direction. Farmers had pledged 39 million pounds in 1904, 55 million in 1905, 61 million in 1906, and 95 million in 1907. As early as 1905 some Association leaders claimed to be in control of the crop in some corners of the Black Patch. In Tennessee the chairman of the Montgomery County Association declared that "everything is going our way. We are masters of the situation." A district chairman described his district as "nearly solid" with only three farmers refusing to join.[1] In the fall Association members celebrated their success with a large rally. Congressmen from both Kentucky and Tennessee made speeches and, as the *Black Patch Journal* later recorded, farmers toasted Ewing for organizing "the greatest farmers' organization the world has ever known."[2]

But the Association faced the danger that its success might not be enough. There were questions about the legality of a "trust" of farmers under the Sherman Anti-Trust Act. And not all farmers joined the organization. If enough stayed out, they would destroy the whole carefully constructed arrangement. Ewing and the planters backing him hoped his farmers' trust would compete on equal terms with business. He hoped to lead farmers into the organizational culture of the twentieth century. But to do so he would have to appeal to Black Patch traditionalists, farmers resistant to modernization. To appeal to such men Ewing would rely on traditional forms of rhetoric, calling upon their patriotism and sense of community. Ewing risked violence with such an appeal: Black Patch

patriotism and communalism had a long association with the region's violent tradition of vigilantism. Ewing took the risk without
hesitation, apparently confident he could control the situation.

The law represented an obstacle to Ewing's plans for a farmers'
trust. Courts consistently ruled against farmers' cooperatives, declaring that they illegally restrained trade. At the end of the nineteenth century Tennessee and ten other states enacted antitrust
laws that exempted farmer organizations from prosecution. But
these exceptions did not stand judicial scrutiny. Courts ruled that
such special privileges for farmers denied nonfarmers constitutionally required equal protection. The Sherman Anti-Trust Act provided no exceptions for farmers' organizations. Senator John Sherman had assured his fellows that the proposed legislation would in
no way interfere with agricultural cooperatives. "To avoid any con-
fusion," he proposed an amendment exempting agricultural associations from prosecution. But when the bill emerged from the Judiciary Committee, it had no such protection for farmers. The fact
that senators considered and rejected such an exemption indicates Congress intended no exceptions to its provisions against
restraints of trade.[3]

Federal courts remained uncertain what business tactics constituted illegal restraints of trade, but they had little difficulty agreeing that strikes, boycotts, and other actions by producers constituted violations of the Sherman Anti-Trust Act.[4] Yet, although
Ewing clearly violated the Sherman Anti-Trust Act, the tobacco
companies never challenged him in court, in part because they
were unable to enlist the aid of the government in bringing the
Planters' Protective Association to court. Politically sensitive prosecutors probably were reluctant to incur the wrath of thousands of
voting tobacco growers and millions of farmers. But the Sherman
Act provided that "any person who shall be injured in his business
or property" as a consequence of acts forbidden by the law "may
sue therefore in any circuit court of the United States . . . and shall
recover threefold the damages."[5] Nonetheless, the trust never took
Ewing and his organization to court. The Italian government probably doubted its ability to get a fair hearing from a jury composed of
Americans in a suit against U.S. citizens. Furthermore, statements
by the Italian ambassador suggest that the Italians only imperfectly
understood U.S. laws.

Popular opinion persuaded the American Tobacco Company not
to pursue the Association in court. Corporations generally fared

poorly in Black Patch courts. In 1884 a Black Patch jury amazed one witness in a suit against a railroad by awarding $500 to the plaintiff because he missed a train that stopped past the platform and would not back up for him to get on. This was $475 more than the defendant's own estimate of the value of his lost time. "Prejudice against a corporation had much to do with the verdict," the witness concluded.[6] Grand juries in Caldwell County so frequently indicted large insurance companies that local businesses, inconvenienced by their inability to obtain insurance, pleaded with them to stop. Their petition led to a summons from an angry judge, demanding why he should not hold them in contempt. When Kentucky's Court of Appeals ruled farmers' associations and pooling arrangements constitutional, the justices demonstrated their hostility to big business by adopting wholesale the language of farmer advocates like Felix Ewing.[7] When Justice Department prosecutors did win a Sherman-Act criminal conviction of burley tobacco Night Riders, popular outrage forced President Woodrow Wilson to commute their fines.[8] Public opinion was far more sympathetic to the victims of business than to the corporate monopolizers.

In 1913 a Union County prosecutor won a conviction of the Imperial Tobacco Company under Kentucky's antitrust law despite an amazingly weak case. Had the Kentucky Court of Appeals allowed this conviction to stand, the Imperial would have lost its Kentucky charter of incorporation. The verdict threatened to put the primary customer for tobacco grown in the Henderson district out of business. Fortunately for Henderson District farmers, the court of appeals reversed the conviction.[9]

In 1905 the tobacco companies were even less popular than the railroad and insurance companies had been earlier. Newspapers all across the Black Patch published articles describing the illegal and immoral schemes tobacco companies hatched to defraud farmers. The low price of tobacco and the arrogant attitude of some tobacco buyers exacerbated anticorporate prejudice. Had the tobacco companies dared challenge the Association in court, no Black Patch jury would have found in their favor.

However, the main reason tobacco companies chose not to attack the Association in court probably was that they had another, more effective strategy in mind. A voluntary association of farmers, the PPA never attracted every tobacco grower in any county in the Black Patch. There were always farmers willing to sell their tobacco outside the Association. The tobacco cartel rushed to reward these farmers, offering high prices in hopes of tempting Association farmers out of the organization. About one-third of the 1904 crop of tobacco in Robertson County sold outside the Association.[10] Those farmers reaped the rewards of high prices. In July 1905, the *Farmers' Home Journal* reported that Association tobacco grown the previous year still sat in warehouses, awaiting sale.[11]

The high prices farmers outside the Association enjoyed tempted Association farmers. Tobacco buyers encouraged Association farmers to sell out. Two buyers visited a Robertson County farmer, for example. He told them he had already pledged his crop to the Association and could not sell it. But the buyers persisted. They offered 2, 6, and 9 cents per hundred pounds for the three grades of tobacco the farmer had grown. Then they boosted their offer to 2, 7, and 9 cents. It would cost him $1.50 per hundred pounds in fees to sell in the Association, the buyers pointed out, and even then the farmer would have to wait a year for his money.[12] Tobacco buyers scoured the country looking for farmers willing to sell. A Davidson County buyer announced he was "not trying to tare [*sic*] down the Association but was after tobacco in the Association or out of it."[13] Tobacco buyers probed the ranks of Association farmers, testing their loyalty, feeling for weak spots.

Organizations like the Planters' Protective Association live or die on the twisting currents of the public mood. When one is perceived as rising in popularity, pressure builds on recalcitrants to join the organization, and it thrives. But when it is perceived as slipping or declining, pressure builds on members to desert the organization, and it withers. Association leaders relied on friendly newspapers to shape the public's perception of events to their advantage. At the end of 1904 the Hopkinsville *Kentuckian* published a list of farmers who had refused to join the Association and who were selling their tobacco at improved prices. The *Kentuckian* promised that in the long run Association farmers would do even better. "If these outsiders are benefited to this extent," the newspaper reasoned, "those who go into the organization and help to make it a success may expect to get still more."[14] It was not an argument persuasive to Association farmers with empty pockets, who saw their non-Association neighbors reaping higher profits resulting from the Association's boycott. The Clarksville *Leaf-Chronicle* advised Association farmers, "Be patient. The Lord blesses those who bear burdens, and wait for his Glory."[15]

Association leaders urged farmers to ostracize their neighbors who refused to pledge their tobacco. Writing in the *Farmers' Home Journal,* "An Up to Date Farmer" declared that anyone unwilling to join the organization "should be drummed out of the country."[16] A writer for the Clarksville *Leaf-Chronicle* applauded an Association farmer who refused to lend a nonmember neighbor surplus tobacco plants for transplanting. Neighbors had traditionally shared the surplus plants from their plant beds, it was true, but now Association men should not do business with non-Association men. "The example of my friend with the tobacco plants, refusing his hillbilly neighbor is mild, compared to what will have to be done to make a clean sweep of the trust." A tobacco farmer not in the Planters' Protective Association, the *Leaf-Chronicle* declared, is a "dead citizen."[17]

PPA leaders appropriated religious forms, turning Association meetings into something resembling religious services. Not only were wavering members exhorted to remain steadfast, but fallen members confessed their sins and begged forgiveness. "George Stevenson made a statement," the newspaper account of one Association meeting reported, "in regard to the sale of his tobacco out of the Association and said he desired to have the Association forgive him, which was readily done as his statement was open and frank."[18] Ben Hollins confessed, "I realized it was not right, but so many false stories had been told on me that I fretted and sold."[19] "Harvey Collier being present was invited to take the stand and stated [that] he sold two crops because of debt, and felt he must have the money, but he [now] felt he had acted wrong." He asked for forgiveness.[20]

Association leaders minimized the significance of defections. According to PPA propaganda, the ranks of the organization remained firm in the face of trust temptations. In March 1905 Ewing assured a rally in Cadiz, Kentucky, that the PPA was a great success. Of a total of seven thousand members, Ewing claimed, only twenty had broken their contracts with the organization, not enough to justify "the establishment of a law department."[21] But despite Ewing's brave words, the PPA had already established a law department. In the very county where Ewing gave his speech Association lawyers filed suit against farmers who broke their contracts with the Association and sold their own tobacco.[22]

Association propagandists warned that the higher prices tobacco companies brandished were designed not only to lure independent farmers away from the Association, but ultimately into wage slavery. If the trust successfully destroyed the Association, it would ultimately force farmers to sell their tobacco at prices below the cost of production—as they had done in 1903. Farmers selling tobacco below the cost of production would be in debt. A decline in tobacco prices would lead to a decline in the value of land, the Clarksville *Leaf-Chronicle* explained. "Finally those lands must be sold and the trust magnates will be ready purchasers, making sycophants and slaves of the former owners, to be hired cheap to raise tobacco under trust instruction and management."[23] Alternatively, according to PPA propagandists, tobacco companies would absorb tobacco production into the trust itself. Thus the independent farmer would be reduced to a mere wage laborer.[24] Like antebellum Republicans and earlier farm organizers, Association speakers considered a wage laborer to be little more than a slave. Such rhetoric seems to be characteristic of the complaints voiced by the victims of industrial revolution everywhere. Workers in England compared themselves with slaves as manufacturers molded their lives to fit the cogs of their new machines.[25]

But despite the efforts of the Association and its allies to counteract it, the tobacco companies' strategy sometimes worked. Thanks to arrangements Ewing had made with Black Patch banks, Association farmers got some money for their pledged crops. But they all knew that their 1904 crop remained unsold even as the 1905 crop ripened in the barns. Meanwhile, their neighbors who had not joined the Association sold their crop for prices higher than the Association had even asked for.

Ultimately, Ewing appealed for government legislation in support of his organization, but only after his membership plummeted. He could hardly ask lawmakers to make it a crime not to join the Association. In fact, his first task was to legalize Association efforts to sell tobacco as agents of farmers. Holding the crops of large numbers of farmers until tobacco buyers had no choice but to offer a more favorable price might well have been an illegal restraint of trade or criminal conspiracy. Progressive Era courts, after all, regularly found against labor unions for "pooling" the labor of workingmen and holding it off the market until the price of labor improved. There is no evidence that any court ruled against the Association, and after 1906 they could not. The Kentucky legislature legalized the sale of pooled tobacco.[26]

Planters also called on legislators to pass anti-enticement legislation similar to that enacted immediately after the Civil War. With emancipation, planters wondered how they could force their ex-slaves to stay on their plantations. The freedmen signed contracts, but how to enforce such agreements? The answer in Mississippi was a law empowering "every person" to arrest freedmen quitting their employer before the expiration of his or her term of service. Georgia forbade the employment of the servant of another, making it illegal to "entice, persuade, or decoy" another man's servants. Alabama and other states had similar legislation. In Kentucky many ex-masters seized black children and made themselves legal "masters" of these "apprentices." The legislature made it illegal to entice away a master's apprentice.[27]

The anti-enticement laws of the so-called "Black Codes" show the pervasive influence of planters in southern legislatures. That influence was still apparent in the Progressive Era. In 1907 Tennessee lawmakers passed a bill making it illegal for tobacco companies even to try to persuade a farmer to sell his tobacco once he had agreed to sell it through the Association. In 1908 Kentucky passed a similar law. The language of these laws, making it illegal to "induce or persuade" farmers to violate contracts, unmistakably recalls similar laws aimed at ex-slaves.[28]

The situation in the Black Patch invited violence. The PPA had successfully defined nonmembership in their organization as deviance. Members belonged to the Association out of patriotism and community loyalty, and thought cultivators outside the organization acted from greed and selfishness. But the tobacco companies had challenged the PPA's stance, rewarding the very deviants the PPA condemned. In 1905 Black Patchers prepared to undertake the same kind of premodern, community-sanctioned violence Americans had traditionally practiced. While Association leaders sought to participate in a more modern world, their followers believed they were defending the traditional moral economy of their community. They viewed the Association as a tool to defend that traditional way of life. Those outside the organization threatened the existing moral economy.

The anger Association farmers felt toward farmers outside the Association ripened in the fall of 1905 with their tobacco. Ewing fanned the flames of farmers' indignation toward outsiders. When his own neighbor sold his tobacco in violation of his pledge to the Association, Ewing heatedly indicated he had no intention of taking the man to court for breach of contract. "The community," he declared ominously, "in which this man lives can prove a stronger court than any other." Ewing instructed his followers to "no longer extend the hand of fellowship" to the traitor. "Side-track him," Ewing commanded, "do not know him when you see him, and he will be a sufferer indeed."[29] Association leaders published lists of farmers who refused to join the Association. In August some "hill billy" farmers found placards warning them to join the Association nailed on their barns. Association leaders disavowed the signs, suggesting that those responsible were non-Association farmers trying to make the Association look bad.[30]

The first step toward community-sanctioned violence took place in Tennessee, at a school in the northwest corner of Robertson County. Stainback School sat close to the center of Robertson County's 17th Civil District in a gently rolling landscape of rect-angular fields punctured with sink holes and frequently interrupted by patches of woods. From the site of the school Kentucky appears to the north as a hazy blue-green line of trees on the horizon. In late October men gathered at Stainback School. They passed reso-lutions calling for "a committee composed of not less than five nor more than two thousand Association members [to] visit each farmer who is not a member and offer him an opportunity to be-come a member . . . and upon the refusal of said farmer to comply with the request the committee may (without violence) proceed to counsel and instruct said farmer, and further that said committee may wait upon the trust buyers and, without violence, counsel and instruct them as to their future course, the public welfare demand-ing it."[31]

Although signers of the Stainback Resolves had taken the first step toward vigilantism, their actions did not make violence in-evitable. Tobacco companies had violated the Sherman Anti-Trust Act, as had the Planters' Protective Association, but the law the Stainback Resolves asserted was popular law of the sort English workers and American colonists had enforced through mob action. The authors and signers of the Stainback Resolves hoped to intimi-date their enemies into submission. They put Black Patchers out-side the organization on notice that they faced a phalanx of their neighbors.

Most of the thirty-two signers of the Stainback Resolves culti-vated small farms in the 17th Civil District. A few came from neigh-boring civil districts to the south and east of the Red River, but the majority lived in the neighborhood of Stainback School. Most farmed a hundred acres or less and had one tenant, if any at all. For the most part the signers were young men. Although William Clay Riley, fifty, took his seventy-three-year-old father with him to Stainback School, over three-quarters of the Stainback signers were in their mid-forties or younger. Half were in their twenties or thirties.

Who did not sign the Stainback Resolves is at least as significant as who did sign. M. L. Bradley, a staunch Association man, a district chairman for the organization in Robertson County and a planter with over seven hundred acres, did not sign. His absence suggests that the Stainback Resolves were not a product of the Association leadership. James R. Young, another Association planter, also refused to sign. The other big planter in the neighborhood, Mose Walls, opposed both the PPA and the Stainback Resolves. However, in at least a couple of cases, the kin of the wealthy supported the Stainback Resolves even though the wealthy themselves did not. Bradley's nephew, W. B. Dye, signed the Resolves. Wash Fletcher, who owned 411 acres and three tenant cabins, did not sign. His brother, Jesse, who owned just 100 acres, did. In this early period, when public opinion remained fluid and minds were still open to persuasion, loyalties proved tenuous. Eventually both Jesse and Wash Fletcher became deadly opponents of many of the men Jesse consorted with at Stainback School. M. L. Bradley, in contrast, joined his nephew and became a leading vigilante.

The men meeting at Stainback School claimed to act on behalf of the Association. They supported the Association's goal of raising the price of tobacco and raged at farmers who negotiated separate deals with buyers. The Stainback Resolves reflected conservative and progressive ideas. The signers both aimed to enforce a community conformity and to compel tobacco growers to join a twentieth-century-style business organization.

The procedure the signers outlined to force reluctant farmers into line had a long heritage in Anglo-American history in that it resembled patterns of intimidation English workers used during the English Industrial Revolution and colonists relied on in their resistance to English authority. In late eighteenth-century England, large crowds of well-organized workers would descend on English towns. Usually peaceful, the workers intimidated by force of numbers.[32] The same process occurred in America. When community interests came under attack, neighborhoods often substituted crowd action for the state. Crowds acting on behalf of the community characterized themselves by their discipline, here again intimidating not with violence but with force of numbers. "In Boston,"

John Phillip Reid wrote, "the favorite Whig persuader was the mass visitation. Instead of releasing a mob, the 'body' would adjourn to reassemble at the culprit's house or place of business."[33] In less dramatic form, community churches relied on the force of mass intimidation to enforce local standards of morality through the nineteenth century.[34] Like English workers, American rebels, and nineteenth-century churches, the Stainback signers derived their authority from the community. No "hillbilly" had ever faced two thousand men; this large number represented the authority of the community.

The Clarksville *Leaf-Chronicle* reporter called the Stainback Resolves "a wild and wooly" circular. Already Black Patch residents worried that "Possum Hunters," as enforcers of the Resolves were called, might turn to violence. Ewing called a special session of the executive committee of the Planters' Protective Association to discuss the Association's reaction. Fifty-five-year-old Will Warfield, a planter with five hundred acres, claimed to have counseled against the Possum Hunters' strategy. M. L. Bradley, a physician, detailed "how he had exercised all his medical skill to cure the 'possum hunting' fever" in his nephew and the other signers. Ewing "deplored violence." Newspapers did not record exactly what the PPA leaders decided to do about the resolves. "We have to be a little meek about what we say," the *Leaf-Chronicle* reporter wrote. "In fact it is against the rules to say anything about the happenings on such an occasion but a newspaper man is just bound to say something."[35]

Although the *Leaf-Chronicle* said nothing about what the executive committee determined to do about the "wild and wooly" resolves, the leaders clearly decided that the Association had no choice but to go along with the circular. Such a neighborhood-based organization stood in opposition to the PPA's "modern" structure, with power concentrated at the top, but someone, presumably the authors, had already sent copies of the circular to every county in the Black Patch. The circulars inflamed the Association rank-and-file against "hillbillies" and tobacco buyers. Shortly after the executive committee met, Association chapters all over the Black Patch officially adopted the "wild and wooly" circular and its "possum hunter strategy."

Association leaders, realizing they could not stop the Possum Hunters, decided to try to control them by embracing them. Ewing instructed county chairmen to find conservative members to serve on the committees called for in the resolves. In Robertson County, the chairman allowed the resolutions to pass, but saw to it that the five men appointed to the committee to canvass nonmembers were older, conservative men. Immediately a member jumped up from his seat and angrily demanded that "younger, stouter active fellows do the service."[36]

In Montgomery County, the Clarksville *Leaf-Chronicle* reported, "The men came . . . fired to the highest tension, saying they were determined to protect themselves, their wives and children and share croppers from the machinations of the trust agents." Roundly condemning Ferigo's "Hopkinsville Scheme" to buy directly from farmers rather than through the Association, the farmers were determined to counteract it. They would commit no acts of violence, the *Leaf-Chronicle* reported, and "these farmers understand that the trust has the right under the law to go into the country and buy tobacco at a higher price than any independent dealer can compete with. . . . They also recognize that the hill-billies or anyone else has the right under the law to sell to them."

The reporter probably knew that the farmers "understood" all these things because he had just heard Polk Prince and the other Association leaders remind them. He also heard what farmers from the floor of the meeting had told their leaders. The farmers were "conscious of the moral law on their side of the question and the right of self protection and preservation and they mean to avail themselves of their rights," he reported. After discussion, the Montgomery County chapter of the PPA passed resolutions copied directly from the Stainback Resolves. Its sponsors announced that the Stainback Resolves should be implemented by "peaceful means, but violent means if necessary." The minutes of the Montgomery PPA noted that those in attendance selected five "leavel headed" [*sic*] men to canvass the county and persuade non-Association men to join the organization.[37]

Similar events took place in Kentucky. The Logan County Association appointed a committee to "wait on" Regie buyers. Alarmed, conservative members worried that such committees were "akin to the 'Ku Klux Klans' of former days."[38] In Trigg County the local chapter also enacted resolutions copied directly from the Stainback Resolves. Association men appointed a "Committee of One Hundred" to "wait on" Regie buyers to demand that they buy the 1904 crop, packed in hogsheads stored in Association warehouses, before buying the 1905 crop.

Latham's warehouse in Hopkinsville after the raid. Photo from *Harper's Weekly,* February 8, 1908, 15.

In contrast to what happened in Tennessee, in Trigg County the county elite embraced the document. Ninety-four members of the Committee of One Hundred can be identified in the 1904 Trigg tax list. In general they owned more property than the average Trigg Countian. Some 64.8 percent of the committee owned more than a hundred acres of land, while in the county as a whole only 25.9 percent of the taxpayers owned more than a hundred acres. Ten percent farmed five hundred acres or more, including one with over nine thousand acres. In all of Trigg County only fifty-six taxpayers owned agricultural implements valued at $100 or more; ten of them were members of the Committee of One Hundred. Thirty-three fathers of members of the committee can be identified on antebellum tax lists. Seventeen held slaves, and four had owned fifteen or more slaves. It seems clear that, in general, the committee represented a wealthy class of Trigg County taxpayers, including planters.[39]

The committee singled out the Regie's representative in Trigg County, Cleland White, as their prime target. Described by the Cadiz *Record* as the richest man in Trigg County, White was a leader in the Cadiz Baptist Church and president of the ten-mile-long Cadiz Railroad. He later told his family that he had arrived at the Association meeting unannounced, sitting in the back while speakers lambasted "trust agents" like himself. Then he strode up the center aisle of the hall to respond to the astonished Association men. He expressed sympathy for the farmers' plight and told his listeners that he had warned Ferigo that the prices he offered Ewing would lead to violence if not improved, but he had to fulfill his current contract. Nonetheless, he promised he would not visit the barn of any Association man to encourage him to break his contract with the Association, and he would turn his warehouse over to the Association when his contract with Ferigo expired.[40]

Five members of the committee agreed to meet privately to consider White's offer. Some demanded that the Association put White out of business immediately. But after insisting that he reiterate his promises not to buy any tobacco next season on the Regie contract, nor rent his warehouse to anyone outside the Association, a majority of the committee voted to recommend accepting White's offer.[41]

Despite his agreement with the Association, Night Riders continued to subject White to threats and abuse. They warned that his property would be destroyed if he did not end his connections with the Regie.[42] White gave in to Association demands. He quit the tobacco business entirely at the suggestion, he said later, of "my friends and the tobacco association," who "thought it was interfering with the interests of the farmers in the county."[43]

After White severed his relations with the Regie, there should not have been any Regie agents around, but the Association constantly had to be on guard against infiltrators. Dr. James H. Lackey remembered later that the Association, in one of its regular meetings at the Trigg County courthouse, had asked him to serve as a chairman of a committee to investigate a report that a Regie buyer had entered the county. Lackey claimed later that he served as a messenger, not a vigilante. "I asked the Association if they merely wanted me to make the request and they said that was all they expected me to do and I agreed." Reports indicated that the Regie buyer was staying with the Vinsons, so Lackey and Peter T. Light, a sixty-year-old Canton area planter with 525 acres, rode to the Vinsons' home. "I hallowed," Lackey said later, "and Mrs. Vinson came to the door." After asking the lady if she harbored a tobacco buyer and being assured she did not, Lackey turned to his companion and said, "Mr. Light, there is no tobacco buyer here." With that the two men left.[44]

Although Lackey and Light eschewed strong-arm tactics, many in the Association did not. Increasingly, those outside the Association found their property destroyed by vigilantes. Since the violent abuse of independent farmers obviously benefited the Association, many believed that Ewing or other Association leaders directed their activities. The court testimony of Robert S. Warfield, son of Association man W. C. Warfield, confirmed the link between the Association and the vigilantes but not Ewing's involvement. Robert testified that he came to the little town of Guthrie, Kentucky, to attend a meeting of the Association's executive committee; when he arrived, he was told that no such meeting was planned but that "we have a little private meeting here—a little secret order, a wheel within a wheel, . . . branch of the Association." This was a reference to the Night Riders. In 1909 a spy claiming to have penetrated the Night Rider organization reported that while Ewing played no role in the vigilantism, his top lieutenants did. Ewing himself confirmed this after the Black Patch war, telling a friend he opposed night riding but could not control it.[45]

One might well question Ewing's physical capacity to control the Night Riders. In November 1906 the Association announced Ewing was suffering from nervous prostration and had entered a sanatorium.[46] Nine months later an Association stalwart described Ewing as a martyr to the cause, "slowly dying in a New York sanitorium." Other reports confirmed that the Association leader lingered near death.[47] But at the end of October, the Association announced that Ewing had improved and would be home in a few weeks.[48] Ewing, apparently recovered, sent a letter to the membership.[49] But during the time the Night Riders were most violently active, Ewing was out of the Black Patch.

Whether or not Ewing directed them, the Night Riders attacked the enemies of Ewing's Association one by one. In May 1906 the vigilantes visited Joseph F. Garnett of Christian County. With over five hundred acres, Garnett was recognized as a major tobacco producer in the area. In 1904 the Hopkinsville *Kentuckian* specified him as an example of a farmer who had benefited from the Association, while not a member. By holding members' tobacco off the market, the Association had forced the price up, but it was nonmembers like Garnett who had profited the most. In December 1904, Garnett sold his crop for a dollar to a dollar and a half more than he had sold his 1903 crop. But in May 1906, Garnett found his plant beds in ruins. Someone had destroyed the young plants in the night.[50]

In Robertson County the Association's committee threatened T. L. Polk with vigilante violence but failed to persuade him to join their organization. The committee consisted of Jim Morris, "a very nice old gentleman" who came alone to talk with Polk. Morris told Polk that the Association wanted him to put his tobacco in the Association. Polk told Morris the tobacco had already been sold the week before. "Well," Morris said, "I understand that, but we want you to go and take that back and turn it over and put it into the Association." But Polk refused. "I have sold my tobacco and I feel like it was mine and I had a right to sell it and I sold it to a man that had a right to buy it." Nonetheless, Polk tried to be conciliatory. "Now you all contend that we few boys that are not in [the Association] here are running [ruining] your business," Polk acknowledged. "I will make another crop of tobacco and I will see if I am satisfied in my own mind that we are what is the matter," he promised, "and if we are . . . I will either put it in [the Association] or I won't raise any."[51]

At about the same time Polk refused to sell his tobacco through the Association, vigilantes attacked Ben Sory, a tobacco buyer for the Italian Regie. Sory was camping with his wife on the Red River in Tennessee. Large numbers of Night Riders rode out to Sory's camp, expecting to overawe him with their numbers. To the vigilantes' surprise, he defied them, forcing even his opponents to concede that Sory had the respect of the community. The men visiting him that night had thought themselves endowed with an authority sanctioned by overwhelming numbers. By refusing to recognize that authority, Sory had denied and limited it. The community—or most of it—must acquiesce for vigilantes to exercise their authority.

Other members tried the same tactics they used on Polk with Thomas Menees, a farmer, merchant, and liveryman in Polk's neighborhood. The Association men warned Menees that his store would be boycotted and he would be entirely ostracized if he continued to refuse to join the organization. Menees was vulnerable in another way too. He had sold his threshing machine to a Mr. Fizer, with a contract promising to stay out of the threshing business for three years. In return, Fizer agreed to thresh Menees's wheat. But after the Association began boycotting Menees, Fizer told the "hillbilly" that he would no longer be able to thresh his wheat. This forced Menees to buy a new threshing machine. But before he could even unload it, Association men told Menees they would destroy it if he tried to use it.[52]

By 1905 the Association had taken several important strides toward control of the Black Patch tobacco crop. Controlling public opinion was the key. Public opinion neutralized antitrust laws. Association leaders claimed to have the public on their side and warned the reluctant that they stood against the weight of public enthusiasm for the organization. Communities mobilized to pressure holdouts into the Association. To insure everyone understood that the Association represented local communities and neighborhoods, Association organizers made certain their meetings resembled neighborhood church meetings. Association men claimed that their enemies had turned their backs on their communities, neighborhoods, even their families. Such individuals should be thought of as "dead" citizens. As traitors they deserved to be ostracized by their neighbors.

Despite these successes, enough tobacco growers had remained independent to cause members of the Black Patch planter class to consider turning to force to drive recalcitrants into their organization. It may be that in such a violent culture as the Black Patch the use of traditional community forms and rhetoric led naturally to violence. By the middle of 1906 it was likely that Menees would be the first to feel this turn toward violence. The Association had defined him as outside the bounds of popular law. He had been sentenced by the Association; his punishment would be carried out by men known as Night Riders.

Night Rider—the image of riders on horseback, silhouetted by burning barns. According to one writer, the "Possum Hunters" acquired their more romantic name in November 1905, when Kentucky Congressman Augustus O. Stanley warned farmers not to resort to violence, to "night riding."[1] To this day residents of the Black Patch surround the name with myth and fable. "They had men in there with guts to do what was right," an elderly resident recalled in 1982.[2] This positive image had its origins in the earliest actions of the Night Riders, when the vigilantes limited themselves to humiliating outspoken opponents of the Association and destroying the property of the hated tobacco cartel. The planter elite leading the Night Riders calculated these raids carefully. This was "politics-out-of-doors," almost bloodless and enormously popular. Moreover, the Night Riders seemed to act on behalf of their communities and at the direction of the Planters' Protective Association, an organization already legitimated by corporate malevolence in the eyes of many.

From 1905 through 1907, Night Rider violence escalated from the punishment of individuals to the destruction of trust-operated tobacco warehouses. The Night Riders turned to violence to shore up an organization which, though popular, was never popular enough. Had enough farmers joined the Association to deny the tobacco companies their crops, there would have been no need for vigilantism. They would carry out their boldest raid when their raison d'être teetered on the brink of collapse. Since they could not prevent some farmers from selling their tobacco to the companies, the Night Riders would destroy that tobacco after the sale, in company warehouses.

Association men in the Night Rider stronghold at the juncture of Lyon, Caldwell, and Trigg counties launched the terrorist organization in Association meetings. A representative of the *Farmers' Home Journal,* visiting an Association meeting in Trigg County, expressed surprise at the intensity members displayed. They seemed, he wrote, "terribly in earnest."[3] Here Association stalwart Dr. David Alfred Amoss emerged as a natural leader. His father, E. N. Amoss, had won the respect of his neighbors, establishing a good practice. In 1848 the elder Amoss and his wife helped found the Wallonia Christian Church, in Trigg County, just a few miles down the road from what would become Cobb. Worshipers elected Amoss bishop at their new church.[4] As the Civil War drew near, Amoss, owner of four slaves, favored secession. "He is," the R. G. Dun correspondent noted in 1863, "a fool rebel but good for all his contracts."[5]

A doctor and son of a doctor, a community leader, David Amoss earned the respect of his friends and patients. In 1910 a newspaper reporter described him as a "quiet-looking, gentlemanly appearing man" with "gray eyes that smile as he talks." The reporter noted that his neighbors thought "nothing between hell or heaven could scare or intimidate him" and idolized their doctor.[6] Like others of his class, this small man with a penetrating gaze believed vigilantism both efficacious and necessary. He had engaged in vigilantism in the past, as a so-called "whitecapper." Whitecapping, the violent enforcement of morality, had long been prevalent in western Kentucky. In 1889 Amoss joined whitecappers in his neighborhood when rumors began to circulate that J. H. Gray had been mistreating his wife. But a cousin warned Gray, and when the vigilantes showed up, he surprised them from behind a woodpile with his shotgun. As the raiders scattered, Gray shot the organizer, who later died of his injuries. Amoss's exact role is unclear, but of seven individuals indicted in circuit court for their part in the episode, he was one of the two who eventually pleaded guilty.[7]

In addition to a proclivity for violence, Amoss may have been a political radical. In 1910, while the doctor awaited trial, the socialist newspaper *Appeal to Reason* approvingly compared him to Eugene Debs. The newspaper quoted Amoss as describing farmers' fight against the tobacco trust as an episode in an ongoing "industrial war," as a class fight between "the plutocracy" and labor.[8] But there is no evidence other than the *Appeal to Reason* article that Amoss espoused socialism, and it is clear that he tailored his rhetoric in hopes of tapping the socialists for funds to help with his legal bills.

Amoss's use of the term *plutocracy* suggests rhetoric employed by Tom Watson in his antibusiness magazine.[9] Watson regularly railed against federal courts for failing to rein in big business. He even came close to advocating exactly the kind of violence against big business Amoss would carry out against the tobacco trust. In 1905, after President Theodore Roosevelt had urged tighter government regulation of railroads, "railway king" Samuel Spencer had compared the proposed legislation to lynch law. Outraged, Watson exploded, "If the people of New York had half the dash and grit which Western ranchmen had when they formed Vigilance Committees and hung horse-thieves by the neck until they were dead, your pals . . . would be swung up to a lamp-post."[10] Watson went on to warn that if people could find no relief from corporate greed, *"watch out for other methods."* He lectured, "IN THE PEOPLE rests the final power of government. FROM THE PEOPLE come all law, all authority, all official power, ALL PUNISHMENT OF CRIME!" He concluded, ominously, "Revolutions have been; revolutions may be again."[11] Watson's radical rhetoric certainly penetrated the Black Patch. Association leader and alleged Night Rider Charles Fort not only read *Tom Watson's Magazine,* but regularly contributed to it.[12]

Although he grew no tobacco himself, when tobacco problems arose farmers looked to Amoss as their leader. At an Association meeting he demanded that every member willing to shed blood and take up arms for the Association stand up. Almost everyone did, and he asked those who did not to leave.[13] All over lower Caldwell County, Trigg County, and southern Lyon County, Amoss called Association men to secret meetings in their local schoolhouses and urged them to form a new organization, "a wheel within a wheel," to "take up arms for the Association." Then Amoss went to work expanding the "Silent Brigade," as the Night Riders came to be called, into surrounding counties.

The planters leading the Night Riders relied on black labor to produce their crop. They were racists, but they imagined their racism superior to the grittier variety practiced by white laborers. They "knew" blacks were inferior, incapable of taking care of themselves. That was their job and they performed it eagerly, demanding only the image of sycophantic loyalty in return. Economic hard times did not turn them against their labor force because they understood that large numbers of apparently contented blacks suppressed wages and contributed to their prosperity.

Amoss himself took a paternal interest in his black neighbors. Clyde Quisenberry, a black former sharecropper in the Cobb area, remembered Amoss as a protector. Blacks in Cobb lived in a cluster of six or seven houses. One day Quisenberry's father and some white residents "had a little misunderstanding and I think he was pretty sassy. He sassed some of 'em." The whites talked about "running us out—all of us." Amoss interceded on behalf of Cobb's black community, telling the would-be vigilantes not to molest the blacks. "Them darkies ain't hurting nobody," Quisenberry quoted him as saying. To defuse the situation he suggested that Quisenberry's father leave town for a while, telling him to "go out and catch a little air." "Yes," Quisenberry concluded, "he was a friend to us."[14]

Night Rider photographed for *Hampton's Magazine* 22 (February 1909): 180.

Amoss's organization successfully buried itself in secrecy. Members took a "blood oath" not to reveal the secrets of the organization. Such secret organizations held a powerful allure for Victorian men. They were community-affirming, creating tightly organized male networks within an increasingly impersonal larger society. And the Night Riders were such a gender-defined organization, allowing men to act on behalf of the larger culture but outside that culture. In many cases, wives and children did not know their men belonged. The daughter of a Trigg County man remembered her father pointing to a place where "I took the awfulest oath," but he said nothing about the Night Riders.[15]

At best, we get a few glimpses at the secret order. Jim Lawrence and his friends decided to go to a Night Rider meeting at Humphrey School just for the fun of it. Jim's friend, Charley Aldridge, the son of a Night Rider leader, suggested the boys throw open the doors and see what happened. When Jim and his friends threw open the doors, Night Rider sentinels grabbed them, put them on their bended knees, and made them take the blood oath of the Night Riders.[16]

Joe Ellis Scott joined the Night Riders in a schoolhouse near Lamasco in Lyon County in 1906, after his friends asked him to

Night Rider photographed
for *Hampton's Magazine*
22 (March 1909): 341.

attend a meeting. Although Scott told his friends he had no interest in vigilantism, they persisted and he did attend and join. The vigilantes told their recruit he would be better off if he did not know anyone he met among the Night Riders.[17] The penalty for knowing, and talking, could be disappearance and death. Organizations like the Night Riders require secrecy for success. The Night Riders had to appear to represent everyone, to be the entire community. Secrecy made them both invisible and persuasive. If anyone could be a Night Rider, then perhaps everyone was a Night Rider. Secrecy fomented their power.

The Black Patch war began December 9, 1905, when an explosion jarred the six hundred residents of Trenton, Kentucky, in southwestern Todd County, from their sleep. Looking out their windows, they saw flames ravaging the large S. D. Chestnut and Company tobacco warehouse, occupied by the local Regie contractors. Regie workers had loaded the warehouse with "hillbilly" tobacco a few days before and had posted guards around the building. But on the night of the attack the guards mysteriously abandoned their posts. Night Rider attacks were often accompanied by reports of disappearing guards—a tribute to the perception of invincibility the vigilantes cultivated.

The Kentucky militia: they are in Lexington, which is outside the Black Patch, but this photograph was taken during the Night Rider crisis. Similar soldiers and a Gatling gun were stationed in Hopkinsville. Photo from *Hampton's Magazine* 22 (February 1909): 177.

The violence did not stop in Trenton. A few days later masked and armed men stopped train number 80 at Bradshaw on the Elkton branch of the Louisville and Nashville Railroad. Five men covered the fireman and engineer with pistols while ten or fifteen others went through the coaches looking for tobacco buyers. They did not find any, but rumors quickly magnified the affair until the word was that over a hundred heavily armed Night Riders had held up the train. Todd County had hardly had time to digest the news of these events when Night Riders raided Elkton, the county seat, dynamiting the three-story frame warehouse operated by the American Snuff Company. Later, one former resident remembered the sound of horses, the explosion, and his grandmother praying beside her bed. The Night Riders had destroyed her building. By first light, local residents found it "blown to atoms." A few weeks later a man called on the old woman and apologized for the destruction.[18]

The raids on Trenton, train number 80, and Elkton excited Black Patchers. The raids seemed big and dramatic, showing that the Black Patch could fight back against tobacco buyers in impressive ways. No one died in any of these early raids and their bloodlessness contributed to the romance and legitimacy of the raiders. Far from being criminal, they fought against wrong and did so without killing anyone; they were so gallant, they even apologized to a lady when they had to destroy her property to get at the greater evil. The Black Patch had a new band of heroes.

Association leaders used the violence to enforce discipline in their organization. The morning after the Elkton raid Tom Ayers, a PPA official, came to Tom Menees's store in Cedar Hill, Tennessee. Ayers asked if Menees had heard about the destruction of the tobacco factory at Elkton. When Menees confirmed he had, the Association man warned him to get in the organization: "You see what the boys is doing." When Menees still refused, Ayers said, "Just wait until we put the torch to you and you will come in after it is too late."[19] Menees stolidly refused to join the Association in the face of threats, ostracism, and a boycott of his store. It was Menees, referred to earlier, who was forced to buy a thresher when none of his neighbors would hire one out to him. Despite the threats, he even hired his machine out to other farmers who had refused to join the Association. Though he found it difficult to find anyone brave enough to operate the thresher in the face of Association intimidation, he finally hired two men, instructing them to stay with his machine at all times. One of the guards, John Johnson, later recalled being awakened one night in the middle of July 1907. Someone stepped on his sore toe and growled, "Get up, old man." Johnson got up as quickly as he could. "I am an old negro, you know, and it takes me a good while to get up," he explained later. On his feet, Johnson found himself in front of a crowd of armed men. He estimated that he faced sixty or seventy gun barrels.

They asked Johnson why he worked for Menees and he explained that he had to work for a living. One of the men told Johnson he would not be able to work on Menees's thresher any more: "I am going to blow hell out of this thing." Another Night Rider sarcastically asked if Johnson had a match. Johnson blanched at the question. Everyone knew how dangerous it was to have anything flammable near a thresher. Steam driven, the contraptions were dangerous enough even when treated with respect. The Night Riders escorted Johnson a safe distance away. Someone else did have a match. An explosion shook the night.[20]

Although direct evidence of a connection between the PPA and the Night Riders may not exist, an Association official had threatened Menees, and the Night Riders made good the threat. The official was not from the top ranks of the PPA hierarchy, but contemporaries did not make fine distinctions between levels of PPA leadership. Association men made threats which the Night Riders carried out. Top PPA leaders probably did not control the vigilantes, but they appeared to be directing every raid.

The next raid came on the other side of the Black Patch. The Night Riders chose Eddyville, an old river town in Lyon County, Kentucky, as their first target in the western Black Patch. Perched on the east bank of the Cumberland River, with a population of 1,400, Eddyville had served as the county seat of Lyon County since its formation in 1854. A few brick and frame buildings with wooden awnings, clustered between an unimposing brick courthouse and the gray mass of the state penitentiary, made up downtown. Like many southern towns, Eddyville seemed a tentative compromise with nature. Houses sat wherever their builders could find space between a long wooded ridge and the river. Observers from the penitentiary's towers had trouble picking out the houses and buildings from among the trees. The streets were dirt paths.

Usually a peaceful village, Eddyville in 1906 braced for attack. With a tobacco warehouse in their midst, residents nervously listened to farmers' angry rumblings. The warehouse's owner, Robert B. Bradshaw, had been acting as agent for the American Snuff Company for two years. Bradshaw and city residents had more cause to fear fire-wielding Night Riders than most. In that Eddyville had only a feeble fire department—eight volunteers, paid one dollar for each alarm—a serious blaze would be hard for the town to handle.[21]

Early in the morning of November 12, 1906, an explosion ripped through the cold morning silence, shattering windows and jarring residents from their sleep. Lyon County sheriff Sam G. Cash left his house on Franklin Street and found Bradshaw's warehouse wrecked.[22] Sheriff Cash was confronted with a huge crime and enormous property loss, but the situation resembled no other Cash had encountered. Most Lyon Countians agreed with Association rhetoric that agents of the Trust, like Bradshaw, were enemies of the people and robbers of women and children. The Night Riders had wreaked considerable havoc on Bradshaw's warehouse, but they had not physically injured anyone. They had functioned in the republican tradition of a united community acting to preserve agreed-upon values. Their deportment confirmed the perception that because they represented the community they had to be well-behaved even in the commission of violence. Onlookers frequently commented on the discipline the Silent Brigade exhibited in these early raids. One eyewitness described them as marching "two by two as neat as soldiers.[23] "They were all well drilled and behaved like gentlemen," another Eddyville resident observed.[24]

Sheriff Cash dutifully borrowed bloodhounds from the state penitentiary and followed the trail of the raiders into Caldwell County, even though Kentucky sheriffs rarely tracked criminals outside their counties. This does not mean, however, that Cash was enthusiastic about the chase. Cash was a politician familiar with the popularity of the Association and the Night Riders, and he valued the good will of his constituents, making loans and signing notes for his many friends.[25] He was not the kind of lawman who isolated himself from his friends and neighbors to pursue some abstract ideal of justice. Moreover, Cash probably accepted the Night Rider image of power. Two men and some dogs, he certainly calculated, had no business tangling with the Night Riders. In any event, he soon gave up the chase.[26] He never identified the raiders and Lyon County never prosecuted them; nor did any property owner sue them for damages. Violence went unpunished.

After the Eddyville raid, following the early episodes in the eastern Black Patch, the Night Riders seemed a vast and powerful force, literally able to strike anywhere at any time with impunity. Many residents of the Black Patch must have eyed their local tobacco warehouses uneasily and wondered when the large, rickety wooden structures might explode in flame. Every sheriff, prosecutor, and judge must have calculated the value of taking on such a powerful force that acted on behalf of the entire community. More than one lawman must have wondered how one man could defend the law against the enraged will of the community.

Less than a month later, the Night Riders struck the tobacco warehouse in Princeton, Kentucky. In the evening of November 30, farmers began filtering into the streets, taking up strategic positions around town. Princeton, population 3,200, was a larger town than Eddyville, but the fire department was only a little less amateurish. There were twelve firemen, equipped with a horse-drawn hose cart. One fireman stayed at the hose house at the edge of town at all times. Six blocks of commercial buildings formed a square about the courthouse, among them two tobacco warehouses.[27]

Shortly after midnight, masked men filled the empty streets from every direction. They efficiently disarmed both of the police officers at their station as well as the guards at the tobacco warehouses. At the telephone office Annie Roche sat alone when, at

12:30 A.M., three masked men broke the glass in the locked door, forced it open, and instructed her not to send any messages. The Night Riders stayed with her for about half an hour. Many calls came in, but she did not dare answer. Roche heard an explosion and then saw a building ablaze. In another part of town, a traveler heard the same explosion, lit a lamp, and peered out his window. A voice in the darkness commanded him to put out his light or be shot. He did as told.[28]

The Night Riders had dynamited and burned the tobacco factory owned by John G. Orr, destroying over 230,000 pounds of tobacco belonging to the British Imperial Tobacco Company, valued at $17,998.41. Five blocks down the same street, they destroyed another tobacco factory, affiliated with the British firm of Gallaher Limited, along with 150,000 pounds of tobacco. Thomas Gallaher protested that the Night Riders had made a ghastly mistake. His company opposed the trust, he declared: "We have been fighting the Imperial Tobacco Company on this side [of the ocean] as the trust policy is to crush all independent manufacturers."[29]

The Night Riders did not restrict themselves to destroying tobacco company warehouses. Both the Association and the Night Riders claimed to speak and act for their communities as a whole. They were an expression of the community will. In fact, this claim to represent the will of the group constituted the chief source of power for both the Association and the Night Riders. Both overawed dissidents by focusing the concentrated wrath of the community on the miscreant. Association men and Night Riders alike made their opponents feel very lonely and isolated. While Night Rider leaders did not believe that every last tobacco farmer had to pledge his crop for the Association to be a success, they did believe dissidents had to acquiesce with their silence. If enemies of the Association and Night Rider violence did not challenge the vigilantes' claim to represent the community, then they posed no threat. The masked men left them alone.

The Night Riders were men firmly rooted in their communities. The twenty-seven of the Tennessee Night Riders whom Menees identified included a teacher, a dry goods salesman, merchants, a mechanic and, primarily, farmers. Most came from families long established in the area, farming in the same neighborhoods as their fathers before them. Some 27 percent held no land. Another 27 percent owned a hundred acres or fewer. Another 27 percent farmed between one and two hundred acres, and 18 percent had over two hundred acres.[30] A study of twenty-eight Caldwell County Night Riders identified in federal court in 1908 reveals that the vigilantes included some of the wealthiest members of their communities. The Caldwell County Night Riders owned large acreage themselves or sharecropped for large landholders. Forty-three percent of the Kentucky Night Riders identified in court owned no land but sharecropped, while another 43 percent had two hundred acres or more. Some of the sharecroppers lived on the farms of fellow defendants. The brothers Firm, Edgar, and Wallace Oliver, for example, worked for shares on John E. Hollowell's farm.[31]

Older men, the Night Riders came from families well established in their community. "The best people in the county," a neighbor described them. "They are the people who pay the taxes, who keep up the churches and schools." Three quarters belonged to the Baptist church, the neighbor claimed. "I can count as many as twelve men charged with night riding who are deacons of Baptist churches."[32] A less friendly source described them as "grim farmers" but also as "toughs stiffened with corn whisky."[33] The Tennessee Night Riders averaged forty-three years in age. The Kentuckians ranged in age from twenty-one to sixty-four, also averaging forty-three. Many, probably most, were married and had children. One once served as sheriff. The son and brother-in-law of a magistrate and the son of a constable joined the "Silent Brigade." The Night Riders also reflected long-established kinship networks in the region. The parents or grandparents of at least twelve of the twenty-eight indicted Night Riders had lived in the same neighborhood in 1850.[34] Undoubtedly some "toughs" joined the Night Riders, but so did many community leaders.

A few additional conclusions can be drawn about the Night Riders and their leaders. First, their neighbors thought them progressive. Many Night Riders practiced up-to-date farming methods. For example, Tennessee Night Rider Jim Tom Matthews introduced burley tobacco to his county. Amoss's alleged socialism notwithstanding, most Night Riders did not have an antibusiness bias. The second-ranking Night Rider in Kentucky, Guy Dunning, became a businessman in 1919. Prominent Night Rider John W. Hollowell also became a businessman and even something of an industrialist after the Black Patch war, producing metal railroad ties.[35]

One of Amoss's most enthusiastic recruits in Trigg County was a black man, John Thomas Wright. His white father, Joseph Parker Wright, had inherited fortunes from both his father and father-in-law. Despite his father's great wealth, though, Tom built his fortune from nothing. Born in 1854 to his father's slave, John Thomas Wright had been his father's slave as well as son. Neighborhood gossips wondered how a former slave had garnered such impressive wealth. To whites he always credited his white relatives for helping him when he needed it. But that may have been palaver. Blacks whispered that he had used a metal needle to locate a treasure buried by a rich "massa" when the yankees came. Whites preferred to believe no black man could build such a fortune without their help; blacks preferred to believe he had done it on his own.

Wealthy, and as light in complexion as most white men, Wright chose to live in a racist culture as an African-American. Although he had servants to wait on him and dressed in clothes superior to what most of his white neighbors could afford, whites respected him as a man who "stayed in a nigger's place." "I know that I am a colored man and I don't pretend" to be anything else, his white nephew, Durwood Wright, remembered his saying. Wright was very aware of the limits his mother's color imposed on his life. He tried to operate a flour mill, but sold it when he realized that whites objected to having a black man price their wheat and keep track of their debts. But he did not advertise the real reason. "I just don't feel like keeping the books," he explained. Once on a cattle buying trip, the would-be seller solicitously greeted Wright, who was accompanied as always by his black driver, as "Mr. Wright" and invited him to spend the night with him. Wright explained, "I know you don't know it, but I am a colored man and I have to stay in a colored man's place." "You don't mean to tell me," the seller sputtered, "you're a damn nigger?" Married three times, Wright always chose the "blackest nigger around," his nephew remembered. He was making a statement, in a manner to which no white could object, about which world he preferred.[36]

Not every Night Rider was white, but almost all their victims were. If race did not distinguish vigilante from victim, neither did economics. Night Rider victims came from a variety of economic backgrounds. Fourteen can be identified from the Cadiz *Record* and other newspapers in District Four. A few owned little property; four had no land. One more, Burnett Humphries, could not be located in the 1904 tax list, but the press described him as "a poor man trying to raise a family on a small place." Yet most of the victims cannot be described as lower class. Their holdings ranged from thirty to 244 acres with most owning farms of about two hundred acres. A recent student of the Black Patch war who surveyed opponents of the Association in Montgomery County, Tennessee, found that about half were renters. Of fifteen victims of Night Rider violence in Montgomery County, ten rented their homes, but seven were wealthy enough to employ help.[37] In the same way that wealthy Night Riders were joined by their poorer neighbors, class mattered less than geography in the determination of targets. Communities rather than individuals enlisted in the fight on the tobacco trust.

Although neither race nor economic status determined whom the Night Riders visited, speaking against the Night Riders guaranteed a violent visit. When Trigg Countian John Wesley Barefield boasted that he had purchased plow line and matches to hang and burn Night Riders, the Riders responded by shooting into his house, forcing him out, and whipping him. Brute force brought some recalcitrants into line, or at least silenced their opposition. Others needed only the threat of violence. In Lyon County's Confederate neighborhood, Night Riders threatened John Cannon when he refused to join their order. Afraid they would burn his house, Cannon hosed the roof down. But the Night Riders never visited Cannon, satisfied with his statement that "I know when to keep my mouth shut and when to open it."[38]

Victims of the Night Riders received little sympathy from their county officials. In Trigg County, local government openly sided with the vigilantes. One citizen who complained that he had received a threatening letter from the Night Riders was advised by local authorities to "get in the Association."[39] In his *Memoirs,* newspaperman Arthur Krock recalled seeing Representative Ollie Murray James, later chairman of the Democratic National Convention that nominated Woodrow Wilson and a distinguished United States senator, "ride proudly and openly in a victoria through the streets of Cadiz . . . at the head of a group of mounted, armed men who, everyone knew, had been burning barns and destroying tobacco crops the night before."[40] The Cadiz *Record* winked at the violence. "Between the trust agent and the night rider, we had rather be the latter," it editorialized.[41]

When the Night Riders did raid black tobacco growers, they indulged in none of the violent "ku kluxing" usually associated with southern night riding. Around Cobb, where farmers almost universally accepted the Association and the Night Riders, every large planter in this neighborhood but one enlisted in the Association.

Only Lee Pollard refused to join his neighbors. While the Night Riders never visited Pollard, they did raid his black tenant, Tom "Bear" Wormelduff. The story of the visit became a part of local folklore, complete with dialogue. The Night Riders came to Wormelduff's cabin just when the tobacco plants, a tender green mass crowded in plant beds, had matured and waited to be transplanted into the fields.

The Night Riders called for "Bear."

"Yes sir, white folks!"

"Come out, Bear, we want to talk to you."

"I ain't got my shoes on."

"You don't need no shoes, just come on."

Bear went outside.

"Where's your hoe?"

"In the corner. . . ."

"Well, get it and go over there." The Night Riders escorted the cropper to the plant beds and made him hack out the delicate young plants. "Now, go up there and tell Mr. Pollard to pay you for scraping your plant beds."

"I—I can't do that, white folks."[42] So the Night Riders confronted Pollard, forcing him to pay his tenant for the labor he had performed for them. These Night Riders were certainly racists and paternalists, but they did not resent Wormelduff. They were after the white landlord, Pollard. Some blacks saw this as a kind of victory. For many years thereafter local blacks enjoyed telling of the time when the Night Riders humbled a big landlord.

In Tennessee, too, public opinion favored the Association and the vigilantes. Dancey Fort, the younger brother of Planters' Protective Association propagandist Joel Fort and Association president Charles Fort, served as the city attorney of Clarksville and also as a state senator. Dancey supported the PPA as strongly as his brothers. "I am with this organization, right or wrong," he told an audience of farmers. "The farmers' ship may go down, but I will go down with you. Don't give up the ship. Do not think that Dancey Fort will ever turn his back on the farmers."[43]

But the violence of which so many approved remained relatively bloodless. The Night Riders destroyed property and humiliated their victims, but they did not kill anyone. Moreover, they only attacked the property of tobacco companies and outspoken opponents of the Association. Approved by the community, the violence was legitimated, making more violence possible later. Approval ran so deep that some Kentucky- and Tennessee-born historians still express approval.[44] Through secrecy and limited violence, the Night Riders had created a powerful aura about themselves. They represented the people against powerful, outside business interests. By the start of 1907, the Black Patch's planter elite had reached a new plateau of success in their efforts to enlist yeomen farmers in their fight with the tobacco trust. They had created an enormously popular guerrilla army to go after every last pound of tobacco grown in the Black Patch and enforce membership in their Association.

Despite the success of the Night Riders and the refusal of the federal government to intervene, by 1907 the Association was in trouble. The Clarksville *Leaf-Chronicle* estimated that 85 percent of growers belonged to the PPA the first year but only 40 percent belonged in 1907. This is certainly false—the PPA's own records show their membership larger in 1907 than in 1904.[45] But the Association did decline after its early successes, though membership in the farmers' organization did not slump in every county at the same rate at the same time. Trigg County farmers remained notoriously loyal to the Association through 1907 and much of 1908. They resented their neighbors in Christian County, where the Association declined more precipitously.

In retrospect it is clear that farmers had slight chance to improve tobacco prices by themselves. They needed governmental intervention to insure a long-term improvement in tobacco prices, and that would not come until the New Deal in May 1933. Even then many farmers would hotly defend their independence, agreeing to adhere to New Deal regulations only because the nation's economic crisis forced them to try experimental and unprecedented legislation. The New Deal's Agricultural Adjustment Act reduced tobacco acreage and implemented a tax to finance payments to farmers, guaranteeing that their incomes would at least equal their costs.[46]

The inherent problems Ewing faced in attempting to maintain a farmers' organization without the powers of the federal government led him into disputes with warehousemen. Some members mistrusted him. Perhaps they would have mistrusted a government-run program as well, but as a private individual, Ewing was particularly vulnerable to complaints of corruption. In the spring of 1906 Ewing became ensnared in a bitter public feud with Clarksville warehousemen when he required Association warehousemen to sign contracts that contained a clause forbidding them from accepting tobacco not pledged to the Association. The warehousemen, led by Charles P. Warfield, railed against the clause, saying Tennessee state law required them to accept all tobacco. Ewing further alienated Clarksville tobacco handlers when he refused to allow their board of trade to inspect Association tobacco. Inspectors employed by the board of trade had always inspected and graded all the tobacco passing through Clarksville, but Ewing insisted that only Association inspectors could grade Association tobacco. It was no small point. A high price for good tobacco does a farmer little good if graders judge his tobacco to be inferior. His feud with Clarksville tobacco men cost Ewing the support of the powerful Clarksville *Leaf-Chronicle,* which always came down on the side of Clarksville's business community. In retaliation, Ewing moved the Association's sample room from Clarksville to Guthrie, Kentucky.

Warehousemen who originally supported the Association now turned against the organization. C. P. Warfield published an especially bitter public attack on Ewing on November 22, 1906. Warfield advised Ewing to stop abusing his best friends, meaning Clarksville businessmen, and accused the PPA leader of "boasting of the men and markets you have destroyed and built up, great sales you have made (triumphs never accomplished)."[47]

Ewing feuded not just with warehousemen, but with the top officers of the Association itself. His falling out with Association president Charles Fort stemmed from politics. Although numerous politicians in both Kentucky and Tennessee eagerly associated themselves with Ewing's organization, Ewing insisted on a nonpartisan stance for his organization. When Kentucky Congressman A. O. Stanley persuaded Fort to break his promise to Ewing not to endorse any political candidate, Ewing erupted in anger. In a bitter letter, Ewing condemned Fort as untrustworthy, all smiles in his presence while darkly muttering complaints in his absence. For good measure, Ewing described Fort's brother as a drunk.[48]

Meanwhile, in the basement of the Association sample room, Association salesmen negotiated secret sales of Association tobacco. Association farmers received no information on how much their own tobacco brought or even who bought it. Critics soon loudly demanded that the sales be made public and statistics published. Even the vice president of the Association came to believe it should change its policy of secret sales. Farmers widely endorsed the idea,

and in May 1906 the *Leaf-Chronicle* reported extensive farmer dis-
enchantment with the Association's sales procedures. Farmers
said they wanted to know when the Association sold their crop,
who bought it, and the price. Ewing refused to compromise. There
would be no end to secret sales. The vice president resigned in
protest.[49]

Even though tobacco prices climbed sharply, Ewing's secretive
methods prompted farmers to criticize him for the prices he
negotiated. Labor continued scarce and expensive, and Montgomery County Association men complained bitterly that the
prices achieved by the PPA were still too low.[50] Farmers disrupted
an Association meeting in January 1906 with demands for better
prices. One farmer shouted, "Close the headquarters and nail the
damn thing up until it is one!"[51] The complaints about the price of
labor indicated that these complaining farmers were not small
growers and tenants.

Many observers recognized that the price of tobacco had more
to do with the size of the crop than anything else. In 1905 the PPA
called on farmers to reduce the size of their tobacco crops to force
the price up. That year spring came late and a scarcity of plants
forced the reduction Association leaders sought. One district in
Dickson County, Tennessee, reported acreage reduced by half.[52] As
a result of the smaller crop, the price of tobacco doubled.[53] But
in 1907, encouraged by higher prices and good weather, farmers
planted a full crop. At the beginning of the year Association advocates again urged farmers to reduce acreage, but they soon
gave up. Farmers thought they had beaten the trust, one Christian
County resident sadly concluded, but "the whole face of the earth
was planting tobacco." With such a large crop, the Association
could not enforce its high prices and had to lower grades, effectively reducing prices, to make sales.[54]

Not only did the Association fail to win the prices it promised, it
found it could no longer finance loans to smaller growers. This
represented a fundamental problem. Reduced to its most basic
terms, the Association was an organization of tobacco planters
with an arrangement with local banks to finance a boycott of tobacco buyers by yeomen and tenant farmers. Tobacco was too
democratic a crop—anyone with three acres and a strong back
could produce a thousand pounds—for larger planters to control
the market by themselves. For smaller producers, the income from
their tobacco crop was too important to be given up. So the suc-

cess of the Association hinged on the ability and willingness of local banks to advance money to small tobacco growers.

The downfall of the Association began in the fall of 1907 when the United States and the rest of the world suffered a short but sharp business contraction. In Kentucky, Louisville banks tried to draw in currency from all over the Commonwealth to cover the big payrolls of the railroads. Money became scarce.[55] Although the Hopkinsville *Kentuckian* congratulated local banks on riding out the crisis, local banks had met all their obligations by hoarding currency, creating what the *Kentuckian* conceded was a "general local stringency." The banks that had allied themselves with the Association, advancing money on tobacco pledged to the PPA, now refused to make any loans at all.[56]

Only recently released from a New York sanatorium, Ewing advised tobacco growers to be thrifty and avoid credit, and he warned against hoarding. He told his followers to maintain their confidence in the banks. W. C. Warfield urged Association farmers not to sell the tobacco they had pledged to the Association, promising that when the Association finally sold their tobacco it would bring a high price and ready cash. Joel Fort, president of the Association, thought the whole panic had been engineered by the trusts to pressure President Roosevelt to ease enforcement of the Sherman Anti-Trust Act. "The banks were full of money," Fort told one audience, "but a panic was needed. The beef trust needed a panic, the Standard Oil Company needed a panic. They sent out and got all the money (surplus) and carried it down to Wall Street and then they shut down. Down went the price of hogs two cents a pound. Then they turned on the tobacco business, and there could not be any advance obtained on tobacco."[57]

When banks stopped advancing cash, many poorer farmers had little choice but to sell their crops outside the organization for immediate cash. The Association lost members. With economic incentives no longer available, the necessity for intimidation grew. The successful raids on Eddyville and Princeton, coming before the contraction, had forced many farmers into the Association, but now some of those farmers deserted. The Night Riders' power constantly had to be reaffirmed. Amoss and his lieutenants decided on a bigger and bolder raid. They targeted Hopkinsville, with a population of ten thousand, in Christian County.

Hopkinsville was a city of tobacco warehouses. Some even held Association tobacco. But other warehouses held the tobacco trust buyers had been busily acquiring from Association deserters and independents who had never joined the Association. If the Night Riders could burn those warehouses filled with "hillbilly" tobacco, they would counter the loss of farmer support. It was easier to burn tobacco in warehouses than in each dissident farmer's barn. The raid would be a naked grab for control of the entire Black Patch tobacco crop and would show that the Night Riders were the law in the Black Patch. By raiding a large, dominant town they would demonstrate their authority to doubtful farmers thinking of deserting.

To mount an attack of the scale necessary to subdue Hopkinsville, the Night Riders had gathered five hundred supporters from a wide stretch of the western Black Patch, chiefly the Kentucky counties of Trigg, Lyon, and Caldwell. Earlier raids pitted neighborhood farmers against the local warehouse, but now men found themselves marching shoulder to shoulder with vigilantes from communities miles away from their home neighborhoods. These men could hardly claim to be defending their homes and neighbors; this was an undisguised bid to control tobacco across the entire Black Patch.[58] Such an alliance of "island communities" was not unprecedented in the Black Patch. Black Patchers from diverse communities had banded together in 1812 to fight Indians in Indiana, and in 1861 many of them had joined the Confederacy or fought in guerrilla bands. But this was different from these wartime episodes. Everyone understood that war temporarily suspended normal rules and procedures; the Association and the Night Riders fought for a permanent change in the rules. By drawing together vigilantes from so many diverse neighborhoods, the Night Riders advancing on Hopkinsville shattered their carefully cultivated image as defenders of community life. Now they seemed more modern and perhaps menacing to the neighborhoods they once claimed to protect.

On the night of December 6, 1907, the Night Riders gathered from Cedar Grove Lodge and Nabb's School; from Wallonia and Caledonia; from Gracey, and such hamlets as Roaring Springs and Humphrey's School. In northern Lyon County, fifty miles from Hopkinsville, Joe Ellis Scott cut holes in his stocking cap for his eyes and put on corduroy pants and overalls to keep warm.[59] He joined crowds of men on horseback.[60]

In Hopkinsville, the masked men broke a window at Latham's warehouse. Inside, they poured coal oil over chairs and piled-up boxes. Someone lit a match. Scott later remembered the explosion and then the storm of fire that engulfed the building from top to

Fire from Latham's warehouse spread to this warehouse which housed, ironically, Association tobacco. Photo from *Harper's Weekly,* February 8, 1908, 15.

bottom. Another squad of Night Riders wheeled south onto Campbell Street toward the single-story, frame "Growers'" warehouse owned by W. T. Tandy and operated by the Italian Regie. Inside, there were 111,295 pounds of tobacco, for which the Regie had paid farmers nearly $10,000. It went up in flames.[61] A crowd of Night Riders singled out tobacco buyer Lindsay Mitchell. They forced him out of his house, beat him, and then hustled him to the center of town to be released.[62] Some of the Riders' shooting went wild and a stray bullet struck Amoss, who collapsed, grazed in the scalp.[63] The masked men loaded their leader onto a buggy and escaped, leaving $200,000 worth of damage.[64]

Community courts had tolerated and encouraged vigilante behavior because the Night Riders appeared to be defending traditional values. How would they react to this new exercise of extralegal power? Previous raids on Princeton and Eddyville had provoked only a minimal response from local lawmen and had the sanction of the community. But with their strike on Hopkinsville, the Night Riders had finally assaulted a profoundly hostile community. These Night Riders came from all over the Black Patch—not just the immediate vicinity around Hopkinsville. This was not a matter of local farmers destroying "their" warehouse. Now farmers

Major Bassett of
Hopkinsville pursued the
Night Riders after the raid
on Hopkinsville. Photo
from *Hampton's Magazine*
22 (March 1909): 348.

from many different communities joined together to attack a warehouse many had probably never seen before. This was something
far more modern than politics out-of-doors. Paradoxically, while
the Night Riders seemed too modern, they also seemed dangerously old-fashioned. Hopkinsville was a far more cosmopolitan
place than Eddyville or Princeton. People chose to live there because they believed in the future, which they usually associated
with business prosperity. They did not appreciate a band of rural
ruffians setting fire to a portion of their city in what seemed like
a throwback to some darker, earlier period. Hopkinsville could
hardly hope to attract industry and business if lawless vigilantes
stood ready to attack and destroy those same businesses.

As a result of Hopkinsville's hostility to the raiders, the first
pitched battle of the Black Patch war occurred only a few hours
after the Night Riders left the burning city. Major Erskine Birch
Bassett, commander of company "D" of the town militia, scrambled
to assemble his men. Bassett's company had benefited so much
from the generosity of multimillionaire philanthropist John Camp-

bell Latham, whose warehouse the Night Riders had just burnt down, that they were originally called "Latham's Guards." Rounding up a dozen of "Latham's Guards," Bassett started after the retreating Night Riders.[65]

Bassett and his men quickly found where the Night Riders had hitched their horses before marching into Hopkinsville. There was a scattering of debris, a hitch rein, papers, the remains of meals eaten, and a fire. Pushing their horses hard, the posse neared Trigg County as dawn approached.[66] They could hear the Night Riders before they spotted three buggies and some horsemen from the top of a little rise. Bassett and his son rode up alongside one of the buggies. Each grabbed a rider and demanded that he surrender. When Bassett's man shrank from his grasp, the buggy's horse lurched into a gallop, pulling away. They fired. The Night Riders returned the fire. Bassett's men hit at least two Night Riders, killing teenager George Gray of Blue Springs and injuring Clancy McCool. Bassett collected a bloody scarf and a cap.[67]

Part of the posse took another road, headed south, and caught up with another party of raiders. The resulting exchange of gunfire killed another Night Rider. He was taken to his home, where his family said he died of "heart failure," and was buried in the family cemetery.[68]

The Night Riders ahead of Major Bassett scrambled down the road with George Gray's body. They reached Reuben Stewart's house, where they were welcomed inside. The next day two of the most prominent men in Trigg County claimed Gray's body and returned it to his parents' house in Blue Springs.[69] Community support for the Night Riders remained solid in Trigg County, where they could easily find safe refuge and support from local government.

A raid on a town the size of Hopkinsville blackened Kentucky's name from coast to coast. Everywhere there were calls for a state response. The New York *Times* put the story at the top of page one, telling readers that anarchy had broken out in Kentucky. The Night Riders impressed the Chicago *Tribune* and the Memphis *Commercial-Appeal* with their careful planning and organization while the Los Angeles *Times* emphasized the raid's destruction. The Atlanta *Constitution* published a more sensationalized account, describing Hopkinsville's population as cringing in terror before the ravages of a "wild mob, shooting right and left." The raid left the *Constitution* and the Memphis *Commercial-Appeal* so jumpy that on December 12 they headlined rumors, later proven false, that the Night Riders had launched a second raid on Hopkinsville.[70]

The Night Riders had fielded an army that made news in newspapers across the nation. They terrified their enemies. Many farmers joined the Association out of fear. The only drawback was that in asserting their force the Night Riders had created contempt and disrespect for the established court system. The Hopkinsville raid was the Night Riders' sharpest challenge to Kentucky's constituted authorities.

Planters had forged a powerful, and popular, army. But however much they represented their communities, the Night Riders operated outside the law, and as they organized, their leaders must have wondered how local prosecutors and judges would react. They had nothing to fear. All over the Black Patch lawmen virtually endorsed vigilantism, making their courts seem powerless and weak in the face of masked men if not an adjunct to lawlessness. This proved to be the most salient characteristic of the Black Patch war.

Black Patch lawmen permitted the Night Riders to act extra-institutionally on the assumption that the normal process of government could not satisfy community needs. Judges, prosecutors, sheriffs, and juries felt that the Association and the Night Riders defended the Black Patch's traditional communities from outside interference; the threat tobacco companies posed justified extra-legal violence. The attitude was essentially the same as expressed by the leader of the mob action in Baltimore a century before: "The laws of the land must sleep, and the laws of nature and reason prevail."[1]

One judge who acquiesced to Black Patch rioting was Charles Waller Tyler, an unusually powerful county leader. By an act of the Tennessee legislature, Montgomery's county court judge had a dual function, presiding over both the county court and the criminal court. Tyler occupied this influential position from 1873 until 1918. In 1985, a retired lawyer remembered Tyler as a benevolent despot who got things done regardless of rules, regulations, or statutes. Tyler oversaw the construction of the Montgomery County courthouse after the great fire of 1878 and revamped the jail and jail system. Boss of Montgomery County, Tennessee, Tyler was the quintessential Bourbon.[2]

Yet, despite his authority, this powerful political boss allowed vigilantes free rein in his county. In this he was not alone, but Tyler differed from other Black Patch judges, sheriffs, and prosecutors in that he had explained the conditions under which he would condone vigilantism, in a novel he published in 1902.[3] Entitled *The K.K.K.,* Tyler's novel argues that vigilantism occasionally was necessary. The novel begins with a murder, but it is a murder without a mystery: the victim identifies her attacker before dying. To bring the murderer to justice, leading citizens form a Ku Klux Klan band. But the Klansmen do not plan a lynching; they exemplify not mob violence, but order, forming a stable "shadow government" of responsible men.[4] Thus, for most of his book, Tyler's fictional Ku Klux Klan assists lawful authorities in a tedious journey toward justice. The chief Klansman tells his followers, "Trust to the law, trust to the law. Let us not advertise to the world that we have evils which our laws are incapable of redressing."[5] Klansmen urge witnesses to attend court and express faith in the proceedings. Apparently vindicating their faith, a jury convicts the defendant and condemns him to hang. But Tennessee's supreme court overturns the conviction on "a quibble."[6] One criminal exults, "I drink to de law. De frent uff de guilty and de terror uff de innocent." But the Klansmen seize the prisoner, try him before their own court, and hang him.[7]

In his novel, Tyler explains why citizens should generally shun vigilantism, but explicitly states the conditions under which it is justified. Citizens should avoid mob law, he contends, because such extralegal action often results in terrible mistakes. Sometimes mobs hang the wrong person. Furthermore, it promotes contempt for the law and encourages disorderly persons. Finally, it proclaims to the world that the community resorting to such measures is incapable of ordering itself through law. But on rare occasions extralegal action is justifiable. Community leaders must turn to mob law only in the face of a terrible miscarriage of justice. In *The K.K.K.* the supreme court's reversal of the conviction for murder represents just such a justification for vigilantism.[8]

The Black Patch war broke out four years after publication of Tyler's novel. Once more, Tyler and other Black Patch lawmen thought events justified vigilantism and did not act to stop it. But in allowing their courts to be perceived as ineffectual against vigilantism, they would damage the fabric of society in a way not easily repaired. When lawmen permitted the Night Riders to overawe local courts, they allowed the vigilantes to appear more powerful than they really were.

Night Riders dominated the Caldwell County grand jury. On April 18, 1907, Night Riders scraped Robert Hollowell's plant beds in Caldwell County. Although his brother, John E. Hollowell, served as an officer in the Caldwell County chapter of the Association, Robert Hollowell had refused to join. Hollowell's wife, Mary Lou, was sure that her husband's brother and his tenants had been responsible. But the grand jury to which she related her suspicions included Association men. The same men who destroyed her husband's plant beds controlled the Caldwell County circuit court.[9]

The grand jury was a conduit to the vigilantes, and after Mary

Lou's testimony the Night Riders tried to intimidate her. Her brother-in-law John shocked her with his knowledge of what she had said in the grand jury room. He assured her he meant no harm but warned her to stop talking against the Night Riders. "You could be killed," he warned her. But Mary Lou had no intention of caving in to vigilantism. Determined to give the Night Riders a dose of their own medicine, she hired her husband's two tenants, Steve Choate and Ned Pettit, to scrape the plant beds of her brother-in-law and those of his tenants.[10]

When Mary Lou's brother-in-law learned who had destroyed his plant beds and retaliated by organizing a raid on the Hollowells and their tenants, she found further evidence that the court system was in the hands of the vigilantes.[11] This was not unique to Caldwell County. All across the Black Patch local courts hesitated to act against the vigilantes, if indeed they were not actually in league with them. When lawmen did bring vigilantes to court, the results usually disappointed advocates of law and order. In Princeton, the Night Riders threatened one witness after he swore out a warrant against one of their number. Onlookers applauded when the witness publicly retracted his earlier positive identification.[12] A Princeton merchant who had watched the Night Riders invade his town bluntly told a reporter that if he served on a jury, "you'd never get me this side of the Eternal to vote any one of 'em into the penitentiary. No sir!"[13] Others shared the merchant's feelings. In Tennessee a Robertson County jury swiftly acquitted five Night Riders in 1906. A juror boasted afterwards: "There was not a 'hill billy' on the jury," meaning no farmer who had refused to join the Association. The judge called one of the defendants to the bench to congratulate him. By this time the victim realized he could not survive in his community outside the PPA. Pledging to join the Association, he thanked each of the jurors who had acquitted his tormentors.[14]

Tennessee officials regularly defended the Association, and even the Night Riders, in court. For example, in August 1907 Night Riders burned a store in Montgomery County, which was within the purview of Judge Charles W. Tyler. Minimizing the Night Rider threat in his county, Tyler told the grand jury investigating the fire that he was "not prepared to believe that these lawless acts have been done by the Association." Calling the fire "an incident to which far more importance has been attached than deserved," he suggested that vandals other than the Night Riders set the "small fire of unknown origin." He theorized that "some thief may have broken in, and burned the house to conceal his crime." Other crimes attributed to the Night Riders, he declared, "are manifestly the work of secret villains prompted by malice." Moreover, the judge opined that the Association "has been of great advantage to the people of this section."[15] The Montgomery County grand jury investigated and indicted a single individual for the crime.

State authorities gave less credence to Tyler's theories. Tennessee's state fire marshal investigated the fire, summoning witnesses and taking testimony. Seven of the witnesses consulted Clarksville city attorney Dancey Fort, and on his advice defied their subpoenas. All were Night Riders. The fire marshal returned to Nashville and again summoned the seven, obviously so he could bring them to trial in a more favorable court than the one in Clarksville. The case against the seven witnesses came to trial in Nashville in January 1908. The Clarksville city attorney argued on behalf of the Night Riders, claiming Tennessee law gave the fire marshal only limited subpoena power.[16]

This episode pitted Clarksville officials against state authorities, with the local lawmen actually defending arsonists. Although this incident is unusual for officials' openness in their surrender to lawlessness, it actually typifies most localities' reaction to Night Rider violence. In Trigg County vigilantism virtually supplanted the rule of law. The Night Riders met in the courthouse in meetings presided over by county attorney John Kelly. Trigg Countians settled their disputes in the courtroom but not in court. For example, when Clarence Wilson acted on a grudge against Alfred Hendricks, persuading Night Riders in Roaring Springs to burn his house down, Hendricks complained to Kelly. Rather than take the case up as county attorney, Kelly had Hendricks make his complaint on the second floor of the courthouse to the Night Rider leadership. After the assembled vigilantes agreed that Wilson had misused their order, Kelly instructed Night Riders to "visit" Wilson.[17]

Kelly and other Trigg County, Kentucky, authorities steadfastly resisted prosecuting vigilantes. In July 1908, the vigilantes shot Walter Goodwin, who had offered evidence against a band of Night Riders in Trigg County. The pistol bullet cut his tongue slightly before plunging downward and erupting out the left side of his neck. Goodwin called E. C. Walker, a militia officer stationed in Trigg County, who told the sheriff that Goodwin had named his assailants, and he offered the assistance of his men in arresting the three suspects Goodwin named. Sheriff W. C. Broadbent rejected the offer, but said he was too busy waiting on the court to arrest the suspects himself. The frustrated Walker found and arrested two of the three men himself. Broadbent angrily complained, demanding to know on whose authority Walker had made the arrests and telling him he did not want the militia "butting in his territory" making arrests. The Trigg County grand jury refused to indict any of the men Goodwin accused of shooting him.[18]

As in Clarksville, Sheriff Broadbent and Trigg County grand jurors openly defended vigilantism, using county resources to protect Night Riders from punishment. Even shooting victims like Goodwin could expect no help from lawmen. When court officers allowed vigilantes free rein, they damaged the credibility of the legal system in their communities. The apparent impotence of the courts contributed to the public's perception of Night Rider power. This left Night Riders free to so thoroughly terrorize their victims that they would hesitate to come forward when courts finally did try to reassert the rule of law.

With the courts refusing to act, opponents of the Night Riders found they had to protect themselves. Several farmers in the neighborhood of Stainback School, determined to oppose vigilantism, organized a neighborhood alarm system. When the Night Riders struck they were ready, sounding the alarm when the vigilantes caught George Cornelius "Neil" Lawrence outside his two-story farm home. The masked men shot Lawrence in the hand. Lawrence and his hired man returned fire, killing at least one raider. Other opponents of the Night Riders in the neighborhood rushed to Lawrence's aid. Ambrose Marion "Bud" Cope, a tenant for two Adams businessmen opposed to the Night Riders, his three sons, and their hired man all ran toward Lawrence's farm, armed with shotguns supplied by tobacco-buyer Ben Sory.

By the time they got there, the Night Riders had already set ablaze Lawrence's barn, filled with a neighbor's tobacco, and left for their next target. There they set fire to L. W. "Wash" Fletcher's barn and visited one of Fletcher's tenant houses, occupied by Mon Lowe, his wife, and three children. They called Lowe out and whipped him with a pistol—then disappeared into the night.[19]

In neighborhoods like Lawrence's, where several farmers opposed vigilantism and could help each other, such resistance effectively blunted night riding. Where the Night Riders controlled or intimidated virtually the whole neighborhood, dissenters found themselves entirely at the mercy of the masked men. Local lawmen rarely offered Night Rider opponents solace.

Cities and towns all across Kentucky and Tennessee posted guards, nervously eyed strangers, and waited for the Night Riders. Clarksville, Tennessee, officials first tried to battle the vigilantes. City leaders convened meetings, armed the citizenry, and formed a Law and Order League. They collected money to hire guards. City Attorney Dancey Fort tried to smooth over tensions between farmers and Clarksville tobacco buyers. On January 6, 1908, he wrote in his diary cryptically only that he "used efforts" to ease frictions, but he was undoubtedly in contact with both sides, trying to persuade buyers not to offend Association farmers and Association men not to stage a Hopkinsville-like raid on Clarksville. Fort straddled the fence for much of the Night Rider crisis, serving as city attorney but also as defense attorney for various Night Riders.[20]

But if Fort was trying to talk Clarksville out of a crisis, other civic leaders were taking more concrete—and more dangerous—steps. A committee of five business leaders, including the mayor, approached Judge Tyler to discuss what could be done to defend the city. In this meeting Tyler agreed to disburse county funds to help hire six extra policemen or guards, probably to appease law-and-order advocates without calling out the militia. Tyler and the businessmen discussed who should take charge of the guards. Someone mentioned the sheriff, but he was recuperating from a lengthy illness. "Better let him sleep," Tyler said. Someone else suggested the sheriff's deputy, but Tyler dismissed him as well: "He's only a Night Rider." Someone finally suggested Ben Sory, the Italian Regie tobacco buyer who had already boldly resisted the Night Riders. Tyler agreed.[21]

On March 9, 1908, Dancey Fort traveled to Nashville to plead the case of some of his clients charged with Night Riding before the Tennessee Supreme Court.[22] Presumably he had no idea that at least three of his seven clients would don masks that evening for a rendezvous with other Night Riders. They met at the Association tobacco factory operated by Henry Bennett in eastern Montgomery County. Then Vaughn Bennett, his brother Earle, and their fellow Night Riders galloped across the county, intending to whip a man for keeping a brothel.[23]

As the Night Riders rode off, two of Sory's allies, Robert and Henry Morrison, were standing guard at their house, north of Bennett's tobacco factory. The Night Riders had repeatedly threatened them for their determined refusal to join the Association. Looking out an upstairs window, Robert saw the crowd of mounted and masked men ride by. He telephoned Will Crouch, another Association opponent. Crouch passed the word to his father, who called Sory in Clarksville.[24]

Sory told the police chief that fifteen Night Riders were headed for Clarksville. The police chief and Sory called the sheriff, but as they expected, he took no action. Sory then assembled his town guards, forming a posse.[25] They rode to Crouch's house, on a little hill with a serviceable view up and down Trough Spring Road. By this time the telephone lines had been cut, so Sory and his men could only guess the Night Riders' movements. Then they heard shooting. After whipping the brothel keeper, the Night Riders had ridden south on Woodson Road, crossing Trough Spring Road.

Sory positioned members of his posse at various strategic points, stationing two men, Walter Hunt and John Gardner, at a crossroads. All nervously watched and waited for their quarry. Gardner saw the Night Riders and called out in the dark, "The Night Riders are coming." Then Hunt saw them too. Both later claimed the Night Riders fired first. In any case, both Gardner and Hunt fired their automatic shotguns five times in rapid succession, blasting two masked men from their horses. One did not get up.[26]

Night Rider Marcellus C. Rinehart, who called himself "Bud the Bull," described what happened. "We were ambushed. Vaughn fell over behind his rifle and said he was shot." Gunfire also struck Vaughn's brother, seventeen-year-old Earle, but he managed to cling to his horse for a time, riding right over his brother's fallen horse.[27] Finally Earle fell. He crawled south on the road until he came to a big double log house occupied by a black tenant couple, "Uncle" John and "Aunt" Jane Woodson. Earle recognized "Uncle" John as the man who barbecued hogs for barn raisings and other social gatherings. The Woodsons saved Earle's life, bandaging him and administering first aid.[28]

Meanwhile, the posse regrouped at Will Crouch's house. Accompanied by Crouch and his father, they returned to the crossroads. One of the Night Riders was still sprawled on the road. Gardner lit a match and held it close to his head. They pulled his mask off. It was Vaughn Bennett. They had shot him in the right eye, the right temple, the back of the neck, and in the right arm near the shoulder. Sory and his men took Bennett to a barn, where he died without regaining consciousness.[29]

Violence then threatened to erupt in Clarksville at any minute. The silence from both sides only increased the tension. Both Sory's men and the Night Riders did and said nothing; the possemen consulted attorneys and were advised to keep silent. Sory wanted to publicize the incident but the other members of the posse and Judge Tyler dissuaded him.[30] For their part, the Night Riders first considered retaliation. After the shooting, a crowd of horsemen reportedly gathered at the home of Vaughn Bennett's disconsolate father. If he wanted them to, they were ready to burn Clarksville, they told the old man. Henry Bennett could be a violent man. In 1906 he had tried to knife a neighbor who refused to join the Association. But now Bennett told the horsemen that there had been enough violence.[31]

But while the Night Riders took no action in response to the killing, the Association did. Although it claimed to have no connection with the Night Riders, Association leaders, enraged by Bennett's death, organized a boycott of Clarksville businesses. Clarksville merchants swiftly capitulated to the pressure and negotiated an agreement. Virtually a surrender document, the agreement severely limited the activities of Clarksville lawmen and citizens, even the militia. There would be no more posses like the one Sory led on March 9.

Some evidence suggests there may have been an unwritten addendum to the agreement, specifying the arrest and perhaps even the conviction of the two men who shot Bennett. Such an unwritten understanding would have been possible because one of the parties to the agreement was Judge Tyler, the same man who had financed Sory's posse and the man who would preside over any trial of Hunt and Gardner, unless he disqualified himself.[32] Soon after the agreement George Albrecht of the Kentucky militia wrote that "the authorities over at Clarksville are bending heaven and earth to secure an indictment of Ben Sory for the killing of Bennett." According to Albrecht they preferred not to convict Sory but to jail him without bail to end his campaign against the Night Riders. "I have been trying to get Sory to come across the [Kentucky-Tennessee] line and perhaps he may if he has time to get the news and beat the officers," Albrecht wrote.[33] The agreement between Clarksville and the Association surrendered local courts to the Night Riders. They would now have the power of the state at their disposal to battle Sory.

Even so, Montgomery County officials never indicted the popular and powerful Sory. However, they quickly indicted Gardner and Hunt. On September 8, Montgomery County's criminal court convened a special session for the trial. William Daniel, Jr., led the defense. Daniel sympathized with the fight farmers waged on the trust—in 1888, his father had been the Montgomery County Wheel's choice for governor. But despite his feelings, Daniel opposed the Night Riders and was deeply upset over the divisions the conflict caused in the county. Daniel owned several farms, which he rented out to sharecroppers. Night Riders had repeatedly raided one of these farms. After they locked two mules in a stable and set it afire, Daniel decided to go after the people he thought responsible. He had grabbed his shotgun, but his father had stopped him.

When the Night Riders learned that Daniel planned to defend Gardner and Hunt, they threatened to kidnap his sister, Eleanor, if he did not withdraw from the case. Once again, Daniel believed he knew who had made the threat. Approaching the man, he told him if anything happened to Eleanor, he would kill him. Nothing happened to Eleanor.[34]

District Attorney General Matt G. Lyle led the prosecution. Although in the Gardner and Hunt case Lyle would be on the side of the Night Riders, he was not really a Night Rider partisan and in fact had earlier hired Pinkerton detectives to investigate the vigilantes. The Pinkertons typically conducted such probes by placing some of their "operatives," as they preferred to be called, inside the organization to be investigated. This procedure had worked well in both urban and rural environments with murderers, bank robbers, and even the close-knit Molly Maguires. So, disguised as tramps, Pinkertons rode freight trains into Montgomery County hoping to collect information on the Silent Brigade.

One Pinkerton agent posed as a fruit tree salesman. Traveling to Clarksville by train and slipping up an alley to the Baptist church across from Lyle's apartment, he made oral reports to the prosecutor. On one occasion, the Pinkerton agent, a convivial man, reported drinking and playing cards with some Night Riders. At the end of the evening's game, the vigilantes told the spy they knew who he was and what he was doing. They advised him to give up "selling fruit trees."[35] But through such agents, Lyle had learned a good deal about the people involved in the case.

The judge presiding over the trial would be Charles Tyler. Although he had helped organize and finance the posse that resulted in the shooting, Tyler did not step aside for a special judge and denied defense requests for a change of venue.

On court day, spectators packed the courtroom, each person having been searched by the sheriff. Each person, that is, except for William Daniel, Sr. The old lawyer told Judge Tyler that he would not submit to a search, but would give his word as an ex-Confederate officer that he was not armed. An ex-Confederate officer himself, Judge Tyler thought that was good enough.[36]

Once the trial began, the defense argued that the defendants had been authorized by community leaders—including Judge Tyler, the chief of police, and the mayor—to put down invading Night Riders. "The defendants were there that night with an officer, performing their duty as custodians of women and children of this city and county," Daniel told the jurors. Gardner and Hunt had acted in self defense, firing only after a Night Rider had fired at them shouting, "Boys, let them have it."

In response Lyle produced five of the Night Riders, all between sixteen and twenty-five, who had accompanied the Bennetts the night Vaughn died. They all admitted to being masked and wearing a white piece of cloth on their shoulders as a Night Rider badge. But all insisted they were simply "out for fun" and committed no "depredations" other than cutting phone lines. One witness said he knew that the Night Riders planned to whip a man that night and simply wanted to watch. Another said he knew how to dress like a Night Rider from reading the Nashville *Banner*. The witnesses agreed that they missed the whipping but saw twenty-five or thirty masked men leaving the house of the man that had been whipped.[37]

Both the prosecution and the defense claimed that a victory for its side would be a victory for law and order. Daniel warned jurors that if they convicted Gardner and Hunt the Night Riders would reign supreme in lawless anarchy. The prosecution similarly warned against freeing Bennett's murderers. To do so would send a message to all of society that any group could pick up guns and make themselves the law. Since picking up guns and making themselves the law was exactly what the Night Riders did, there was some irony in Lyle's argument. His oral attack on vigilantism may have been as much directed against the Night Riders as against the defendants. Like Daniel, he was calling for the imposition of a rule of law and an end to lawlessness.

After the prosecution and defense made their final arguments, the judge charged the jury. Tyler explained to the jury that self-defense was "a situation where he [the defendant] has good reason to apprehend grave and imminent danger. . . . The danger must be real or honestly believed to be so." He told the jurors that it was not necessary for the Night Riders to have fired first for the defendants to be acquitted, if they fired only when they "saw the band . . . making hostile demonstrations and apparently about to fire upon them." No one can appoint a citizen to act in lieu of the sheriff, Tyler said. However, the statutes did allow any officer or citizen to make arrests, without a warrant, for offenses committed in their presence.[38]

With both sides claiming to act for law and against anarchy and lawlessness, in essence, the jury had to determine who represented their community. The jury decided for the Night Riders. They found Hunt and Gardner guilty of murder in the second degree. Tyler sentenced the two men to ten years in the penitentiary.[39] The verdict and sentence meant that the Night Riders had actually used local law-enforcement institutions for their own purposes. Vigilantism supplanted local law-enforcement structures.

At the well-publicized Gardner-Hunt trial Sory's men fought the Night Riders for legitimacy. Lyle had real doubts about the Night Riders, but in this trial he, too, went along with lawlessness, championing the Night Rider claim. The presence of such a respected community leader on the side of the Night Riders cannot be overestimated. Such an endorsement convinced many observers, who knew nothing of Lyle's connection with the Pinkerton investigation, that the vigilantes really represented their community—not Sory and his lieutenants. Tyler's position in this case is remarkable. As the man who authorized Sory to defend Clarksville, he clearly should have recused himself from the case. But he did not and even sought to imprison the very men he had dispatched against night riding. That he turned on his own men demonstrated the force of public opinion on behalf of vigilantism.

This surrender by lawmen to vigilantism distinguishes the Black Patch war from other episodes of vigilantism. Urban laborers, midwestern grain farmers, and Deep South cotton growers all expressed anger at trust plundering. Tobacco growers all over Kentucky and Tennessee sold their crop to the same tobacco trust for precisely the same low prices. An area of Virginia produced the same crop as the Black Patch for the same customer. Violent episodes occurred in all these geographic regions. In fact, Night Riders in central Kentucky were so prevalent that a recent student has urged scholars to discard the term "Black Patch war," which refers only to western Kentucky and Tennessee, and substitute "tobacco wars" instead.[40] Yet only in western Kentucky did vigilantes become powerful enough to seize whole towns. Only in western Kentucky did the local court system surrender to vigilantism. In Kentucky many officials saw warehouse-burning crowds as practicing "politics-out-of-doors." Just like the Revolutionary-era Whig mobs, these crowds pursued popular justice in the absence of effective law. The capitulation of Kentucky lawmen to violence allowed the Night Riders to remain a powerful force even as the Association declined. Amoss's men began with a narrow mission. But in the atmosphere of toleration for lawlessness he helped create, vigilantism would become its own justification. Masked men attacked people not because they threatened the Association, but because they challenged the Night Riders.

The Hopkinsville raid alarmed Black Patch traditionalists. By joining together so many men from so many different communities, the Night Riders clearly sought control of the entire Black Patch tobacco crop. The Association had always presented itself as a defender of the traditional order. But by 1908 it was apparent that despite their claim to represent tradition, the Association's leaders were engaged in a very modern enterprise. More and more the Association appeared to be a radical force determined to centralize control in the hands of a few planters led by Felix Ewing.

It became clear that despite their apparent popularity, the Night Riders represented only one interest in the Black Patch—that of a narrow group of tobacco growers—rather than the whole community. As time passed the class dimension to the Association became more and more apparent. Landlords dominated county-level Association meetings with their constant complaints of "Labor is scarce," "No extra labor to be had," "If labor is not secured crop will be ruined," and "not enough labor to plant a full crop."[1] The voice of employer rather than employee held sway at Association meetings. And the intense strength of the Association in some neighborhoods masked the fact that the organization never controlled the entire Black Patch. After the Hopkinsville raid many people reconsidered the legitimacy of the Night Riders as "politics-out-of-doors." They began to see the Night Rider movement as illegitimate, usurping and challenging the Black Patch's network of autonomous communities rather than protecting it. In the Kentucky Black Patch most still thought the Night Riders acted for their communities, but doubts surfaced and some state authorities moved to restore order. Nevertheless, despite their emerging misgivings regarding the Night Riders, many Black Patchers still mistrusted the state government as an outside force.

Kentuckians had long disputed the proper role of their state government in promoting trade and industry.[2] Some still championed the Jacksonian ideal of a minimalist government while others preferred an energetic government working on behalf of business. This tradition of bitter divisions over exactly the issues the Night Riders raised paralyzed Kentucky's Democratic governor, John Crepps Wickliffe Beckham. Beckham tried to straddle an issue that really could not be straddled. Republicans and "New Departure" Democrats warned against the antitrust clamor against businesses "which are daily and hourly giving employment to thousands of laborers . . . and [have] strengthened and consolidated the power, the civilization, and the true greatness of the human race." They often opposed even limited business regulation.[3] Regarding vigilantism as incompatible with their vision of Kentucky's industrial future, New Departure Democrats and Republicans advocated laws to stop mob violence. It was at the urging of a New Departure governor that Kentucky legislators passed the state's so-called Ku Klux law after the Civil War. Moreover, New Departure Democrats opposed union activity, damning union violence as the work of "thieves, dead-beats, and bummers."[4] If Beckham listened to these voices, he would come down hard on the Night Riders.

But conservative Bourbons, who advocated local autonomy and condemned trusts, took a more tolerant attitude toward such violence. They opposed federal intervention in state affairs, voted against legislation designed to end vigilantism, and never hesitated to appeal to white voters' racism. Democratic governor John Y. Brown had rationalized lynchings as justified by "the most atrocious crimes" blacks committed.[5] If Beckham heeded men like Brown, he would take a tolerant view toward the Night Riders.

But as a Democrat, Beckham would be most unlikely to act against the Night Riders as decisively as many Republicans would prefer. More than either wing of the Democratic party, Kentucky Republicans favored using the power of federal and state government to pacify local passions, paving the way for business expansion. When Kentucky experienced a spasm of lynchings after the Civil War, thirty-six in 1870 alone, some Republicans had urged direct federal rule over the Commonwealth to end racial violence.[6] Kentucky Republicans also tried to use state power on behalf of black citizens, pushing a tough antilynching law through the legislature in 1897. Republican governors not only opposed lynchings but also regularly pardoned blacks sent to prison by mob-dominated courts. In the years after the Civil War, these issues won few elections for the Republicans. Republican John Marshall Harlan, for example, had run a strong race for governor in 1871 against inept opposition, but went down to defeat anyway. Many—perhaps most—voters regarded the Republicans as the champions of blacks and big business. Rural whites found one as distasteful as the other.[7]

Until the 1890s Kentucky Republicans had remained on the sidelines. People used the phrase "when Kentucky votes Republican" the same way others used "when hell freezes over."[8] But in the 1895 gubernatorial campaign the Democrats split into hard-money and free-silver wings, each with a candidate for governor. As a result, Kentucky elected its first Republican governor, William O'Connell Bradley. The following year the Commonwealth stunned observers by voting for the Republican presidential candidate, by the narrow margin of 281 votes. This first victory whetted the appetites of Republican politicians, many of whom dared hope that they stood on the brink of making Kentucky a solidly Republican state.

But the prize remained just out of reach. After Bradley moved into the governor's mansion, he faced a Populist-minded legislature. Lawmakers ignored Bradley's pro-business agenda and passed legislation intended to regulate corporations operating in Kentucky. Vigilante violence designed to make Kentucky toll roads free also marred Bradley's term. Angered that private corporations profited from public roads, these raiders destroyed toll-collection facilities. Their violence, and bloody feuds in Appalachia, confounded Bradley's efforts at mediation. Although he had promised in his campaign to curb lynchings, during his term extralegal executions took the highest toll since Reconstruction, and he left office with few accomplishments.[9]

The Republican nominee following Bradley, William S. Taylor, faced a dynamic opponent in the Democrats' William Goebel. Goebel electrified Kentucky farmers and laborers with a Populist-style campaign against trusts, particularly the powerful Louisville and Nashville Railroad. Although he failed to propose any concrete steps he might take against it as governor, Goebel vigorously attacked the tobacco trust. This made him popular with many farmers, but historians now agree that he lost to Taylor by 2,500 votes statewide. Nevertheless, the Democrats claimed victory and protested when Taylor took the oath of office and assumed the duties of governor. Tensions ran high, and in the excitement a sniper shot and critically wounded Goebel in front of the capitol building. The Democratic-controlled legislature voted to overturn the official election results and made the dying Goebel governor and, when he died, installed his lieutenant governor, John C. W. Beckham, in office. For a time Kentucky had two governments. Rival militia camped in the capital and Taylor declared a state of insurrection. Finally the courts ruled for the Democrats, and Taylor yielded, averting civil war.[10]

The experience left Beckham shaken. As governor, he tried to calm emotions rather than stir them and avoided waving the bloody shirt of Goebel's murder—although most Kentuckians believed that prominent Republicans had ordered the killing and Taylor fled the state to avoid prosecution. Moreover, Beckham proposed little reform legislation. A determined middle-of-the-roader, he made overtures to both the warring wings of his party. He did little to antagonize business but also avoided acting against Black Patch vigilantes.[11]

In the 1907 gubernatorial campaign Republican candidate Augustus E. Willson challenged Democrat Samuel Wilber Hager. The Democrats charged that Willson was a regularly employed attorney for the tobacco trust. Willson first admitted the charge, bluntly demanding to know "if . . . that fact is against my doing my duty as Governor of Kentucky." But after consulting his advisors the next day and assessing the public impact of the charge, Willson took a sharply different approach to packaging the same set of facts. Republican papers headlined Willson's "denial" of the charge. Though still admitting that he was the attorney in the two cases the Democrats offered as evidence, he now declared, "I am not and never have been the retained attorney of the Tobacco Trust." Willson then counterattacked, "Beckham, Hager, and Company have not yet denied and I am informed cannot deny . . . that the Tobacco Trust had contributed $15,000 to Beckham, Hager, and Company's 1903 campaign." Soon Republican papers trumpeted this new charge across the state.[12]

The Democratic charge that Willson was a trust lawyer missed reality by a wide margin. Willson actually sympathized with farmers and tried to arrange financial relief for tobacco growers while he was a candidate, asking the secretary of the treasury to lend money to tobacco farmers. Willson probably hoped to avert further Night Rider raids by financing farmers too poor to put their tobacco in the PPA. He never publicized his effort, which suggests his concern was more than mere politics.[13] In fact, Willson said as little as possible publicly about tobacco. Reports of his speeches in Henderson, Owensboro, Murray, and Paducah in western Kentucky are curiously devoid of references to local tobacco troubles, clearly the most important issue in that part of the state. In Hopkinsville, Willson's speech did deal with the Association and the Night Riders. Willson endorsed the Association, but added that he was for law and order too.[14]

Willson made public morality the general theme of the campaign, condemning Hager and Beckham as representing the "ring" or the "machine." It was a phony charge, but effective among rural Ken-

Governor Augustus
Willson vowed to crush
the Night Riders. Photo
courtesy of The Filson
Club.

tuckians. Successful Republican candidates in Kentucky always ran
quasi-nonpartisan campaigns. Willson did so by boasting that his
campaign had meant the end of the Republican machine, and that
he was now after the Democratic machine. It was all nonsense. If
there was a Republican "machine," Willson was more its product
than its opponent. But it worked. Rural Democrats hesitated to
vote for the tarnished Hager, urban Republicans turned out, and
Willson squeaked into the governorship by 18,000 votes.[15]

When the Night Riders staged their spectacular raid on Hopkinsville they confronted newly elected Willson with the specter of
anarchy. With only days left in his term, Beckham finally acted,
dispatching a militia company. Three days later Willson began his
gubernatorial career.[16]

Kentuckians elected Willson by the narrowest of margins, but
Republicans hoped he could move Kentucky decisively into the
Republican camp. To do it, he had to establish a record of accom-
plishment in office.[17] Furthermore, Willson had to repair the Republican party's image, tarnished by the Goebel affair. The alleged
involvement of Republican politicians in the assassination deprived the party of its best issue—immorality and corruption—
against the Democrats. If the party of murder tried to run against
the party of scandal, it ran the risk of being tagged the party of
hypocrisy. Willson needed to establish a law-and-order record to
cleanse his party of Goebel's blood.

Willson felt other pressures to follow a hard law-and-order line.

City officials in Hopkinsville made strong requests to him for military help. Unlike Clarksville officials, Hopkinsville's leaders had never opened channels of communication with protest leaders in the countryside; unwilling to negotiate with their foes, they relied on armed resistance. They looked hopefully to their new governor for help, since Willson had publicly expressed outrage at the Hopkinsville raid. His first reaction had been to sharply condemn it, vowing a thorough investigation as soon as he became governor. "The guilty ones shall be punished," he had promised. "Law and order must prevail."[18]

True to his word, immediately after his inauguration, Willson plunged into the Night Rider controversy. With the intention of acting quietly and discreetly, he dispatched Kentucky State Guard general Roger Williams to augment the state's investigation of the Hopkinsville raid. But Willson hoped to avoid using force against the Night Riders. He registered surprise when Williams told a reporter that the governor considered the situation critical and intemperately promised that the administration would break "the mob spirit prevailing in many sections of the state . . . if it required the entire state militia to accomplish it." Such inflammatory talk was exactly what Willson wanted to avoid. He angrily wrote in the margin of his copy of the newspaper report, "I did not tell him I thought situation critical." Confronted by the furious governor, Williams denied he had spoken to any reporters. But the newspaper told Willson's private secretary that the information came directly from Williams.[19]

Later that same evening Willson received a telephone request from Hopkinsville militia commander Erskine Bassett asking for more troops and claiming that another raid was imminent. Willson hesitated and instead of immediately sending troops he asked his new adjutant general to investigate. If he was hoping for a report that no troops were needed, the governor was disappointed. After telephone conversations with panicky Hopkinsville officials, the adjutant general urged Willson to send the troops, and Willson ordered another company of state guards to Hopkinsville.[20]

Although he believed that the local government in Trigg and Caldwell counties sympathized with the Night Riders, Willson never declared martial law.[21] Inhibited by Republican governor Taylor's near-catastrophic attempt to use the militia to hold his office, which had led to the Goebel shooting, Willson insisted that he was constitutionally prohibited from doing so unless rioters threatened the central government. Moreover, he knew that southern Republicans had been identified with the use of military force to retain office since Reconstruction.[22]

Willson spent his third day in office meeting with tobacco growers and state officials. He received conflicting advice. George W. Long, who as United States marshal for the western district of Kentucky had investigated the Night Riders for the Justice Department, advised Willson that large numbers of soldiers were not needed to maintain order. But others suggested that Willson follow the example of Theodore Roosevelt in the 1902 anthracite coal strike, somehow compelling the tobacco companies to negotiate a fair price with farmers. Chief among those advising Willson to take military action stood John Stites. Reared in Hopkinsville, Stites now practiced law in Louisville, where he also served as chairman of the board of directors of the Fidelity Trust Company. He implored Willson to send a "sufficient force" into Night Rider-plagued counties and arrest vigilante leaders. Stites even advocated Willson's personally leading the militia into Hopkinsville.[23]

But Willson disappointed Stites. He seemed to prefer conciliation, conceding in a public statement that "there must be some genuine cause at the bottom of these troubles" and promising to avoid "drastic measures until all peaceful possibilities have been exhausted."[24] Willson called for a "peace conference" between the companies and the Planters' Protective Association and other growers' organizations. He included James B. Duke of the American Tobacco Company, but failed to invite Joseph Ferigo of the Italian Regie, indicating that he still did not fully comprehend the basics of the conflict.

Stites was sharply disappointed in the governor's call for a peace conference, but actually Willson was considerably less conciliatory than he appeared. The statement calling the peace conference had been prepared by Judge Edward O'Rear, who sympathized with the farmers. Willson signed it as he hurried from his office to a train. Not until the next day did he realize with dismay that the statement included the comment about "some genuine cause" and a promise to eschew "coercive or drastic measures." However, Willson's old mentor, Supreme Court Justice John Marshall Harlan, approved of the announcement. "This is a good move," he wrote Willson, "kindness and firmness combined will settle that trouble."[25]

Remembering his earlier experience with Williams, Willson instructed his new adjutant general not to talk to reporters, telling him that all information should come from the governor's office. To create a positive atmosphere for the forthcoming conference, Willson optimistically claimed Night Rider violence had ended. The Louisville *Herald* echoed that there would be no more trouble in Hopkinsville. The Louisville *Courier-Journal* reported that the governor was "growing more sanguine daily" about the Night Rider problem.[26]

Some two hundred people attended the peace conference, held in the court of appeals chambers, but it proved to be a disaster. Things started badly when Ewing and Duke both refused to attend. Ewing claimed he was reluctant to discuss Association business frankly with competing farmer organizations. Moreover, Willson was unable to set the tone of the conference. To loud applause, Judge O'Rear attacked him for using troops in the Black Patch, charging that the troops were there only because the trust wanted them. "What we need is a physician who will treat the causes instead of the symptoms," he insisted. The tobacco companies present were no more cooperative than farmer representatives, refusing to negotiate with farmers' organizations.[27]

Not long after the peace conference, fifty to one hundred Night Riders swept into Russellville, Kentucky, from the southwest. With oil and dynamite they destroyed the independently owned Luckett-Wake factory and the American Snuff Company's factory, incinerating 465,000 pounds of tobacco. These were the only two warehouses in the city not serving the Association. Newspapers estimated the total damages at $50,000. After burning the warehouses the Night Riders left with military precision, in a double column with pickets and file closers trailing to prevent the kind of straggling that occurred after the Hopkinsville raid.[28]

Having tried the path of reconciliation without success, Willson now focused his efforts on punishing the Night Riders for raiding Hopkinsville. He urgently needed to take some action.

The Russellville raid put new pressures on opponents of the Night Riders to punish the marauders. To try the Night Riders in their home counties was an impossibility. The government and courts of Trigg County were so sympathetic to the vigilantes that one militia officer there calculated that "To kill the whole civil machinery of Trigg County would be to kill just so many Night Riders."[29] Even in Hopkinsville's Christian County indicting and prosecuting them would be difficult. One law-and-order advocate in Hopkinsville wrote, "No one can expect any relief from the ordinary course of the law." He reported that many suspected both the county sheriff and the commonwealth attorney of involvement in the Hopkinsville raid.[30] In fact, Night Rider opponents even suspected the judge of harboring Night Rider sympathies. Rumors circulated that both had sworn allegiance to the Silent Brigade.

One cannot know the truth about these charges, but the prosecutor and judge did block prosecution of the vigilantes. Commonwealth Attorney Denny P. Smith of Cadiz may not have been an actual member of the Silent Brigade, but he harbored political ambitions, and he knew that the base of his support lay in rural areas where voters remained sympathetic to vigilantism. Judge Thomas P. Cook of Murray may not actually have been a Night Rider, but like Smith he unquestionably sympathized with the masked men. After retiring from the bench he would figure prominently among Night Rider defense attorneys. At minimum, local lawyers considered Cook a weak judge. Since their circuit included both Trigg and Christian counties, Cook and Smith held almost complete control of the court where any Night Riders would be tried for the Hopkinsville raid. By controlling the composition of grand juries, Cook could prevent them from indicting or convicting Night Riders.

If a would-be defendant did find himself under indictment, his accusers still had another hurdle to clear before his case reached trial. As prosecutor, Smith examined indictments to weed out those based on insufficient evidence. Since the sufficiency of the evidence amounted to a judgment call, he had wide latitude in determining who went to court and who did not. And, in the event a case reached the trial stage, no one could compel Smith to prosecute enthusiastically or control what he chose to say to the jury.

As circuit judge, Cook had a variety of devices at his disposal to delay or prevent convictions of Night Riders. Under Kentucky law the judge could almost handpick petit jurors. The process required the judge to select three jury commissioners, who met only one time in their year of service, filling the jury wheel with names selected from tax lists. The judge kept the keys to the wheel in his personal possession. Observed only by his clerk, the judge pulled names from the wheel for jury duty. In an interview, former circuit judge Ira D. Smith said, "Of course, [there was] a good deal of responsibility on the judge and the clerk. No doubt about that. They could almost, if necessary, control the selection."[31] It would be a simple matter for Cook to make sure that jurors were farmers

Thomas Cook, the circuit judge who later defended Night Rider Amoss. Photo courtesy of King Library, University of Kentucky.

unsympathetic to the trust and its agents. Nor could anyone control what instructions Cook gave to the jury. If he found the Commonwealth's case not proven, he could direct a not guilty verdict. More subtly, he could evaluate the quality of evidence and the veracity of witnesses in his instructions to the jury.

To remedy the situation, Willson attempted to get both Smith and Cook to step aside. He had no power to remove either man, since both were elected, but he made overtures to each. The irresolute Cook initially agreed to allow Willson to appoint a special judge. But he quickly changed his mind, declaring that to recuse himself from Night Rider cases "would be a reflection on me." Smith, whose hostility toward Willson increased as the governor's term progressed, made it clear from the start that he had no intention of disqualifying himself.[32]

Although forces for law and order had received a setback, Cook and Smith did agree to call a special term of the circuit court to investigate the Hopkinsville raid. Even before Cook empaneled the grand jury in Hopkinsville, officials arrested the first man to be identified publicly as one of the invaders, Herman Richard Crenshaw of Trigg County, the nephew of former state senator and Association advocate Judge Robert Crenshaw. But when Judge Cook announced the grand jury, only two of the jurors lived in the city of Hopkinsville and half belonged to the Association. Nevertheless, the Hopkinsville *Kentuckian* expressed optimism that at last the law was in motion. The paper thought Cook's instructions to the jury were "strong and exhaustive," and Smith impressed reporters by vowing to "do his whole duty." The state fire marshal turned over evidence he had gathered about Crenshaw and also George B. Powell of Hopkins County. But he held back evidence against other Night Riders, waiting to see what the grand jury would do.

The grand jury moved only reluctantly. On January 4, 1908, the fire marshal turned over a list of witnesses, but the jurors said they wanted transcripts of his interviews before they would subpoena anyone. Yet after receiving copies of the transcripts, the grand jurors still refused to act, saying they lacked enough evidence to make a charge. Smith advised the grand jury that the fire marshal's evidence against Crenshaw did not warrant indictment, and they did not charge him. But the grand jury did indict Powell on the testimony of Lindsay Merrick, the tobacco buyer beaten during the raid, and John Smith, a black man. When Commonwealth Attorney Smith prosecuted Powell five months later, jurors acquitted him despite witnesses' positive identification.[33]

By the regular February term of court in Hopkinsville Willson had identified David Amoss as the leader of the raid on Hopkinsville. Amoss later asserted that state militia officials plotted to assassinate him, but no evidence of such a plot exists in Willson's surviving correspondence. It is clear that officials targeted him for arrest. The commander of militia forces in western Kentucky promised to "try hard to get an excuse to run him in."[34]

Night Rider opponents found the Christian County grand jury an insurmountable barrier to vigorous prosecution of the Hopkinsville raiders. Jurors never considered indicting Amoss. They indicted some accused Night Riders, but only four minor figures. When they indicted Crenshaw, James M. Weaver, and Gano Warder, Smith claimed the evidence insufficient to justify a trial and declined to prosecute. When grand jurors indicted Matt Gholson, Smith took him to trial but lost his case.[35] Smith applied a stiff standard of proof to witnesses testifying against the Night Riders, and at least one observer claimed the jurors sympathized with night riding.[36]

Willson could have fought the Night Riders with his own vigilantes. Cook and Smith frustrated Hopkinsville citizens so much that they turned to vigilantism themselves, organizing a law-and-order league. The league lobbied Willson for further prosecutions, more troops, and even a Gatling gun for its own use. Governor Willson appointed one of its members Christian County judge.[37]

But Willson did not intend to rely on Hopkinsville citizens to combat the Night Riders.

In 1908 Willson chose a military strategy, one fraught with problems. The Night Riders waged a hit-and-run war. Submerged in an indigenous population, they chose their battles. "Not one band defies the State's authority," the governor complained. "In every case they strike and then run and hide."[38] Worse, committing conventional military forces against an unconventional enemy risked alienating the local population. Nonetheless, Willson ordered Spanish-American War veteran Major George Albrecht and fourteen men from Louisville's Company "H" to Hopkinsville February 4. In March, he added fifty men from the Whitesburg militia to Albrecht's force.[39]

The governor also sought to penetrate the Night Rider organization with spies. In January 1908 Willson asked the federal government for agents, but Secretary of State Elihu Root refused. By March Willson had his own spy, referred to in correspondence as "John Smith," but in reality Ziba O. King of Central City. Willson paid "John Smith" in part with Commonwealth funds but also with money raised by John Stites of Louisville.[40] Albrecht also attempted to recruit informers, and some of his men traveled in plain clothes. However, because he and the governor had lost confidence in local judges and their juries, he never manifested much enthusiasm for gathering the kind of information that could be used in court. Instead, Albrecht hoped his spies would locate a Night Rider force so he could attack it. Albrecht stationed squads of men in places where he hoped the Night Riders would strike. Armed with a Gatling gun, which he called a "perfectly competent man killer," Albrecht planned to "try and bring on trouble." It would take killing to stop the Night Riders, he told Willson.

Albrecht's rhetoric undoubtedly reflects an amateur's thirst for military glory, but his strategy was not unsound. Willson and Albrecht were engaged in a struggle to reshape the public image of the Night Riders and reassert the law in the face of vigilantism. Their raids on Eddyville, Princeton, and Hopkinsville had made the Night Riders seem invincible. The failure of local courts to prosecute them for their crimes made them seem all the more so. A defeat at the hands of the militia—with some deaths—might change that image.

Willson gave Albrecht a free hand. "I desire to treat every man in a mask as an outlaw and as a burglar entering a house by night is treated," he assured his commander, "and I shall not permit any prosecution to continue against any man for shooting or killing any man in a mask." He considered Trigg County enemy territory, under the control of the Night Riders. "Mount ten men," Willson ordered, "march to Trigg line at night soon—then back. No explanations or talk. Don't shoot until you see the masks."

Albrecht ordered his men first to "be sure of the masks" and second to "pour on the lead." In a firefight, Albrecht hoped to "kill all possible, until hands were up." When Willson ordered Albrecht to send troops through Trigg County, Albrecht "let it slip that they would go straight through Cadiz." He planned to shoot any Trigg County lawmen trying to stop him.

For all his belligerent talk, Albrecht proved unequal to his task. Willson's strategy of defeating the Night Riders with troops failed. The Night Riders continued to carry out raids. Furthermore, a murder in Princeton, Kentucky, would signal an intolerable breakdown of order. Although his presence may have prevented a second raid on Hopkinsville, the Night Riders humiliated Albrecht. They burned a house only half a mile from the militia camp, and Albrecht's forces proved too disorganized to respond. Of course the locals saw it as further proof of the omnipotence of the masked men. Albrecht himself was "deeply chagrined at our failure to give chase" but begged the governor not "to relieve me or send me help I don't want." Still hoping to entice the vigilantes into a trap, he feared too many soldiers would scare them off. "I will have horses ready tonight," he promised.[41]

Albrecht's horses in Hopkinsville did him little good, because the Night Riders next struck in Crittenden County, forty-five miles away. Only the southern half of Crittenden County, which bordered Caldwell County on the north, lay in the area claimed by the Planters' Protective Association. Two independent tobacco dealers operated in the area covered by the Association, Henry Bennett at Dycusburg and A. H. Cardin in View. Night riding had not been much of a problem. But in December 1907, the diminutive Bennett crossed the Association by buying a wagonload of tobacco. The farmer delivering the offending tobacco probably had pledged it to the Association and then decided to get a higher price from Bennett. The Night Riders first threatened Bennett by leaving bundles of switches at his house several times.[42] In response Bennett went to an Eddyville saloon, where he openly, and perhaps drunkenly, challenged his tormentors. He knew Night Rider leaders patronized the saloon, and he offered to fight them one at a time. According to his daughter, "the Night Riders slipped out the back door of that saloon like rats leaving a sinking ship."[43]

On February 4, 1908, at 1:00 A.M. the Night Riders raided Bennett's house at Dycusburg. Bennett's sister-in-law saw them first. She went out on a veranda, but the vigilantes cursed her and ordered her back into the house. Bennett woke his wife, who got his gun and shells. But his wife never let him use them, pleading that their son was sick and the Night Riders might set fire to the house.[44] About 2:00 A.M. the main force arrived and began to line up in front of the house. Bennett's wife and sister-in-law begged the raiders not to molest them, but the masked men told them they would burn the house if Bennett did not come out.[45]

"They shot on the front porch and I heard my wife weaken and I knew I would have to face the music," Bennett remembered later. Bennett's daughter, who witnessed the raid and wrote an account of it in 1977, insisted her father came out unarmed. But according to the Night Riders' account, Bennett brandished a gun and vowed to kill the first man through the door. That turned out to be big Hyland L. "Hi" Coleman of Lamasco, who crashed through the door and snatched the gun out of the surprised Bennett's hands. Once they got outside, both raiders and victim agree, the Night Riders hauled Bennett to a tree where they beat him with thorn bushes. As the defiant Bennett silently bore their beating, his tormentors vowed to beat him until he cried out. Told he would be beaten to death if necessary, Bennett at last broke down and screamed. The Night Riders set fire to Bennett's tobacco warehouse and the distillery next to it. They left singing "The Fire Burns Bright in My Old Kentucky Home." A few days later the Night Riders assembled again and raided View, destroying Cardin's warehouse.[46]

The beating he sustained damaged Bennett's kidneys and left thorns embedded in his flesh. The thorns became infected, forming boils. His injured kidneys no longer able to carry off the poison, Bennett died of his wounds in 1910.[47]

Some two to three hundred men participated in the raids on Bennett and Cardin. From Caldwell County and the Lamasco section of Lyon County, they traveled more than sixty miles in winter over roads so muddy their horses sometimes sank to their knees. To secure an avenue of retreat, a party of raiders seized the town of Fredonia, holding it while the main body destroyed the warehouses in Crittenden County. They passed through Eddyville twice, watering their horses in Saratoga.[48] It was an impressive operation, mounted three months after Willson's militia declared all-out war on vigilantism.

In March Night Rider violence offered further proof that Willson's militia had failed to reestablish law and order. Bennett's cousin, Henry Wilson, had identified the leader of the Dycusburg raid as Orbie Nabb, a member of a prominent southern Caldwell County family. Nabb's uncle and guardian, community leader Ninian E. "Doc" Nabb, was a justice of the peace. Fanatical about the Association, the Nabbs refused to compromise with anyone they perceived to be an enemy of the PPA. Because he was unmarried and had no attachments, J. Orbie Nabb became a leading Night Rider and a member of the "inner circle" that met at Nabb's school. Some said he liked to lead the Night Riders in daylight processions dressed in a gaudy military-like uniform that included a feather in his hat and a gold-fringed sash.[49]

After Wilson informed on Orbie Nabb, the Night Riders forced Wilson to flee his farm. A hunted man, he took a job with the Henrietta Theater in Princeton. But the Night Riders quickly found him. Because of their threats Wilson spent his nights in a stable, afraid to sleep in his own bed. On the night of March 26, Orbie Nabb and Leech Guess came to the back door of the theater. The frightened Wilson hid. "It's Orbie Nabb, and they are trying to kill me," he told his employer. When he suddenly met Nabb on a stairway, Wilson shot first, killing the Night Rider. He fled the state.

By April and May 1908 the failure of Albrecht's strategy had become clear. The vigilantes proved too nimble for the militia to catch. Not only were the vigilantes winning the cat-and-mouse game they played with Albrecht, the raids into Crittenden County and the Nabb-Wilson incident showed that order continued to deteriorate. Reluctantly, the governor concluded that he could not expect his militia troops to tame the Night Riders. And Willson realized that Clarksville's defensive strategy had worked while Albrecht's attempts to launch an offensive against the Night Riders had failed. This encouraged Willson to return to a strategy he had earlier abandoned, once again pinning his hopes on the court system. He began stationing troops deeper into the Black Patch to defend likely targets of Night Rider raids. Albrecht resisted the decision, knowing the presence of troops would discourage raiding. But now Willson no longer hoped to trap the vigilantes into a battle. Soldiers set up camps in Lamasco, Cadiz, and Cobb—the very heart of the Night Rider district. David Amoss fled his home in

Cobb, convinced the soldiers meant to kill him. They planned nothing so dramatic—or outrageous. But they expected to discourage raids and to encourage witnesses to step forward so that the Night Riders might at last be brought before the bar of justice.

The Night Riders raided Hopkinsville just before the leader of the political party most alarmed by their activities took office. But while the Hopkinsville raid enraged Willson, he proved himself unable to crush its perpetrators with state power. Although he first rejected panicky cries for military force in Hopkinsville, from February 4 through April Willson authorized his militia to try to pick a fight with the vigilantes in hopes of drawing blood. This scheme failed—the Night Riders continued to strike at will, successfully dodging the militia. By using troops ineffectively, Willson undoubtedly contributed to the public's perception of the Night Riders as more powerful than government. And his failure to use the law consistently to combat vigilantism probably delayed restoration of local respect for the state judiciary.

As Kentuckians, including some planters, became increasingly uneasy over Night Rider violence, they wondered who could restore law to the Black Patch. Given the region's geography of close-knit communities, could outsiders do the job? After Governor Willson's military campaign had succeeded only in bringing his efforts into disrepute, some Black Patchers began to favor calling on the federal government to restore order. Such calls once again reveal the complexity of Black Patchers' relationship with outsiders. Most saw federal intervention as an unwelcome intrusion to be resisted, but not all.

Willson himself wrote the federal government asking for detectives. In the spring of 1908 city, county, and federal forces would each get a chance to reinstate the law in various places in the Black Patch. But the most successful challenge to vigilantism came from a state judge in Calloway County. Calloway County Night Riders had organized only slowly. Not until the spring of 1908 did the first series of threatening letters sent to non-Association farmers raise tensions there. The pro-Association editor of the Murray *Ledger,* O. B. Jennings, established an understanding with Night Rider leaders that no serious violence would occur in Calloway County.[1] Therefore Jennings suppressed news of the threats. However, local Night Riders were determined to break the agreement. They compelled one of their victims to acknowledge publicly the threatening letter he had received by publishing a "card" in the paper. The man forced Jennings finally to print the card by telling him his life and property were at stake. After this incident, more Night Rider victims appeared in Jennings's offices insisting that their cards be printed as well. Jennings believed that the publicity encouraged Night Rider violence.[2]

On April 1 Al Perry rode into the county seat of Calloway County, Murray. He had been whipped by the Night Riders and instructed to go to town and warn a non-Association warehouseman that if he put up any more tobacco he too would be whipped and his warehouse burned. The warehouse operator retorted that he intended to put up all the tobacco he had contracted to buy.[3] The next day another farmer came to town with a second warning for the warehouseman. In fact, Night Riders later testified, 250 Night Riders decided to burn all of Murray.[4]

After the second warning Judge A. J. G. Wells decided to call for troops. Willson promptly dispatched a group of state guards to Calloway County.[5] When the troops arrived, Willson placed them under the command of Wells rather than a militia officer from outside the community. Willson had sized up Wells. In contrast to panicky city officials in Hopkinsville, Wells seemed determined and resolute and this shaped Willson's strategy in Calloway County. Albrecht—an outsider in Christian County—wanted to "bring on trouble" rather than guard Hopkinsville. He fervently hoped the Night Riders *would* raid Hopkinsville again. Wells followed an entirely different strategy. He hoped to avoid bloodshed and used the troops to protect witnesses he planned to use to break the Night Riders in court.

This community-based strategy resulted in the Night Riders' first defeat. Rumors flew that 150 men had assembled to march on Murray but had disbanded when the Kentucky State Guards arrived.[6] Once assured of protection, witnesses began to come forward. One farmer told Wells that he had decided to avoid trouble by raising no tobacco but the Night Riders ordered him to raise a crop. Another told of being forced to join the Association. A third witness could identify some of the men who had beaten him. Another identified two men who had coerced him to take the Night Rider oath. Another witness told of being forced to disconnect telephone lines during a raid. A few Night Riders turned against their colleagues and offered evidence. The most spectacular witness was W. B. Stewart, who, confirming the worst rumors, detailed the Night Riders' aborted plans to raid and burn Murray.[7]

Wells traded charges with Night Rider partisans who claimed he had betrayed his community and sold out to outsiders. Murray *Ledger* editor Jennings accused Wells of working for the tobacco trust, attacking him as "my trust-y critic." The Law and Order League was the "championed ally" of the "robber trust," he alleged, and even claimed that the trust funneled money into Calloway County to pay for the fight on the Night Riders. Wells hotly denied Jennings's charges. Wells avowed that his fight against violence was a local matter—that far from betraying the community, he represented it. He denied receiving money from tobacco companies. He had collected only a small sum, he said, contributed mostly by local Association men who requested anonymity.[8]

Most important, Wells challenged the notion carefully cultivated by the Night Riders that they were more powerful than the law, indeed represented the true law of the Black Patch. With evidence provided by witnesses protected by the militia, a Calloway County grand jury indicted dozens of Night Riders in April 1908. Consequently, the masked men called off a planned raid on Murray. Newspapers reported Calloway County Night Riders fleeing their homes to escape arrest.

Although Calloway County jurors ultimately refused to convict the Night Riders whom Wells indicted—punishing Night Riders was still virtually impossible—local officials had identified and exposed the masked men to public scrutiny. Judge Wells provided the newspapers lengthy interviews with Night Rider turncoats, which they eagerly printed. By arresting Night Rider leaders and shielding victims willing to testify against their attackers, Calloway County lawmen projected an image of themselves as stronger than the vigilantes. Judge Wells's efforts demonstrated that determined local officials could suppress vigilantism more effectively than federal authority. As a result, Calloway County escaped much of the violence that gripped many parts of the Black Patch.[9]

While Wells battled the Night Riders in Calloway County, the tobacco trust turned to the United States government for relief. The Italian government's tobacco monopoly, a principal buyer of tobacco in the Black Patch, pressed the federal government to act against the vigilantes, hiring a lawyer in 1905 to lobby the government for protection. The lobbyist assured the Justice Department that the Italians did not actually want to prosecute the vigilantes. The mere presence of a federal marshal, they hoped, would deter the offenders. But federal authorities proved as reluctant to intervene as local courts. The Justice Department responded only when the Italians reported that the Night Riders had stopped a train carrying mail. When the marshal investigating the incident reported that the train holdup had not delayed mail delivery, federal officials in Louisville and Washington expressed relief.[10]

Emboldened by the federal government's timidity, the Night Riders warned the Italians' agent in Logan County, J. W. Scott, to quit receiving tobacco. Scott tried to compromise with the vigilantes by suspending business for twenty days. Shortly before Christmas the Night Riders rejected Scott's try at a compromise. After dark, a crowd of masked men gathered at his house to give him three choices: quit the tobacco business, leave the county, or die. Night Riders followed this visit with a letter signed "The Game 65 Men," threatening to hang Scott if he did not quit the tobacco business. Scott wrote his employers that he had to quit buying tobacco. "It is just more than I can stand," he explained.[11]

Again the Regie complained to the Justice Department. Department officials ordered Ben L. Bruner, the chief deputy United States marshal for the Western District of Kentucky, to Logan County. Bruner interviewed Scott as well as the vice president of the Planters' Protective Association, who reassured him that the Italians would be able to receive tobacco without molestation. Bruner returned to Louisville naively predicting that the trouble would end.[12]

Unable to secure protection, the Italians asserted a right to bring claims against the United States government for tobacco the vigilantes destroyed. This caused concern in Washington, and on January 26 Bruner's superiors ordered him back to Logan County. Arriving in Olmstead, he found the situation more serious than he had encountered on his first visit. Scott's successor had incensed local citizens by hiring guards to protect the Regie's tobacco. Bruner again interviewed local leaders of the PPA. They claimed to be working to reduce violence but suggested he visit Felix Ewing. On January 31, he arrived at Glenraven, the Association leader's palatial estate in Robertson County, Tennessee. Learning that Ewing had addressed a letter to his membership only a few days earlier claiming the United States had no right to interfere in the Black Patch, Bruner concluded that Ewing was insincere in his promises to discourage violence.[13]

When Bruner returned to Louisville, Assistant United States Attorney Maurice H. Thatcher called Ewing by telephone. The attorney warned that United States interests could be involved if Night Riders destroyed Italian property and the Italians filed claims against the United States. Ewing agreed to do all he could to prevent the destruction of property, promising to write a circular letter to his members in Logan County. He seemed sincere, Thatcher reported. But when Ewing wrote the letter, he dismissed the Italians' complaints as imaginary.[14]

Ewing's letter so dismayed the Justice Department that, concerned about possible Italian claims for destroyed property, it considered permanently stationing a marshal in Olmstead. But in a letter to the chief U.S. marshal in Louisville, the acting attorney general decided that such a presence might only aggravate a delicate situation.[15] Moreover, the chief marshal soon discovered that the threatened tobacco belonged to W. G. Dunnington and Company, under contract to the Italian government, not to the Italians themselves. Therefore the Italians had no claim against the United States.[16] In the end, the State Department told the Italian ambassador that his government was free to pursue the Night Riders in court, but the federal government had no intention of protecting the property of their contractors or representing them.[17]

The British, too, pressed the federal government to protect their American tobacco. In December 1906 attorneys for the British-owned Imperial Tobacco Company of Kentucky, which had lost tobacco to raiders' depredations, met with the United States attorney in Louisville, George DuRelle. The tobacco company urged DuRelle to prosecute the Night Riders under the Sherman Anti-Trust Act. The Night Riders had prevented the Imperial from buying tobacco from non-Association farmers who had already contracted with the company, the English complained. Clearly, the lawyers told the prosecutor, this was conspiracy in restraint of commerce, not just across state lines but across international boundaries.[18]

The argument impressed DuRelle. Writing the attorney general, he described the destruction of the Imperial's tobacco in Princeton and other Night Rider depredations. He reviewed Section One of the Sherman Anti-Trust Act, which declared "Every contract, combination . . . or conspiracy in restraint of trade or commerce among the several States, or with foreign nations" illegal.[19] Since the Night Riders had destroyed tobacco awaiting shipment to England, DuRelle reasoned that the federal courts might have jurisdiction under the Sherman Act, as construed in cases the Cleveland administration had brought against striking railway workers.[20] DuRelle argued that the Night Riders, like the railroad workers, halted commercial traffic across state lines—the test applied by federal judges to determine federal jurisdiction in Sherman Act cases.[21] But despite DuRelle's entreaties, the attorney general never allowed the prosecutor to pursue the vigilantes in federal court.

It is clear that the federal government preferred not to pursue the Night Riders. Surviving correspondence indicates that federal officials constantly sought excuses to avoid intervention. Yet in other instances, as when strikers halted interstate rail traffic, United States attorneys prosecuted.[22] The apparent inconsistency was rooted in the Roosevelt administration's attitude toward farmers. Theodore Roosevelt urged both workers and farmers to counteract the power of business by organizing, but he did not view workers and farmers in the same light. Roosevelt was more sympathetic to farmers, whom he regarded as independent entrepreneurs, than to labor.[23] While Roosevelt sometimes expressed suspicion of unions, his administration actively promoted farming cooperatives.[24] But he did not believe the United States government should side with cooperatives when they quarreled with business. If farmers organized like business, then they could compete in the market on equal terms and it would not be right to tip the scales on their behalf. Roosevelt's bias in favor of farmers predisposed him not to intervene on the side of their enemies, but it did not incline him to help them in a fight. Farmers, after all, had organized—just as Roosevelt had urged. His solution in place, Roosevelt patiently waited for the market to work out a just resolution.

Moreover, federal officials intervened in disputes among rival economic organizations only when they thought they endangered the national welfare. A great railroad strike, for example, threatened "our great cities" with "ruin, famine, and death."[25] Likewise, in the fall of 1902 Roosevelt intervened when a strike threatened the nation's anthracite coal supply. But, he recalled later, he stepped in only when a winter coal famine seemed imminent, raising the prospect of "misery and violence in acute form in our big cities." It would have been "a crisis only less serious than the civil war."[26] In that confrontation Roosevelt had hesitated to take sides. Although mine operators urged him to use the Sherman Anti-Trust Act against the workers, the president sympathized with the miners and appointed an arbitration commission sensitive to their interests.[27] In sum, federal officials acted only when economic disputes endangered large segments of the population, and they did not want to interfere in ways that aided only one side. Federal intervention to stop Night Rider violence in the Black Patch would have placed Roosevelt on the side of the tobacco trust.

One family of Night Rider victims did bring suit in federal court, persuading a federal judge to intervene in the Black Patch on behalf of order. Although they won, their victory proved less enduring than Wells's achievement in state court. The suit grew out of the 1907 whipping of Robert Hollowell. Characteristically, after the whipping the vigilantes had ordered the Hollowells to leave Kentucky. The Hollowells left, as the vigilantes demanded, going to Oklahoma. But they soon returned to Kentucky to live in Paducah, where they approached lawyer John G. Miller. They told Miller they could positively identify twenty-nine of their attackers, including Hollowell's brother. Miller had no confidence in local courts and determined to sue the twenty-nine in a court "which even . . . Night Riders could learn to fear."[28] He told the Hollowells that he would accept their case only if they established residence in some state other than Kentucky. "Our purpose," Miller explained, "was to cause a diversity of citizenship that would give the federal court jurisdiction of a civil action of our clients against citizens of Kentucky, who had assaulted them." Although employed in Paducah, Hollowell moved to Evansville, Indiana, and then filed his suit.[29]

Miller filed the Hollowells' petition in federal court on March 2, 1908. He described the shooting and beating the Hollowells endured and claimed the Night Riders "did force and threaten said plaintiff against his will and make it necessary for him to leave and forsake his said home and residence and flee the country to save the lives of himself and family." The Hollowells asked for $50,000 in damages. They might have sued under federal civil rights statutes, but they used ordinary tort instead. At the bottom of the petition someone—probably Miller—wrote, "This is an emergency case."[30]

Federal Judge Walter Evans called the Hollowells' suit to trial in April, less than a month after Miller filed the original complaint. In qualifying witnesses and jurors, federal courts usually followed the procedures of the forum state. The main advantage for the Hollowells in federal court was that Evans would be the judge. Though born in Hopkinsville, Evans represented an outside force in the Black Patch. A life-long Republican, Evans held court in a Democratic stronghold. Although western Kentucky had been the most pro-Confederate part of Kentucky, he had served as an officer in the Union army.[31] As an outsider, he sympathized little with local passions. DuRelle joined in the effort, acting as co-counsel with Miller.[32] Like Evans, Louisville Republican DuRelle was an outsider in the Black Patch. In contrast to Wells's community-based strategy in Calloway County, Miller planned an intrusion of federal power into the Black Patch.

One signal that Miller and the court represented an outside force was their inability to penetrate the inner workings of the Night Riders. Only members of the Hollowell family testified about the night the Night Riders whipped Robert Hollowell, and the trial turned on the persuasiveness of their testimony. They secured no corroborating testimony from locals or turncoat Night Riders. Unlike the trials in Wells's court, they offered no insights into the inner workings of the secret order. The Night Riders responded by attacking the Hollowells' credibility. The defendants all produced alibis, and their lawyers maligned the moral character of Mary Lou Hollowell.[33]

In his charge to the jury, Judge Evans ridiculed the testimony offered by the defense, saying that the precision of the alibi witnesses's memories was so remarkable that it made him ashamed of his own. The judge endorsed the testimony of Hollowell's son, who had offered a graphic description of his father's whipping. "I put my money on the boy," he told the jury.[34]

Today such instructions would be grounds for an appeal. But for most of the nineteenth century federal judges enjoyed considerable latitude, dispatching justice with a sometimes heavy hand. Supervision by way of judicial review is a measure of the decline of judicial independence. Until the passage of the Criminal Appeals Act in 1889, defendants convicted of capital offenses had no right to appeal their cases to the Supreme Court. In 1908 the process of standardizing judicial review was still not complete. Hollowell brought his case to federal court at a time Evans's dictatorial style was becoming anachronistic, but it had yet to be prohibited.[35]

Despite Evans's instructions, the jury deadlocked, with two men holding out against the Hollowells. The frustrated judge dismissed the jury. He no doubt suspected Night Rider influence on the jury—suspicions confirmed by an anonymous letter written by someone inside the Night Rider organization. Had there been only one holdout he would have ordered him investigated, the judge fumed. Evans immediately set the case for retrial on May 11, insisting that the welfare of the state as well as the parties demanded a quick verdict. Determined that the next jury would be from a part of the state undisturbed by Night Rider excitement, he called a jury from Louisville, 220 miles from Paducah.[36]

At the second trial, the Hollowells produced a new witness. Lyon County Attorney Walter Krone turned Night Rider Sanford Hall into a witness for the Hollowells by threatening him with prosecution for moonshining. Hall had seen the defendants rehearse their false alibis in Night Rider "schools for perjury." But this trial again turned on the credibility of the Hollowells, producing no insights into the inner workings of the Silent Brigade. The Louisville jurors heard Evans again denounce night riding and criticize the defendants' alibi testimony. Alibi testimony, the judge said, is at once the best defense and the most easily fabricated. Reviewing each defendant's alibi, the judge stressed the remarkable coincidence that every defendant had been talking with some relative at the particular day and particular hour the Riders raided Robert Hollowell's farm. All the elements of a typical fabricated alibi seemed "carefully and completely" in place. As he derided the testimony of the defendants' witnesses, Evans again endorsed that of the Hollowells' son. "It would be impossible for me not to believe the boy," he told the jurors.[37] The jury deliberated just forty minutes before awarding Hollowell $35,000 in damages.[38]

It seemed a great victory, but despite Miller's later claims that his suit against the vigilantes ended "aggressive Night Rider activities," the Hollowell verdict failed to restore order to the Black Patch.[39] Since there were no sensational revelations about the secretive vigilantes, contemporary Black Patch newspapers did not consider the trial a mortal blow to the Night Riders. The press covered the Hollowell trial carefully, but not in the obsessive detail they would later devote to the climactic state trial in Hopkinsville. The Clarksville *Leaf-Chronicle* headlined the result in the same size type devoted to a neighboring headline, "MEN SMOKE AT CHURCH SERVICES."[40] The Cadiz *Record* headline, below an advertisement for Wilson's Busy Store, was simpler: "$35,000."[41]

But the Hollowells received less than half the money the jury awarded them, and much of what they did receive came from public donations to help defray the defendants' losses. The donations demonstrated the continued community support for the Night Riders. In fact, the trial left the Hollowells more shaken than their assailants. "Robert Hollowell," Miller remembered later, "had not recovered his nerve after his shocking experience, was still shaky; . . . he greatly dreaded the long delay of an appeal . . . he labored under a vague apprehension he could not himself explain, and was really eager for an adjustment."[42]

The prestige of the Night Riders could not be diminished by a verdict against them in a federal court delivered by a jury of Louisville citizens. Louisville, two hundred miles east of the rural counties where the Night Riders predominated, represented a different world than the vigilantes and their supporters occupied. To them, the Hollowell verdict constituted an outside attack. The Night Riders' honor and respect depended upon their neighbors and kin. An outside verdict could not deprive the Riders of it.

A measure of Black Patchers' persistent resistance to outside authority may be found in their continuing violence after the Hollowell verdict. Six months after the federal court in Paducah had imposed fines on Caldwell County Night Riders, Governor Willson would still deplore violence. He was to declare that "Kentucky has reached a stage of lawlessness where the constituted authorities are unable to make headway for the preservation of law and order" and urged private citizens to counter Night Rider violence by arming themselves.[43] Violence would spread beyond the Black Patch as outbursts occurred in central Kentucky and even other states.[44] A year after the federal trials and Governor Willson's commitment of state troops in the Black Patch, *Hampton's Magazine* still observed that "Night Riding is by no manner of means ended. . . . The local courts are unable to meet the emergency."[45] A year after that the socialist newspaper *Appeal to Reason* would assure its readers that the Night Riders' war against capitalism was still in full swing.[46]

In 1908 both state and federal courts had attacked the Night Riders. In Calloway County a state judge failed in his efforts to punish his masked opponents, but he did manage to rob them of much of the secrecy they required. Exposed to public scrutiny, the "Silent Brigade" became less effective. Federal Judge Walter Evans also challenged Night Rider power and secrecy. Evans acted quickly and decisively, persuading a jury to assess damages, and some historians credit him with ending the Night Rider crisis. Miller himself made this claim in his 1936 memoir of the case, *The Black Patch War*. In his book Miller describes the Night Riders as "so drunk with their sense of importance" that they underestimated the power of the federal judiciary.[47] Miller wrote that suits in federal court forced the defendants to give up their night riding to earn the money necessary to pay damages. "What're you doin' these days?" Miller quotes one vigilante as asking another. "The answer was, 'Plowin' corn for Mary Lou.'"[48] In fact, Miller exaggerated Evans's impact on the Black Patch war. Night riding continued after the Hollowell verdict, and community fund raising on behalf of the raiders again demonstrated the public's support of the Night Riders. Finally, the Hollowell verdict did nothing to restore the authority of local courts. And the Black Patch war was most of all a crisis of local authority. Local lawmen legitimized lawlessness, tarnishing state and county institutions. Only when those local courts again asserted their authority would peace return to the Black Patch.

More important than the concrete achievements of these two judges was the fact that they dared stand up to the Night Riders at all. Other lawmen had refused to do so and fueled the vigilantes' power. But now, for the first time, legal authorities dared confront the Night Rider challenge. They took the first steps toward reasserting law in the Black Patch.

Racial and ethnic violence is timeless. Traditionally, though, elites manipulated such mischief, often channeling popular energy in what they saw as useful directions. But when political, economic, racial, or ethnic divisions cut across community lines, destroying the bonds that connect neighbor with neighbor, they can lead to a kind of unfocused, uncontrollable violence that historians have come to call "modern." Early in the Black Patch war, David Amoss organized communities in disciplined attacks on property. But after the raid on Hopkinsville Amoss lost the community consensus he once enjoyed and Night Rider violence became bloodier and more racial—modern. Evidence that the Black Patch's planter elite had lost control of the movement it launched appears in the nature of Night Rider violence. Masked men began to assault blacks and whites they saw as immoral, targets unconnected with the tobacco industry. Perhaps nothing symbolizes the change better than the departure of the planters' leader from the head of the Night Riders. The final wave of violence of the Black Patch war came at a time when Amoss no longer provided the leadership his Kentucky vigilantes needed in order to remain a coherent force. Without Amoss, scattered bands of vigilantes attacked targets at will. A list of the victims of mob violence reveals no pattern; nothing ties these scattered incidents together. Some Night Riders became almost puritanical, punishing prostitutes and bootleggers. Others whipped blacks. Others settled personal quarrels.

When Willson stationed troops in Cobb and Amoss fled, the vigilante leader first traveled into Trigg County, then left the state, eventually finding his way to Charles Mill's farm in Stewart County, Tennessee. In 1983, Elizabeth Mill Durrett still remembered the day Amoss came to her father's house in a buggy. Durrett described the fugitive as "loveable, kind, compassionate," becoming one of the family. Some slave cabins still stood on the Mill farm, occupied by the descendants of the original occupants. Amoss provided medical services to them, delivering one woman's baby. He did it "beautifully," according to Durrett, as though he were expecting a fee of a million dollars. But Durrett knew Amoss had been shot during the raid on Hopkinsville. "I remember very distinctly that little scar above his ear," she said.[1]

Amoss had viewed black labor as a resource to be guarded and steered his followers toward appropriate targets. But not everyone in the Black Patch viewed blacks as Amoss did. While all whites shared the same racial slurs and stereotypes, they had profoundly different economic interests in black labor. Some whites met blacks as economic competitors. White workers prospered when blacks were scarce; white employers were happiest when the black labor pool was large, driving down the price of labor. For their part, African-Americans perceived some whites as competitors and others as patrons, and they spoke and acted accordingly. And because of all this white employers and white employees developed different ideologies. There is nothing to admire in upper-class white racism, but it was not the same as lower-class racism. One group wanted to exploit; the other, to exclude.[2]

Amoss was a member of the group that employed black labor. While he might resent insubordination from those he regarded as racially inferior, he saw them as a necessary part of the economic landscape and opposed efforts to drive them away. But Amoss had created an atmosphere of tolerance for vigilante action and then left the scene. In a culture where racial hatreds always ran close to the surface, Amoss had made such attacks virtually inevitable by leaving Kentucky. While he was in Tennessee, the planter elite lost control of the vigilantes they unleashed. In Trigg County residents called disorderly vigilantes "shirt-tail" Night Riders. They represented the "shirt tail" of the initial impulse for vigilantism, capitalizing on the toleration for lawlessness that had been created. Residents identified one band as local "bad boys." In one example of mindless violence, juveniles admitted getting drunk at a dance before riding to a cabin occupied by Newt Crenshaw, a black tenant farmer. Crenshaw fired his shotgun at the teenagers and they scattered.[3]

"Shirt-tail" Night Riders directed much of their violence at the tenants and sharecroppers planters relied on. Planters had organized the Planters' Protective Association and the Night Riders to preserve their black labor force. Now the lawless climate they had created inspired attacks on the very labor force they sought to defend. While "shirt-tail" vigilantes viewed blacks as competitors for jobs, planters needed a pool of black labor. Attacks on black labor by white laborers were indirect attacks on the planters themselves.

The most serious shirt-tail violence occurred in a region of western Lyon and Trigg counties called Between the Rivers. Located between the Cumberland and Tennessee rivers, the area was long known for the manufacture of pig iron, of which Kentucky had been the leading southern producer in 1860. After the Civil War the industry had declined, but it revived briefly around the turn of the century.

The iron industry never led to much settlement between the rivers. As late as 1879 a visitor described the area as "still so densely wooded and so nearly void of human habitation they might as well have described it as no-mans-land." In 1900 only 17 percent (3,979 persons) of the population of Lyon and Trigg counties lived in the Between the Rivers area.[4] While most residents there farmed, some worked in and around the pig iron furnaces. In 1910 about a quarter of those persons listing their occupation as "laborers" worked in and around the furnaces.[5]

The companies operating the iron furnaces between the rivers represented the same kind of alien, modernizing force as the tobacco companies. But while the tobacco companies represented a largely theoretical threat to yeomen farmers, furnace operators offered a working model of a hellish future. The work in the fiery furnaces was hot and unpleasant; African-Americans constituted the majority of the laborers there. Whites worked in the vicinity of the furnaces, destroying the landscape by mining iron ore, driving mules, and chopping wood. The men who hacked and clawed at the environment did not form any sort of community in the traditional sense. The majority came from outside the Between the Rivers region. Moreover, the 1910 Lyon County census does not identify a single iron worker as owning the house in which he lived. White, Dixon, and Company, operating Center Furnace, built what one worker later described as "some shacks" for laborers to live in. Many wood choppers lived in the woods, sleeping where they worked, connected to their neighbors by mud roads nearly impassable even in summer. It took four mules to pull wagons laden with charcoal over such roads. White, Dixon, and Company paid their workers in scrip redeemable only at the company store. This exploitative labor milieu differed dramatically from the paternalistic, quasi-plantation economy where Amoss's organization flourished.[6]

Boyd Hudson was one of these rootless laborers, cutting wood for Center Furnace. Cords of wood, eight feet long and four feet high, sold for fifty cents. Workers thought a dollar a day was a very good wage. As a teenager, Hudson had worked on farms in the summer and cut wood in the winter. He soon gave up farming to work for the furnaces all year.[7]

Workers like Hudson were eager recruits for a vigilante army.

Hudson first heard of the Night Riders while hauling coal with a friend. "How'd you like to join an organization that don't cost you anything?" the friend asked. Hudson asked what the organization was. "Well," the friend vaguely explained, "it don't cost you anything to join it . . . it's just a kind of an organization." The Night Rider persuaded Hudson to join by telling him that local leaders as well as his friends had already joined. Most prominent among these community leaders was Dr. Emilus Champion, a respected and well-liked local doctor, who led the organization. Undoubtedly many residents of Between the Rivers joined his organization because of Champion's association with it. But Hudson joined because his friends joined. It was the thing to do. "I don't know of a man or a boy that didn't join if they asked 'em to," he explained. Even "an old nigger drawing coal for us—he was a Night Rider too."

Hudson and his fellow furnace workers, isolated and exploited, lashed out at the rich men who owned the homes they rented and the furnaces where they labored. Unlike Amoss and the tobacco Night Riders, they did not seek to defend a way of life or an existing community structure. They wanted to overturn the existing structure, which they regarded as corrupt and immoral. Champion argued that the iron industry's waged labor system was corrupt because it treated black and white labor too equally. Whites competed with blacks for similar jobs and, if they were lucky enough to find employment, lived in shacks little different from those occupied by blacks. Waged labor was immoral because it tolerated the lazy, paying those who worked little the same as those who worked hard. It also promoted employer indifference toward those who would not work at all; no one counseled them or urged them to work. Champion's Night Riders hoped to establish a traditional sense of community. The first characteristic of nineteenth-century community structures was uniformity of thought. Joining the Night Riders promoted that kind of homogeneous society among the disparate iron workers of Between the Rivers.

Hudson's initiation into the secret order was remarkably casual. One night Hudson's Night Rider friend simply asked him to go to a Night Rider meeting. "Well, we're going to have a meeting, at the furnace," he said. "Wasn't going to be at nobody's house," Hudson recalled later. It was going to be held at the furnace hill. "So, there was a bunch of us young guys, you know, and older ones too, met down there on that hillside," Hudson remembered. "There was a big rock and we sat down there on the big rock. So, we joined the organization, didn't cost us anything. . . . They says you don't have to do anything." The informality of initiation suggests the difference between the original Night Rider organization and the vigilante groups that organized in its wake. Amoss's Night Riders attached great importance to the formal oath they administered to recruits. According to Hudson, Champion did not. "We didn't take no oath," he explained. The Night Riders merely told him, "Keep your mouth shut."

Champion encouraged his men to police Between the Rivers, telling Hudson and the other recruits to report "if somebody wasn't working or wasn't treating their family right." Even many years later, Hudson thought this vigilante-imposed discipline had a propitious effect on some workers. "There was one fellow worked there at the furnace. He'd come out on Monday morning and work a Monday, maybe, and look up and see the sky, you know, 'I hope it don't rain this week, I ought to work all week.' Well, maybe you wouldn't see him until payday. That kind of a fellow. They put him to work. He made a pretty good hand. And he had a right smart family, too. He was just too lazy to work." This kind of neighborhood watch resembled nineteenth-century white caps more than Amoss's Night Riders.

Champion, the leader of these Night Riders, had been born in 1858 in Livingston County and had practiced medicine with his father for three years there before moving to Lyon County. He was a graduate of Vanderbilt, a member of the Populist party, and owner of the first car in his neighborhood.

In 1907 Champion's son murdered his sister's husband and his mistress. According to later testimony, after a Lyon County grand jury indicted Champion's son for murder, Commonwealth Attorney Denny Smith advised the elder Champion to see Amoss to get his son out of trouble. In exchange for Amoss's help, Champion joined the Night Riders, and organized Between the Rivers.[8] It is possible Amoss and Champion entered into such an agreement. Champion's son left Lyon County and authorities never prosecuted him for murder. Henry Bennett's family believed Champion accompanied Amoss's raiders into Dycusburg.[9] But while it is possible Amoss had a connection with Champion, it is unlikely. One must wonder why Amoss would want to organize Between the Rivers, an area where farmers produced little tobacco.

A comparison of the composition of Champion's Night Riders with Amoss's men suggests the two groups had little in common.

Through suits in federal court seventy of Champion's men can be identified in Lyon County and in Marshall County on the west side of the Tennessee River. Of this number, thirty-nine have been located in the 1900 census. They ranged in age from fifteen to fifty-seven; while they averaged thirty, 60 percent were thirty or younger. About half were not yet the head of a household in 1900, living, in most cases, with their parents. Most of the seventy had no land. Those with land generally had a hundred acres or less. In contrast, Amoss's men averaged forty-three years of age and most had wives and children. About a third of Amoss's men were landowners with nearly two hundred acres or more, sometimes a lot more. In general, Amoss and his men were heads of households, well-established in their communities. Mature men, they had families and a long-term commitment to the local economy. Champion's men had yet to stabilize themselves in society.[10] Amoss's men fought to preserve their communities; Champion's men fought to establish one.

A comparison of the activities carried out by the two organizations reveals that Amoss and Champion had different objectives. Between the Rivers night riding had nothing to do with tobacco; at first they settled neighborhood disputes and tried to enforce prohibition. Ultimately, they would turn on the black minority living in Lyon and Marshall counties.

In October 1908, a band of fifteen masked men came to Tandy W. Ferguson's house in Linton in Trigg County. Ferguson owned no farm land and only one lot valued at $150. He was an annoyance to his neighbors. He had had a minor brush with the law, the Commonwealth attorney having unsuccessfully prosecuted him for violations of the local option law. He filed a civil suit against his neighbors. This was enough to make him the target of Champion's vigilantes. When the masked men fired a volley over his house and called him out, Ferguson scrambled out the back, leaving his wife to talk to the Night Riders. She learned they had no interest in tobacco or the PPA. Instead, they threatened to return and hang her husband if he did not settle his differences with his neighbors. Mrs. Ferguson relayed the message and Mr. Ferguson quickly settled his lawsuit.[11]

Champion's men also singled out John Collins in the little community of Golden Pond located between the rivers in Trigg County. Collins sold liquor from his store and campaigned against local prohibition; grand juries regularly indicted him for selling liquor without a license, selling liquor to minors, and other violations of the liquor laws. In January 1908, seven masked men came into his house and poured out his stock of beer, whiskey, cider, ale, and even vinegar. Collins valued his losses at $100.[12]

Collins's brother, Robert L., living at Rock Castle, on the east side of the Cumberland River in Trigg County, also sold liquor illegally. In addition, Robert quarreled with his neighbors over property at Rock Castle. At the end of 1907 and the beginning of 1908, two mysterious fires wiped out much of Rock Castle. Some blamed the Night Riders for the destruction. On March 8 twenty or twenty-five men shot into Collins's house. Armed with short switches, the Night Riders whipped Collins twenty-five or thirty licks.[13]

The same vigilantes that visited the Collinses also targeted area blacks. But they manifested their racial hostility in the form of moral regulation. The Night Riders blamed White, Dixon, and Company for giving black men jobs that the Night Riders wanted reserved for whites. But when they visited Zabe Miller at Empire Furnace, the masked men accused Miller of gambling and whipped him. Miller got the message; he promptly left for Louisville. Night Riders next called Tom Weaver "impudent" and murdered him.[14]

Authorities tolerated these activities. As several historians have suggested, a desire to preserve the existing hierarchy—more than racism—motivated elite toleration of subculture violence. White-trash rowdiness reinforced the existing hierarchy by demonstrating the difference between the top and bottom of society. Moreover, the white elite often tolerated lower-class white crime to preserve order. Acceptance of minor misdeeds vented frustrations that, improperly channeled, might threaten the established order. And the upper classes expected nonelites to serve as shock troops in the war against disorder by serving as militiamen, jurors, and constables. Thus Trigg County Attorney John Kelly excused the murderers, blaming it on a "crowd of boys, meaning to have some fun out of him." Such forbearance was a necessary accommodation of a potentially dangerous class.[15]

Encouraged by the toleration of local law enforcement authorities, Champion's Night Riders began to threaten Eddyville blacks in anonymous notes. But the notes stirred the enmity of the elderly county judge, William L. Crumbaugh. Like David Amoss, Crumbaugh epitomized the Black Patch planter elite's attitudes toward blacks. Born in Logan County in 1835, he had traveled to Missouri with his parents when upper South slaveowners were trying to

Former slaveowner and Lyon County Judge William L. Crumbaugh armed himself to guard Eddyville blacks. Photo from *Hampton's Magazine* 22 (March 1909): 347.

expand slavery west of the Mississippi. Returning to Kentucky, Crumbaugh settled in Lyon County and prospered. At the outbreak of the Civil War he was a twenty-six-year-old tobacco grower with a wife, two babies, and eight slaves.[16] His experience as a master taught him the paternalistic ideal, and he regarded blacks as wards of whites to be punished when necessary but more often protected from life's tribulations. For many years Lyon County voters demonstrated their respect for old Will Crumbaugh, electing him magistrate in 1866, sheriff in 1868 and 1870, county surveyor in 1886, and county judge since 1890.[17] Although Kentucky counties had no formal administrative head, Crumbaugh sometimes functioned as the boss of Lyon County.[18]

When Champion's Night Riders threatened Lyon County blacks, Crumbaugh naturally came to their defense. But the seventy-three-year-old judge found that the paternalistic ideal he still believed in no longer appealed to many twentieth-century whites in Eddyville. When he tried to enlist his neighbors in this effort, he found them to be more in sympathy with the lawless Night Riders than with the blacks he believed whites had a duty to defend. They refused to rally with Crumbaugh against the vigilantes. But in the center of Night Rider power, Crumbaugh took his moral obligation to defend local blacks very seriously, telling his neighbors that he intended to use force to defend Eddyville blacks and showing them his Remington automatic shotgun and stock of buckshot shells.[19]

Crumbaugh was sure that even if Sheriff Sam Cash felt no responsibility to protect blacks, he would stand up for law and order. And, when he met with the sheriff, Cash agreed to help guard the threatened blacks. Crumbaugh recruited four other Eddyville whites in his effort. The four agreed to meet at night and station themselves around the section of town where blacks lived. When the raiders came, Crumbaugh and his men would surprise them from ambush.[20] But when the agreed-upon time came, Cash and the other men did not show up. Crumbaugh stood guard alone. As he sat within shooting distance of the house he thought the Night Riders most likely to attack, the judge realized that although he had long held office in Lyon County and was a respected member of the community, some of his neighbors would kill him if they knew what he was doing.[21] The Night Riders did not appear that night, and Crumbaugh returned home alone.

When Champion and his men did appear, on Sunday morning, February 16, just after midnight, there were too many for even Crumbaugh and his shotgun to repel. Tom Cash, the eleven-year-old son of the sheriff, remembered dreaming that someone was beating on the woodbox of their home in Eddyville. But the noise was no dream and awoke Tom with a start. Tom realized that someone was shooting downtown. His father was already up. "What's that—what's going on?" he asked. The elder Cash instructed his son, "Just raise the window there, raise the blind, look out there, you'll see."[22] It was a moonlit night. Tom could clearly see the men marching, perhaps five abreast, on the street some forty feet from the house. Then some of the Night Riders knocked on the front door. "And my Daddy went to the front door," Tom remembered later. "He stayed there, I don't know, five minutes, came back in, and I said, 'What—what—who was it?' He said, 'I don't know.' I said, 'What'd they say?' 'They told me that if I knew what was good for me, I'd better stay in the house.' "[23]

The raiders whipped ten people, six of them black; they forced a local ruffian to surrender his guns and commanded the operator of a pool room to change businesses.[24] The pool-room operator had trouble comprehending the new turn vigilantism had taken. "I am a good association man and have never broken a rule of the organization," he told the masked men. "To hell with that," a Night Rider shouted back at the astonished Association man. "We don't care nothing about what you are doing except that you are running a pool room and you've got to stop."[25]

The Night Riders looted buggy whips from a hardware store and wore them out on their black victims. Then they used sticks and clubs. One victim died less than a month after his beating.[26] After they whipped their victims, the Night Riders took them to the town limits and released them, telling the blacks to leave town. As they left, the raiders promised to return for a third raid on Eddyville.[27]

Night Rider partisans claimed to see a logic in the raid consistent with patterns established by Amoss's organization. They insisted that the Night Riders "were all well drilled and behaved like gentlemen."[28] But even though they praised the conduct of the raiders, they themselves could not discern a strategy behind the raid. In fact, the second Eddyville raid represented a descent into chaos. Several observers puzzled over the "peculiar feature" of the raid. "None of the victims . . . is connected with the tobacco business," they remarked. A lawyer in Hopkinsville indicated the raid was "worse than anything yet done in the matter of whipping men." "Anarchists in Russia are no worse," he concluded bitterly.[29]

The Eddyville raiders succeeded in dispiriting community leaders. The Night Riders did not whip Crumbaugh, but the judge's spirits sagged nonetheless. He walked the familiar streets of Eddyville much as he had before the raid, but now he looked into the faces of his friends and neighbors knowing he could not trust any of them. Formerly a community leader, Crumbaugh was now outside his community. The judge believed that if he could have rallied just ten men, he could have fought off the mob and asserted the rule of law in Lyon County. No one had been willing to stand with Crumbaugh. The local postmaster had been a staunch ally, but he too had refused to stand up to the Night Riders.[30]

The mob prevailed, threatening unbridled lawlessness, chaos. At this point, Crumbaugh wrote, masked men could have ridden into Eddyville and openly robbed the bank and businesses and no one would have dared resist. Crumbaugh's efforts to enforce the law had failed. Courage had not been enough. Yet, even in his despair, he remained resolute. "I have clews," he wrote, "that I shall investigate personally and secretly because I dare not trust a man here. I am alone."[31]

Within a week of the raid, Crumbaugh's spirits revived when he found four men he believed he could trust. All lived outside the Eddyville community in Kuttawa, a little town just two miles away. They were County Attorney Walter Krone, Town Marshal W. H. McCollum, rural mail carrier C. E. Braswell, and a Mr. Smith. Krone was a small man, much younger than Crumbaugh. McCollum, described by his daughter as the Gibraltar of the Republican party in overwhelmingly Democratic Lyon County, was a fearless man, perhaps too fearless. He had killed several men, more or less in the line of duty. Children hid when they saw him coming. These four men gave Crumbaugh more than just moral support and additional firepower against the Night Riders. Braswell offered Crumbaugh something he sorely needed: information. He had a friend inside Champion's organization, who would tip him off on the next raid on Eddyville.[32]

Crumbaugh sought order in Lyon County. He decided to do so first by imposing order with state troops. He made preparations for a violent confrontation with the Night Riders—asking Willson to have about fifty soldiers ready in Hopkinsville to swoop into Eddyville by rail in the event of a third raid.[33] Crumbaugh also searched for order by trying to decipher a logic in the chaos he faced. He identified a local politician whom he thought could influence the vigilantes: the head of the Association in Lyon County, Confederate captain and hero William Stone. Crumbaugh warned Stone that "if even the meanest negro is molested or harmed we will hold him . . . responsible to us, not financially, but physically." Stone, a man of transcendent influence, a church leader, former Speaker of the Kentucky House of Representatives, United States congressman, and candidate for governor, promised Crumbaugh that no more outrages would occur.[34] At the same time, Albrecht reported from Hopkinsville that he believed the Association had put the word out to stop all violence.[35] Crumbaugh decided that "the modern and unique reformers," as he described the Night Riders, "can be controlled by the officers of the County Association."[36]

But Crumbaugh and Albrecht were mistaken in thinking Stone and the Association could rein in the chaos threatening the Black Patch. The Night Riders continued to be a powerful presence in Lyon County. Moreover, they seemed determined to defy Crumbaugh's authority. Intending to frighten potential witnesses, Crumbaugh thought, fifty men rode into Eddyville on March 7 in military formation. Boldly riding down the main street, they dismounted at the courthouse. They assembled in the circuit court room, which had been made available for their use by the jailer. Crumbaugh wrote Willson that it was imperative he provide protection to would-be witnesses.[37]

Eddyville Night Riders also brutalized black residents of Birmingham, Kentucky. Visiting the homes of black families, the attackers roused them out of bed and cruelly whipped them. In an exchange of shots, the raiders murdered two people, one of whom was a two-year-old child.[38] In August a mob lynched four blacks in Russellville in violence the Earlington *Bee* blamed on the climate of lawlessness created by the Night Riders.[39] Once again, the raiders showed no interest in the tobacco trust or the Planters' Protective Association. They took advantage of the toleration of lawlessness Amoss's men had engineered to launch an orgy of racial hatred. In Birmingham they succeeded in driving blacks out of the area. Blacks fled in such haste they abandoned their belongings. One riverboat alone took seventeen black families out of Kentucky after the Birmingham raid, unloading over one hundred blacks in Tennessee.[40]

Unlike the authorities in Trigg, Marshall County authorities quickly acted to counter Champion's activities. With testimony from Night Riders-turned-witness Otis Blick, the Commonwealth indicted three men, including Champion. At the trials, Blick produced his mask and showed that a hole in it corresponded to a scar on his shoulder, where he had been shot during the Birmingham raid. The defense countered with Blick's father, who testified that his son lied habitually. Jurors convicted only Champion, sentencing him to one year in Kentucky's penitentiary, ironically located in Eddyville.[41]

The Eddyville raid and the Birmingham murders introduced a new phase of Night Rider violence—less massive but more vicious.

While some of the vigilantes carrying out this new wave of violence had no interest in the tobacco troubles, others acted to dissuade witnesses from testifying about their illegal activities on behalf of the PPA. In the spring and summer of 1908, as Between the Rivers vigilantes inaugurated a new wave of violence, Governor Willson and his allies moved to challenge Amoss's Night Riders in court in Trigg, Crittenden, and Lyon counties. Willson's efforts yielded only a few convictions, but his use of a Night Rider turncoat launched the vigilantes on a bloody hunt for spies in their own ranks.

After the Hollowell trials, county attorneys in both Crittenden County and Lyon County, Kentucky, asked Sanford Hall, who had

Night Rider Otis Blick rode with Dr. Champion but later testified against him. He struck this smug pose for *Hampton's Magazine* in 1908. Photo from *Hampton's Magazine* 22 (April 1909): 465.

Lyon County Attorney Walter Krone, his wife, and guards pose with their house plants. Krone engineered a state-court strategy to subdue the Night Riders. Photo from *Hampton's Magazine* 22 (April 1909): 463.

testified on behalf of the Hollowells about Night Rider "schools for perjury," to identify vigilantes. In Crittenden County the men Hall identified were outsiders, living in Lyon and Caldwell counties. County Attorney Carl Henderson personally led a militia company into Caldwell County, where he rounded up thirteen defendants. In Lyon County, Sheriff Cash and Marshal McCollum arrested the defendants named by Hall and brought them to the Crittenden County courthouse in Marion, where they immediately made bond and returned home. But Henderson's legal effort ran into delays, and no trials resulted from the indictments until 1910, when a jury convicted a single defendant and sentenced him to one year in the penitentiary.[42]

In Lyon County, County Attorney Walter Krone had even less success than Henderson. In part this was because of Kentucky's unnecessarily cumbersome criminal justice system. Each county has a county attorney and each judicial district has a commonwealth attorney. Both offices prosecute crime. The county attorney, who has several legal functions besides prosecution, handles misdemeanors and the preliminary work of felony cases. In a felony case it is the county attorney who writes the initial warrant and pursues the case until it reaches the grand jury. In the grand jury room the commonwealth attorney takes over. Such a system can work only when the county attorney and the commonwealth attorney cooperate.

Krone arrested and placed on bond the men Hall identified as Night Riders. But those arrested had every reason to feel optimistic about their fate.[43] In Lyon County the working relationship necessary to make the complex prosecutorial system work did not exist. Krone was a forceful opponent of the Night Riders determined to prosecute them no matter what the political cost. But Denny Smith, politically ambitious and sensitive to public opinion, proved difficult to work with. In August 1908, Smith made a fiery speech to the grand jury, demanding they indict Night Riders, including Night Rider leaders. Despite his earlier record of sympathy for the vigilantes, the speech impressed the Hopkinsville *Kentuckian*. The newspaper predicted that "every guilty man . . . will be indicted" with "some sensational indictments . . . expected."[44] Rumors reached Governor Willson that the Night Riders feared the Lyon County proceedings. According to one report, Amoss and 150 hand-picked men planned to arrive in Eddyville when Hall testified to "put a quietus" on his "testimony and . . . existence."[45]

It is extremely doubtful that Amoss actually planned such a dramatic raid. He almost certainly remained in Tennessee through this period and probably saw no need for a raid when his own men were on the grand jury. One man serving on the grand jury would be a defendant in a suit brought by two different Night Rider victims in federal court. More important, Captain William J. Stone, head of the Association in Lyon County, served as foreman of the grand jury. Later the judge would allow Stone to resign his jury duty to tend to Association business in Guthrie.[46]

The Association certainly had more influence on the panel than did County Attorney Krone. The Paducah *Sun* reported soon after the grand jury began meeting that Commonwealth Attorney Smith took charge of the panel, entirely ignoring Krone. Krone ruefully told the reporter that he did not even know what the grand jury was doing.[47] It had been Krone, not Smith, who had been working to persuade Night Riders to testify against their fellow vigilantes. Krone had located Hall, first sequestering him in a Paducah boarding house and then moving him to Louisville. Instead of working through Krone to arrange for Hall to testify, however, Smith sent a telegram to the sheriff in Louisville asking him to arrest Hall. Distrusting Smith, Krone moved Hall out of Louisville, to Indiana.[48] Not surprisingly, when the grand jury made its final report on August 25, it returned no indictments, "sensational" or otherwise, against the Night Riders, and all the men Hall had identified were released.[49] The Night Riders triumphed in Lyon County.

Unable to defeat the Night Riders directly, Willson in 1908 next tried a more circuitous avenue of attack, targeting John W. Kelly, leader of Trigg County Night Riders. As Trigg County attorney, Kelly had been annoyed by legal troubles unrelated to Night Riding for two years. His troubles stemmed from his service as Trigg County master commissioner from 1898 until 1906. Appointed by the circuit judge, Kentucky master commissioners settled insolvent estates and "perform[ed] such other duties as the court may require." Once an estate fell into the hands of a master commissioner, he had authority to sell it to settle debts. He was not to make a personal profit from such sales, but otherwise his power to dispose of such property was virtually unlimited.[50] Such power gave rise to disputes between master commissioners and heirs, and in 1906 the heirs of an estate Kelly was managing accused him of defrauding it of about $500. The heirs filed suit, and the grand jury brought criminal charges against him for the same offense.[51] Kelly's friends, Judge Cook and Commonwealth Attorney Smith, both recused themselves, which meant Willson would appoint the judge and prosecutor in the trial of the leader of the Night Riders in Trigg County. Willson quickly took advantage of the opportunity, appointing two ardent law-and-order men to the positions. He made James Sims of Bowling Green judge and John Stites special prosecutor.

Although the facts of the case had nothing to do with Night Riding, Stites introduced the issue by alleging that Kelly was a Night Rider and that no Trigg County jury would convict a Night Rider of anything. He requested a change of venue, and Judge Sims ordered a hearing on the matter. Such hearings are more informal than trials. There was no jury; Sims himself would hear the evidence and make a decision. Since "common knowledge," accurate or not, can affect a jury's objectivity, the rules of evidence are considerably relaxed in such hearings. Stites need only prove what was "common knowledge" about the Night Riders and Kelly's relation to them. This worked to the advantage of Stites and the Commonwealth and against Kelly. In Night Rider trials, the defendants had relied on strict interpretation of the rules of evidence to escape punishment or even official notice. Masks were not designed to conceal the identity of the wearers so much as to allow witnesses to plausibly deny recognizing them. Legally everyone could "not know" what was common knowledge, and thus the Night Riders remained invisible. If required to do so in the case of *Commonwealth* v. *Kelly*, it would be hard for the prosecution to prove that there were any Night Riders in Trigg County at all. But it would be impossible for Kelly persuasively to deny that most people in Trigg County believed he led the Night Riders and that people—including would-be jurors—feared his power.

To prove Kelly's Night Rider status, Stites offered an affidavit sworn by Sanford Hall, claiming that the county attorney had responded to Night Rider signs and signals. Stites then introduced witnesses to prove that Trigg County was the axis of Night Rider violence. With a friendly judge and no jury, Stites's strategy worked and he won his change of venue. But in the end the hearing proved a fruitless exercise. It secured little publicity, and few Kentuckians considered Kelly to have been "proven a Night Rider." So Willson did not achieve his ultimate objective. Perhaps annoyed that their suit had been converted into a Night Rider spectacle, or perhaps pressured by the Night Riders, the heirs settled with Kelly and declined to prosecute.

The Kelly case certainly did not deter the Night Riders. Shortly after the hearing the masked men carried out new raids on Illinois Central railroad depots in Gracey, Otter Pond, and Cerulean Springs. In Gracey, on the western edge of Christian County, twenty men in light buggies carried out the raid. They knocked a plank from the bottom of the depot, produced kindling and coal oil, and set the frame building ablaze. It was a minor incident, and would have scarcely been noticeable in 1906 or 1907. But after the Hopkinsville raid and Willson's determined efforts to crush the Night Riders, it garnered nationwide attention.[52]

But the Night Riders perpetuated more serious violence than the depot raids. Despite his lack of success in court, Governor Willson had succeeded in shaking the vigilantes. Fearful of spies and traitors in their own ranks, Amoss's vigilantes engaged in a new wave of violence as bloody as that between the rivers. Amoss himself had returned from Tennessee by the fall of 1908 and participated in violence directed at witnesses against his organization—but by this time no one man controlled events. One of the first victims of this new eruption of violence was a Trigg County tenant farmer, Leonard Holloway, who lived near Cobb. Apparently Holloway had spied on the Silent Brigade. His motives are unclear, but the Night Riders intercepted a letter written by Holloway claiming to "have found two more Night Riders." Soon thereafter, on May 15, Amoss cornered Holloway in a Cobb store and asked him about an account for medical services. After a short talk, Amoss maneuvered Holloway to the store's back door, where ten or fifteen men waited. "Here's the damn rascal," Amoss said. The men grabbed Holloway, blindfolded him, and took him to a dimly lit room where he was questioned closely about what he knew and what he had disclosed regarding the Night Riders. Holloway guessed the room was Amoss's medical office, but could not see it clearly. The Night Riders finally took Holloway away and released him with a warning never to leave home at night.[53] Two nights later Night Riders entered Holloway's cabin, seizing Holloway and telling his wife, "You take care of yourself, we will take care of your husband." She never saw him again. Rumors circulated around Cobb that the Night Riders destroyed his body in a barn fire some weeks later.[54]

A month after the Holloway incident, the Night Riders killed another potential witness. Sanford Hall had identified his twenty-nine-year-old brother, Herbert, as one of forty-six Night Riders he knew in Lyon County. Sanford told lawmen he was particularly anxious that his brother be found to corroborate his testimony. He probably feared his own well-publicized cooperation with lawmen would lead the Night Riders to take revenge against his brother. He hoped lawmen would quickly put him beyond the reach of masked assassins. Lyon County issued a warrant for Herbert, but lawmen never found him. According to a Louisville *Times* story Herbert left home at 7:00 A.M. on June 7, telling his family that he was going to help plow a nearby farm. According to the newspaper, "the [Night Rider] captain in Trigg County ordered his lodge to kill him" and "a dozen waylaid different roads." Herb Hall walked away from his house, crossed the crest of a hill, and was never heard from again. A Night Rider indicated the vigilantes had carried Hall "several miles with half his head shot off, and put his body in an old well." "We've gotten rid of him," the *Times* quoted him as saying, "and we will kill Sanford Hall on first sight."[55]

Hopkinsville state guard officer E. B. Bassett investigated the murder and visited the site where Hall was killed. He thought "no French novel ever depicted a spot more harrowing." He learned that the day after the killing Night Riders took Hall's body out of a swampy pond and delivered it to Amoss's chief lieutenant, Guy Dunning. Dunning carried the body to a hole in a field on his farm said to be bottomless.[56]

Rumors about the killing circulated through the little hamlets and neighborhoods where Lyon County joined Caldwell and Trigg counties. Seventy years later Clyde Quisenberry, who as a child held a lantern while his father cut the hair of his Night Rider neighbors, recalled them as saying "[a] fellow . . . by the name of Arnold Oliver . . . killed him."[57] Charlie Merrick, a young boy at the time Hall died, also reported the stories seventy years later. "Well, he left this road. Went across the field a huntin'. He had some good huntin' dogs. . . . So they followed him and got way over there in an old place called the Green Briar Swamp. He got over there on a gate and they shot him off. And, of course, killed him. Killed his dogs. And they take him and threwed him in what's called this old brush pond. It was a great big old pond with lots of dead trees and things that fell in there and a lot of brush. That's in Lyon County. Now, they, the next day—they got together that day—they got—what are we gonna do with him? Well . . . that pond wasn't very deep and they knowed they'd find him. So, they got together and they went back and they taken him out of this pond and carried him down in Lyon County. There was an old well there. And they threwed him in this old well."[58]

In Caldwell County the Night Riders murdered Julian Robinson. Robinson, residents remembered later, was "a rover," who liked to break up parties, and had once killed a train engineer by hitting him with a brass spittoon.[59] "He was about half mean and the best-hearted fellow that ever was . . . he'd do anything for you but you couldn't put a bit of dependence in the world" on him. He was so poor "he didn't have fifteen cents" and lived in "a little old shack" with his wife and children.[60] He liked to ride with the Night Riders: "That just tickled heck out of him to get into something like that— he thought it was about half mean."[61] Robinson's grave is unmarked because he was held in such low regard by the community; "that's what got him killed."[62]

Why a man like that would decide to become a witness against David Amoss is hard to fathom. One Caldwell Countian explained later that "there was a lot of people in Caldwell County that were wanting to get out of it. They felt like they'd done wrong" night riding.[63] So the pro-Night Rider sheriff of Caldwell County hired an anti-Night Rider deputy, Wylie Jones. Jones made inquiries, privately probing the ranks of the vigilantes. In the course of doing so, he contacted Robinson, a distant relative of his wife. In the little community of Otter Pond, where Robinson lived, residents had access to only one telephone, in a store. On June 9, 1910, Robinson walked from his house to the store and called Jones to tell him that he had agreed to testify against the Night Riders.[64] In such stores there were always a few men hanging about. Robinson probably chatted with them as he waited for a summer thunderstorm to pass. That day, after Robinson had made his phone call and left, two of them bought shotguns. They followed the would-be witness.[65]

When Jones found Robinson he was sprawled in the mud near a little creek, about half a mile from his house. His head had been nearly blasted from his body. In the mud Jones could see the murderers' footprints; the shooter wore a small shoe. With this information, his knowledge of the neighborhood, and some well-placed inquiries, Jones soon learned who committed the murder.[66] Although committed to restoring law and order, he had close connections to the vigilantes and respected their leaders. He had no intention of pursuing Robinson's murderers. Nor did he tell his family which respected member of the community had turned to murder. "I was always glad he didn't," Jones's son, Bernard, said in 1982. But later, when Bernard was stripping tobacco leaves at night in a barn, one of his uncles, who had been a Night Rider, told him who killed Robinson. The knowledge haunted the younger Jones for the rest of his life. "Well, I knew the man well. I knew his wife and family. His children. And I'd wish a million times I'd never . . . never heard who he was. A lot of his family is living today around in the neighborhood. I see 'em every little bit. It's the first thing I think of, of course I shouldn't." His face shiny with tears, the elderly son of a deputy sheriff sobbed that the murder "left a stain on this part of the country."[67]

Night Riders also turned to murder in Tennessee. Montgomery Countian Reuf Hunter, a loyal Association man, believed the Night Riders hurt the Association cause. He spoke against the masked men and collected money to help their victims. Hunter responded within the norms of southern folk justice. When he received threatening letters, he read them in his Sunday school class, saying he could not believe his neighbors meant him harm. Then the Night Riders stepped outside the bounds of community justice. In June 1908, a crowd of men on horseback called Hunter to his door. When he appeared, they cut him down with a hail of gunfire.[68]

The original Night Rider organization had mobilized because planters feared losing their tenant labor force. But this second wave of violence targeted men like the Collins brothers and Tandy W. Ferguson for illegally selling liquor or some other misbehavior. These raids were really a critique of local authorities. By whipping the purveyors of alcohol whom local prosecutors had tried and failed to put out of business, the vigilantes demonstrated the supposed superiority of their methods over more conventional methods. And the "shirt-tail" Night Riders whipped and even murdered blacks in the Between the Rivers region. The very labor force planters had mobilized to defend now fell victim to the latest violence. The new Night Riders made their contempt for traditional authority clearest in their feud with Judge Crumbaugh and in their murder of Sunday-school teacher and Association supporter Hunter.

Authorities fought back, struggling to restore order. Crumbaugh established a plan to defeat the Night Riders militarily. In an effort to discern some order in the chaos he faced, he falsely concluded that Association leader Stone could end the violence. By this time the Night Riders had shaken even Stone, and he readily agreed to use his influence. But the "shirt-tail" Night Riders held the Association in contempt, as is evidenced by their cry "to hell with the Association" during their raid on Eddyville. Stone could no more control the mob than Crumbaugh.

Willson had no more luck when he tried to curb the violence with the legal system in Trigg County. He could prevent massive raids like the one on Hopkinsville, but the Black Patch remained in the grip of terrible violence. The murders of Leonard Holloway, Herbert Hall, Reuf Hunter, and Julian Robinson document the more deadly and diffuse violence that now permeated the Black Patch. In communities scattered across the Black Patch, planters who had tolerated and even sponsored and encouraged the initial Night Rider movement now realized that the monster they had created had veered out of control. William Faulkner called the violent class of whites determined to overturn their society's traditional leadership after the Civil War "Snopeses." In the Black Patch these Snopeses threatened to subsume the top of society. In parts of the South they did, threatening to drive away black labor. White planters did not want black labor made scarce; they wanted it plentiful and cheap. Something had to be done.

By the end of 1908 many of the same men who had originally supported the Night Riders had become alarmed by their murderous
raiding. Before 1908 the Night Riders seemed highly disciplined
gentlemen as they conducted almost bloodless raids under the
leadership of local elites on behalf of their communities. But Black
Patch whites split on the question of racial violence. Some white
laborers saw themselves entering the ranks of twentieth-century
waged labor and saw no reason to permit black competition for
available jobs. Others—like David Amoss—expected to continue
nineteenth-century labor arrangements and wanted a large available pool of black labor. It was some of these planters who began to
realize that they had inadvertently encouraged violence by lower-
class whites. Vigilantism had careened dangerously out of control.

Moreover, violence aimed at improving the price of tobacco was
no longer necessary when the average price paid for tobacco all
over the United States approached ten cents a pound. Such prices
were almost unheard of before 1907. Since the price rise was a
national phenomenon, the Association could not credibly claim
credit. Suddenly both the Association and the Night Riders seemed
anachronistic. In 1908 the organ of the Planters' Protective Association, the *Black Patch Journal,* condemned Night Riders as an
"engine of destruction." "Rider," the *Journal* urged, "turn the rope
reins of your mule[,] head homeward[,] and there dwell in peace."[1]

But many riders refused to turn their mules homeward and the
violence continued. In the fall of 1908 Governor Willson was still
frustrated in his efforts to suppress vigilantism in Kentucky. Despite the successes law-and-order advocates had won in federal
court in Paducah and in Calloway County, courts in the heart of the
Night Rider district still refused to act decisively against the vigilantes. In 1908 the violence spread as "shirt-tail" Night Riders exploited the courts' toleration for violence.

In October Willson toured western Kentucky, trying and failing to
cow the lawless and their leaders. In Cadiz, in the heart of Night
Rider territory, he made a belligerent speech taunting them. He
condemned the Night Riders as "masked villains," threatening
them with prison or "the noose." "There shall be order here," Willson declared. "If you believe I will tolerate your lawlessness, you
are mistaken." Although he had praised the Association during his
gubernatorial campaign, Willson now ridiculed farmers who ad-
hered to the organization, reminding them that they had to wait for
their money while their neighbors had money to spend. He chal-

lenged the manhood of vigilantes, praising the bravery of forces for law and order while condemning the Night Riders as cowardly. Just five militia men could "turn the tails of any band of night riders in the State." The governor wanted his listeners to know that he knew who led the Hopkinsville raid. While not mentioning Amoss by name, Willson revealed that "the general who led the Hopkinsville raid left the town with his hair clipped by a bullet instead of a barber."[2] But Willson's efforts failed to shake Trigg County's support for the Night Riders. The Cadiz *Record* denigrated Willson by counting only twenty-eight whites and seventy-six blacks in the crowd that met his train and escorted him to his hotel. When Willson spoke, white listeners remained sullen or hostile.[3]

As Willson toured western Kentucky, his allies continued their efforts to persuade Black Patchers to cooperate in criminal prosecutions of Night Rider leaders. Lyon County Attorney Walter Krone pushed ahead with his efforts to punish the Night Riders in court. When the grand jury convened in December, Krone recognized among its members three men who he believed had participated in the Eddyville raid. He asked each juror individually for the names of anyone who could be helpful in proving criminal offenses in their respective neighborhoods. When Krone reached the Night Riders, he asked directly, "Now, gentlemen, does either of you know any person who could give up any information about Night Riding?" The jurors remained stone silent. "You could have heard a pin fall several yards away," he recounted later, "and no answer came." Exasperated, Krone complained that it was useless to pursue Night Riders with such a jury.[4]

However, Black Patch communities finally came to resist the hegemony the Planters' Protective Association had tried to establish in their community. Felix Ewing had founded the PPA with the aim of forging a farmers' trust. He urged farmers to surrender their traditional independence and community clannishness to compete effectively in the new organization-dominated economic environment. Ewing had won a majority of Black Patchers to his side, forging a new alliance between town and countryside, but at the end of 1908 his coalition began to fall apart. In 1907 Association inspectors blundered in grading tobacco. First they graded it too high. Then, unable to sell it, they had to admit their error and regrade farmers' tobacco lower. This presented critics of the Association with an effective weapon. They charged Ewing with unnecessarily delaying tobacco sales by grading Association tobacco too high.

Because banks no longer supported the Association as they had before the recession of 1907, the failure to sell their crop left farmers without money to pay their debts. And, when Ewing regraded Association tobacco to make it more saleable, his critics could accuse him of taking money out of farmers' pockets.[5]

Under economic pressure, Association unity broke down. Dissidents began to assert the same traditional localism Ewing had warned was inimical to an effective farm organization. At the end of 1908 five hundred Lyon County farmers met in Kuttawa to cheer as Association leader Hugh Lyon demanded that each county chairman be allowed to sell the tobacco crop instead of going through the Association hierarchy. In effect Lyon urged an end to Ewing's "trust of farmers" and its replacement by more traditional community leadership.[6]

Ewing responded lamely. He condemned Lyon as a "trust agent," and warned farmers not to follow "the fellow with a hat full of reforms." One of his arguments against Lyon resembled what tobacco companies had said to explain low prices in 1904.[7] Then Ewing had ridiculed the notion that the quality of the crop varied from year to year, but in 1908 he found himself insisting that the low price of tobacco was due to the bad condition of the 1907 crop.[8] Ewing's arguments did not satisfy Lyon County farmers or stop the contagion of dissent from spreading to neighboring counties.

In the first days of 1909, rumors circulated that hard-pressed Lyon County farmers had sold their 1907 crop without authorization from Ewing. When newspapers published an authoritative report of the sale at the end of January, the news for Ewing was even worse than anticipated. Not only had Lyon County dissidents sold 400,000 pounds of tobacco, but farmers in northern Caldwell County had also deserted. They had sold 1,500,000 pounds of tobacco, and Crittenden County tobacco growers had bolted with another 300,000 pounds.[9]

The Hopkinsville *Kentuckian* headlined that growers were "ON VERGE OF OPEN REVOLT."[10] Following the successful sale of the 1907 crop outside the Association, farmers met and decided to sell the 1908 crop outside the organization "at once." "The tobacco is going to be sold with or without Mr. Ewing's permission," the *Kentuckian* reported with satisfaction.[11] On February 11, Ewing met with rebelling Christian County farmers and agreed to their demands.[12]

As news spread of Ewing's agreement allowing Christian County farmers to sell their tobacco outside the organization, Trigg County farmers decided they too wanted to sell their tobacco themselves.[13] Ewing tried to resist but could not halt the tide. He announced that he had gone along with independent sales in other counties only because he felt he had no choice. Association leaders scrambled to repair the damage by announcing prohibitions of further loose sales and even prevailing on Christian County authorities to secure indictments against the Imperial Tobacco Company and its buyers for buying tobacco contracted to the Association. They secured further indictments of farmers for selling pledged tobacco beyond what Ewing had agreed to. Kentucky law made it a crime for farmers individually to sell a crop they had agreed to put in a pool. Violators could pay as much as $250 in fines for each offense.[14] When farmers complained that it was not fair for the Association to allow some growers to sell their crops loose while others had to wait, the Association answered that "the line had to be drawn somewhere."[15] But nothing availed. Demands by local elites for control of crops led to the collapse of the Association. At the height of its success in 1907, the PPA had sold 95 million pounds of Black Patch tobacco. In 1909 this total dropped to only 36 million pounds.[16]

Another, more ironic blow befell the Association when the Supreme Court broke up the American Tobacco Company in 1911. Although critics have since criticized the Supreme Court's decision for not going far enough in breaking up the gigantic tobacco combine—and it did nothing to the Night Riders' chief enemy, the Italians—at the time it seemed to many a great victory for farmers. The Clarksville *Leaf-Chronicle* triumphantly headlined, "PLAIN LAW LAID DOWN FOR AMERICAN TOBACCO TRUST."[17] It hardly seemed necessary to continue fighting a defeated enemy.

As the Association disintegrated, Tennessee officials moved to restore order by arresting the murderer of Reuf Hunter. Montgomery County Judge Charles Tyler took the lead. Tyler had first sympathized with the Night Riders in their battle with the tobacco trust, but by 1909 the violence—no longer directed primarily at the tobacco trust—alarmed him. In March 1909 the Clarksville *Leaf-Chronicle* announced that "after months of hard work on the part of county authorities, the mysterious murder of Reuf Hunter is about to be cleared up." Authorities arrested Marcellus Rinehart, described by a newspaper reporter as having "a wild look out of his eyes."

The nature of the evidence against Rinehart raises doubts about his guilt. A year before Rinehart's arrest, while Hunter lingered at the edge of death, the sheriff had led a frantic search for the bullet. Although the dying man directed the searchers to look in the fireplace, the sheriff had not been able to identify the fatal bullet. Since the Night Riders had filled the house with bullets, finding a bullet was no problem. The problem was finding the right bullet, the one that had passed through Hunter's body, and at the time of the murder that had not been possible. Nevertheless, a year later, on the eve of the trial, the entire prosecution team visited the murder scene, searching for the bullet that had eluded the sheriff a year earlier. Now they easily identified a steel-jacketed .32 caliber bullet that they now said was the bullet that killed Hunter.[18] Only after officials had arrested a suspect, seized his gun, and learned its calibre had they found the "right" bullet.

But Rinehart was probably a scapegoat.[19] In a letter written from a rest home in 1982, seventy-three years after his arrest, Rinehart still claimed prosecutors had framed him. "A man Mr. Hunter was killed and no body knew who killed him[.] So [prosecutor Matt] Lyle bring the murder on me[.] I didn't know Hunter[.] Lyle hire[d] evidence[,] he got [a] guy to tell all kinds of lies on me."[20] At least one resident of western Montgomery County later agreed that county officials framed Rinehart. In 1985 Robert Holt remembered hearing talk in his neighborhood that Rinehart was with the Night Riders who killed Hunter but that he had not committed the murder. The actual killer was a Robertson County man who left Tennessee the night of the shooting. If this tale is true, then Rinehart did aid and abet the murder of Hunter. But authorities preferred to accuse Rinehart of the more spectacular crime of the murder itself. Perhaps they regarded a trial for murder as more dramatic—and therefore more likely to help end Night Riding—than a trial for aiding and abetting. They certainly realized that whatever the law said, juries disliked sentencing a man to hang merely for being present when another man committed a crime. Moreover, they were trying to bring an episode of violence to an end. Arresting someone for aiding and abetting murder rather than murder itself would leave too many questions unanswered.[21]

Testimony began on June 28, 1909. Spectators crowded the courtroom. Local newspapers devoted pages to the trial, employing stenographers to copy the testimony of each witness.[22] The sheriff identified the bullet the lawyers had dug out of the woodwork at Hunter's house. An ordinary pistol could not fire such a bullet, the lawman testified; it could only be fired by a .32 Colt automatic like the one Rinehart owned. The prosecution called witnesses from the hardware company that sold the bullets and the express company that delivered the pistol to Rinehart.[23] The jury returned a verdict of guilty. Judge Tyler sentenced Rinehart to hang, a sentence confirmed by the Tennessee Supreme Court.[24]

The willingness of a jury to convict a Night Rider and a judge to sentence him to death signaled the end of official toleration for vigilantism. In Tennessee, the Night Riders hastily acceded and mob violence ended. The response to a drive in 1910 by Montgomery Countians for a commutation of Rinehart's death sentence indicated that local officials believed Rinehart's conviction had restored order. It also indicated that Rinehart's judge had doubts about the sufficiency of the evidence that convicted him. Judge Tyler wrote Governor Malcolm R. Patterson that he thought the conviction and sentence had served its purpose: "Lawlessness in this community is now a thing of the past. Good order among us has been restored." But it would not do for the governor to publicly declare the verdict unjustified. "I suggest," he wrote, "that you express no opinion as to whether the evidence justified the verdict. You know how difficult it is to obtain a conviction in a case like this." Tyler warned Patterson that if he criticized the verdict as unjustified, "it would, I fear, have a most unhappy effect on a lawless class here that at one time defied the courts." "They have been taught a lesson," he wrote, and it was best not to weaken it.[25] Tyler's argument impressed the governor. He commuted Rinehart's sentence to life in prison without comment. When one of Rinehart's prosecutors, Austin Peay, won election as governor, he commuted Rinehart's sentence to time served. Years later, Rinehart explained, "Peay . . . knew I was framed so he turn me lo[o]se[.]"[26] The readiness of two governors to ameliorate Reinhart's sentence at least suggests that they understood that prosecutors designed his conviction as a signal of a change in official attitude.

Although the Rinehart trial brought order to Tennessee, Kentucky Night Riders continued to enjoy support in their state. One measure of this can be found in politics. Kentucky newspapers attributed considerable power at the ballot box to the Night Riders. In 1908, the Clarksville Leaf-Chronicle predicted that Calloway County Night Riders would vote as a bloc, and Governor Willson expressed fear that Night Riders all over western Kentucky would vote en masse. A year later the Paducah Sun reported that Night Riders remained a "political force" in Lyon County.[27]

In November 1909, law-and-order candidates challenged Night Rider power and all of them lost to candidates silent on the Night Rider issue. Normally Republican Crittenden County astonished political observers by going Democratic after Republicans allied themselves with law-and-order proponents. The law-and-order candidate for county attorney in Lyon County glumly wrote after the election, "We have met the enemy and we are their meat." A year later he complained that Night Riders controlled the local county courthouse. They were "collecting taxes, dispensing justice . . . controlling the county schools, maker and custodian of all public records."[28] For at least two years after the Hollowell verdict the Night Riders remained a political force in western Kentucky, controlling courthouses in Caldwell, Trigg, and Lyon counties. In fact, they exercised a tighter control of county government in those three counties than they had prior to the federal trial in Paducah.

Some opponents of the Kentucky Night Riders still hoped to defeat the vigilantes in federal court. Three survivors of the Birmingham raid filed suits in federal court, one of the victims winning a judgment of $24,000 in 1909.[29] But that figure proved virtually meaningless. The only property marshals seized from the defendants was a farm appraised at $500, and when they auctioned it at the courthouse door in Marshall County, bystanders made "ugly threats" against anyone daring to make a bid. The plaintiffs' lawyers bought the land, for $400, to keep it from reverting to the Night Rider owner.[30] The community could blunt the effectiveness of the federal court even when it awarded the plaintiffs a substantial judgment.

Nonetheless, opponents of the Night Riders continued their war against vigilantism in federal court. In the first months of 1909 three white victims of another Night Rider raid filed suit. All residents of Eddyville, Kentucky, they not only sued vigilantes they could personally identify as having beaten them, but also every man identified as a Night Rider in previous legal actions and all the leaders of the Planters' Protective Association. All were co-conspirators and equally guilty for the actions of any Night Rider anywhere, the plaintiffs argued. They named over a hundred defendants.[31]

Ultimately few of these defendants ever had to face a federal jury. In November 1910, when the first Eddyville plaintiff's suit against the Night Riders came to trial in federal court, Evans would dismiss charges against all but three of the defendants. The jury would find against two of them, including Amoss, and award the plaintiff

$10,000 in damages.[32] Although it proved Amoss a Night Rider, the trial received scant newspaper coverage. As had been the case in other federal trials, the jury found against the defendants chiefly on the testimony of outsiders. No Night Rider secrets emerged. Evans would ultimately dismiss the remaining two Eddyville suits when the plaintiffs admitted they could not identify any of their attackers.[33]

But the federal suits filed by the Eddyville plaintiffs represented a community-based strategy to vanquish the Night Riders. The federal court cases were not what they seemed. In each case Lyon County Attorney Walter Krone was the plaintiff's attorney. The cases were not designed to suppress the Night Riders through federal law enforcement, but to probe the ranks of the Silent Brigade for weak links, men who could be persuaded to testify against their erstwhile colleagues. Krone could offer Night Riders a choice between paying heavy fines or testifying in state courts.

Krone was not the only Lyon County lawman trying to derail the Night Riders. In Eddyville Judge Crumbaugh continued his efforts. Crumbaugh concentrated on collecting evidence against Amoss and his Night Riders, even after he lost his office in the elections of 1909. In the spring he was able to recruit the head of the Between-the-Rivers Night Riders as a spy. Champion had completed his term in Eddyville penitentiary April 8, only to face more indictments in Livingston County. Hoping to avoid additional jail time or a fine, Champion contacted Crumbaugh. Champion claimed that he could gain entree to the very top of the Night Rider organization, and Crumbaugh hired him "to do some secret service work." In the fall Champion traveled through the east end of Lyon County and into Trigg and Caldwell counties, where he claimed to have met Amoss and to have "hobnobbed with the worst devils of the lot." Amoss was too busy to talk much to Champion, but told him to come back in about ten days. Nonetheless, Champion was able to report that Amoss had told him he had attended a large gathering in Clarksville where "one of the 'biggest elders' in Tennessee" was sworn into the Night Riders. Champion advised Crumbaugh that Charles Fort was a member of the inner circle but that Ewing was not. Crumbaugh hoped to have Champion take a friend with him to corroborate his testimony.[34]

It is, of course, impossible to authenticate Champion's story. Crumbaugh believed him, but it was in Champion's interest to try to sell as good a story as he could cook up. He wanted to make his testimony as valuable as possible in hopes of avoiding further time in jail. Champion wrote directly to Governor Willson in October and made it clear that further "secret service work" was contingent on a pardon from the indictments in Smithland. In December, Champion wrote another letter pleading for a pardon and complaining that Otis Blick, the chief witness against him at his trial, "one of the worst characters we ever had in this county," had received a pardon.[35] Willson wrote Crumbaugh that Champion's letter was "so wrong in its statements that I do not think I ought to have any correspondence with him." But Willson did concede that he had second thoughts about the pardon of Blick, because he was a "pretty bad man."[36]

But slowly local law enforcement officials began to move against the Night Riders in Kentucky. In 1909 the Law and Order League's candidate for judge of the circuit that included Hopkinsville had been defeated by John T. Hanbery, who had been determinedly noncommittal on the Night Rider issue. But shortly after the election, Hanbery unexpectedly made overtures to the League and, in February 1910, the League informed Willson that the new judge intended to move against the Night Riders. Night Rider partisans had long used their control of the jury wheel to prevent a serious investigation of the Hopkinsville raid. With a judge sympathetic to the Law and Order League, this was about to change. As the League told Willson, Hanbery would see to it that the "right men" would serve on the next grand jury.[37]

Hanbery hoped the trial would result in a peaceful settlement of the Black Patch war. Anyone with a mask could call himself a Night Rider now and murder and assault with impunity. Rumors circulated that a band of men planned to rob banks, confident they could escape justice simply by identifying themselves as Night Riders. Something had to be done. Even Amoss agreed that state courts had to reassert themselves. Former circuit judge Ira D. Smith, who served forty-two years in the same seat occupied by Hanbery and began his legal career in the midst of the Night Rider crisis, said in 1982, "I believe that—after the election—I think the Association people and Amoss's friends got together and thought maybe the best thing to do was to have a show and have a trial. It might satisfy the Law and Order people. And that's the reason he was indicted. . . . They wanted to make a show, you know—that they were trying to clear the thing up."[38]

On February 28, 1910, Hanbery began a new term of circuit court in Christian County's recently remodeled courtroom, decorated with carnations and roses. Spectators commented on the warm, pleasant early spring day. The new judge took a seat at a table facing the grand jurors and charged them for over an hour. The Hopkinsville *Kentuckian,* ardently opposed to the Night Riders, praised his demeanor. The grand jury included such Law and Order notables as tobacco handler Elisha M. Flack and W. T. Cooper, whose warehouse the Night Riders had destroyed during their 1907 raid.[39]

The grand jury went to work, systematically summoning persons identified as Night Riders in federal suits in hopes of turning up a confession. On March 7, they summoned Night Riders Milton Oliver, Oscar Oliver, and Tom Jones.[40] All three had been successfully sued in United States District Court by their victims.[41] Thanks to Krone's dragnet strategy of suing anyone suspected of being a Night Rider, over a hundred persons in all, the three knew they faced additional trials in Paducah if they failed to cooperate. Milton Oliver had already paid a fine of $1,000 as a result of the judgment against him in *Hollowell* v. *Hollowell, et al.* Krone could have promised a favorable settlement in the outstanding suits naming him as a defendant if he cooperated and guaranteed no settlement if he refused.

Although Milton Oliver had been secretly cooperating with Crumbaugh for a year, he hesitated to testify publicly against the Night Riders. By March 10 it had become clear that the three witnesses were not going to appear voluntarily, so the grand jury issued warrants for their arrest. But the sheriff and his deputy reported that they could not find the three men. When grand jurors issued a new warrant March 15, the county coroner managed to serve it on Jones, but he escaped while pretending to change clothes for the trip into town.[42]

Milton Oliver proved the key to winning indictments against Amoss and other leading Night Riders. He had hoped to avoid testifying in public against the Night Riders. He spoke only after being forced to appear and even then under the threat of additional fines in federal court.[43] At last Oliver broke down and gave the grand jury a full confession, identifying Amoss and five others as leaders of the raid.[44] As a result, the grand jury issued indictments charging Amoss and his co-defendants with violations of Kentucky's Reconstruction-era Ku Klux Klan act, which prohibited disguised or armed men from confederating and banding together to intimidate others.[45] Grand jurors issued a warrant for Amoss's arrest.

The indictment and warrant the grand jury directed at Amoss

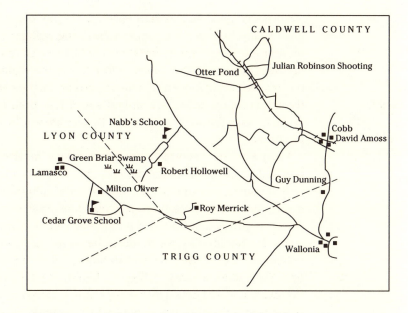

challenged Amoss's carefully constructed public image and with it the mystique of the Night Riders. In the parlance of the honor-oriented society in which they lived, the grand jury "gave the lie" to Amoss. They announced that his public nature was a lie in two ways. He was not, they charged, as strong as he claimed. Second, Amoss and his Night Riders did not really represent their entire community. Southerners attached no dishonor to donning a mask or projecting false images. Everyone recognized the value of fooling an enemy and that successful trickery demonstrated a kind of superiority over an adversary. But the grand jury's indictment nonetheless embarrassed the top Night Rider. Dishonor lay not in trickery, but in trickery exposed.[46]

Presenting this challenge was a delicate matter. The Christian County warrant had to be served on Amoss in Caldwell County, by the same officials known to be in league with the Night Riders. Caldwell County Sheriff Henry Towery passed the warrant to his new deputy, Nathan Wylie Jones. Towery's choice of Jones was no accident. Inasmuch as Jones had been sheriff before the Black Patch war began and had established a record of opposition to lawlessness, he was unemployable as a law officer as long as county officials gave the Night Riders free rein. But in 1910, as county leaders finally became alarmed by the spread of lawlessness, Towery hired Jones as his deputy.

Jones occupied an awkward position. Despite his opposition to night riding, he had close connections to the vigilantes, in that his brother had joined the organization and Night Rider Tom Jones was his first cousin. But despite such close ties to the vigilantes, Jones had resisted Night Rider intimidation and earned their enmity. Only the intervention of his cousin had saved him from a whipping. When he gave the warrant to Jones, Towery knew it would actually be served.

Jones took the train to Cobb, found Amoss, arrested him, and released him when he posted bond.[47] Thus a crack appeared in the wall of community support for Amoss, wide enough to admit one deputy. But it was only a crack. In Lyon County, lawmen offered Milt Oliver no protection from retribution. He lived in a sea of hate, in terror for his life. Unable to sleep, he feared his food might be poisoned. He eschewed medical attention, afraid the doctor might be a Night Rider assassin.[48] Meeting him during his ordeal, Judge Crumbaugh was shocked by his appearance. Normally a large, vigorous man, Oliver now appeared broken, "completely prostrated" by the constant dread of death or attack. He "cried like a great whipped school-boy."[49]

The Night Riders offered Oliver a way out of his hell. John W. Hollowell, Robert Nabb, and Guy Dunning summoned him to a meeting in Princeton. They had an affidavit repudiating his testimony. The affidavit, purporting to be written by Oliver, said Krone and Bassett had taken him to Hopkinsville and threatened him with prison if he did not testify against Amoss. Despite his terror, Oliver would not sign.[50] The Night Riders kept up their pressure, sending a doctor named Sutton to ingratiate himself with Oliver by offering kindly advice. If he signed the Night Riders' paper, he would be safe, the doctor assured him; if not, his life was in danger. On April 20, the Night Riders summoned Oliver to a second meeting. Sutton joined the Night Riders at a livery stable, trying to persuade Oliver to sign their affidavit. Finally they grew menacing. "Now it's up to you," they told him. "Sign this and we will guarantee your safety." Oliver decided his only chance to get home alive was to sign the bogus statement.[51]

Despite Night Rider assurances, Oliver's capitulation did not guarantee his safety. On the night of May 25, 1910, two men accosted Oliver in his yard and shot him in the hip with a shotgun. Oliver's family immediately called Crumbaugh, but Crumbaugh was not at home. Next they called the sheriff. Although they

Milton Oliver and a guard in his tobacco patch. Photo courtesy of The Filson Club.

called at 9:00 P.M., it was not until 9:00 A.M. the following day that the sheriff, county attorney, and county judge started for Oliver's house, twelve miles away. They were not much help when they got there, though the sheriff offered to furnish as many bodyguards as Oliver could afford to hire.[52] When Governor Willson heard of the assassination attempt, he dispatched troops to establish a camp on Oliver's farm.[53]

Although Oliver could not identify the two men who shot him, he suspected a Night Rider named Roy Merrick of involvement. For some time before the shooting, the Night Riders had hidden around Oliver's house and watched him. Oliver identified one of the spies as Merrick, of the Blue Springs neighborhood. Merrick's younger brother, Charlie, later denied that his brother had anything to do with the actual shooting. "My brother hadn't bothered those people none whatever. He wasn't the man that shot old Milt Oliver."[54] But Charlie also admitted that his brother "wasn't no angel." In September 1907, Roy's mother had recorded a notice in the county records declaring she had "set free my son Roy Merrick to do and act for himself, to sue, and be sued." She added, "I am not to be in any way responsible for any of his said acts or doings or otherwise."[55]

Charlie Merrick, eleven at the time of the shooting, recalled that the Night Riders had given him the job of reloading shotgun shells. "I had a fifteen-cent Barlow, a knife, with a sharp point. . . . I'd take this sharp-pointed knife and I'd pick this wadding out of this shell and pour the little fine [bird] shot out in a pan. . . . I'd put nine BBs in a shell and put the wadding back. Then I'd put seven bucks—that's all I could get in a buckshot. They's bigger." When Dr. Z. T. Cunningham dressed Oliver's wound, he found seven buckshot.[56]

Oliver's troubles continued. His injury delayed Amoss's trial. The Night Riders could not get at Oliver—he holed up on his farm, guarded by the Kentucky militia. But on July 30 Oliver's son, Noah, and his hired hand, Axiom Cooper, went to a barbecue. A dancing ring and a fiddler's stand had been set up, and many in the neighborhood attended. Perhaps Oliver and Cooper ventured out because they were tired of being virtual prisoners of their own protection. Perhaps they imagined that the Night Riders were only interested in Milton Oliver and would not bother them. Or perhaps they were filled with resentment for their tormentors and went looking for trouble. Charlie Merrick remembered later that "they was going around there saying they had a pardon in their pockets to kill a night rider and there was some on the ground there." Noah Oliver recalled later that the trouble started just as he and Cooper reached the barbecue. Luther "Spunk" Creekmur "called me off," Oliver observed, "and said someone called him a son-of-a-bitch and I told him there was a mistake and asked him who told him and he said Cooper, and Cooper said to him, 'I never said it; you are just hunting trouble.' "[57]

Then Alonzo Gray hit Cooper twice with brass "knucks," cutting him around his eye. In the next instant Fraud Murphy, Vilas Mitchell, Bart Creekmur, and Spunk Creekmur all shot Cooper. Roy Merrick later told Charlie that he had been the first to shoot Cooper, after Gray staggered him with his "knucks." "It was self-defense," Merrick contended, because Cooper had drawn his pistol and shot at Merrick, putting a hole in his sleeve.[58]

By the time the Kentucky State Guards arrived from Milton Oliver's farm, only about six persons remained at the scene of the shooting. Cooper said Gray had knocked him down, after which Merrick, Mitchell, Bart Creekmur, and finally Spunk Creekmur had shot him. Someone recorded the statement on a small piece of paper. Cooper signed with an "X" before dying the next day.[59]

Militia soldiers rushed off to arrest the killers. They seized Gray,

Mitchell, Murphy, and two accomplices, Jim Bozarth and Bryant Hawkins, but they could not find Merrick; the Blue Springs community had hidden Merrick from the inquiring soldiers. Immediately after the shooting, he had rushed home in his buggy. His father had died a few years previously, but his mother still lived in the big, old log house built in 1810 by Merrick's grandfather. Merrick and his wife lived in a nearby tenant house. As he rode toward the house, the family came out to see what was the matter. Not taking time to get out of the buggy, he told them that the Cooper boy had been killed. Someone asked who killed him. "Well," he answered, "they accused me and Mitchell of doing it and some more of us boys." Merrick hurried off and spent the first night with his brother-in-law.[60]

Soldiers soon appeared in the neighborhood, searching for Merrick, but found the community stolidly uncooperative. Major E. B. Bassett and some of his men went to the house of S. H. Lester only to learn that Merrick had spent the night with him. As the soldiers left, Lester rang his farm bell, in answer to which farm bells began ringing all over the neighborhood, signaling Merrick that the soldiers were looking for him.[61] The soldiers met Merrick's sister on a road and ordered her to open their barn. "My brother's not around here," she said, pulling open the large door. Looking back, she could see the soldiers creeping through the barn, pointing their weapons toward the loft, nervously trying to look in all directions at once. Merrick was not in the barn, but he was close by. Dressed in a woman's skirts and bonnet, he was with his wife's family, "working out" with the women.[62]

For most of the time that the soldiers sought him, Merrick hid in a wheat field. Men in the neighborhood kept him supplied with food and ammunition. One man gave him his old army rifle so his firepower would more nearly match that of a soldier. In 1982 Charlie Merrick still believed that if the soldiers had found his brother, they would have killed him on the spot. While held as prisoners at Bassett's camp on Oliver's farm, the men arrested immediately after the killing overheard soldiers plotting to kill them as well. However, the talk was a ruse. Bassett deliberately allowed the prisoners to "overhear" such talk in hopes of frightening them into a confession. To heighten the effect, he even had his men dig graves within view of the arrested men. But the "old men" of the neighborhood took Bassett seriously. Fearing Bassett planned to hunt down and kill Merrick, they decided that the fugitive should give himself up to the civil authorities. They arranged for Merrick to keep his guns, even after he surrendered, until he got safely to town. Merrick gave himself up to the Caldwell County sheriff. Bart and Spunk Creekmur also surrendered.[63]

Lyon County officials then demanded that Bassett turn over the men he had arrested. When he refused, Crumbaugh's successor as Lyon County judge, Thomas Parker Gray, sent a telegram to Willson insisting that he order Bassett to turn over the persons he arrested. On August 1, the adjutant general, by order of the governor, commanded Bassett to turn over the four prisoners to civil authorities. Bassett still refused, telling a newspaper reporter that he was tired of turning men over to civil authorities only to have them released. Trying to get the order reversed, he sent a telegram to Willson asking "in the name of humanity and civilization to establish safety and law in that section." He "refused delivery to the criminal authorities who would not arrest" the culprits themselves and would turn the prisoners loose "on a straw bond."[64]

Willson's informal advisor on the Night Rider crisis, John Stites of Louisville, also pleaded with Willson. Allow Bassett to hold the prisoners until "they . . . breakdown and [provide] a complete story of the murders," he urged. "Unless sharp and decisive action is taken, there is no telling what will be the outcome." The governor could expect little justice from Lyon County authorities, Stites warned, as they were in sympathy with the murderers.[65]

Willson turned aside Bassett's plea and rejected Stites's advice. He had no doubt Lyon County officials were in sympathy with the Night Riders, but it was unconstitutional for the soldiers to hold civilian prisoners. He explained to Stites that giving the prisoners to the Lyon County court would put Lyon County on trial before the people of the state. On August 3 Bassett reluctantly turned his prisoners over to the Lyon County sheriff.[66]

That same day, Lyon County officials held a coroner's inquest into the death of Axiom Cooper at the site of the shooting. They decided to use the inquest to argue that the shooting had nothing to do with Night Riding but resulted from a drunken feud. Sam Cash, the retired sheriff, served as jury foreman. Again and again, he asked witnesses, "Was there a good deal of drunkenness here that day?" One witness obliged by testifying that he had been too drunk to know what was going on at the barbecue. The testimony of Noah Oliver and Tom Litchfield and his wife, however, did establish that someone had murdered Cooper and even suggested who had done it.[67]

The Lyon County grand jury indicted five men for murder, Roy Merrick, Vilas Mitchell, Luther "Spunk" Creekmur, Bart Creekmur, and Fraud Murphy, and three more, Jim Bozarth, Alonzo Gray, and Bryant Hawkins, for aiding and abetting the murder. The defendants secured Trigg County Attorney John W. Kelly to represent them; he persuaded the court to set Bozarth and Hawkins free on bail. The sheriff and Bassett escorted the other six to jail in Hopkinsville. Bassett complained later that the sheriff failed to handcuff the prisoners and allowed Kelly to accompany them.[68]

In December Lyon County tried the eight defendants in two separate trials, four at a time. Prosecutors hoped that if local jurors acquitted the first four, they could persuade the judge to grant a change of venue or enlist jurors from a different county. Interest in the trials was keen. Reporters came down from Paducah to write accounts of the proceedings. But Bassett recognized men he thought sympathetic to the defendants in the jury and judged the chance of a conviction as small.[69] Even Commonwealth Attorney Smith seemed disappointed in the jury. He told the Paducah *News-Democrat* that two or three of the jury had already made up their minds. The paper added, "It is even hinted that one is a close friend of the defendants." Smith indicated that the best he could hope for was a hung jury so he could request the judge to call in a jury from another county.[70]

At both trials the prosecution summoned a crowd of witnesses from the barbecue who testified the defendants had knocked Cooper down and then shot him. Axiom's brother, Arthur, testified, identifying his brother's blood-stained clothing. Each of the defendants took the stand and professed ignorance of the murder. Each claimed to have been some distance from the shooting. None had seen any of it. Not one reacted in any way when he heard gunfire. Vilas Mitchell heard eight or twelve shots fired, but he stayed by his lemonade stand, a few steps away, making no comment about the shooting to the four or five men with whom he chatted. Fraud Murphy claimed not to have noticed anything out of the ordinary as the murder occurred.[71]

Although he had admitted his role in the shooting to his family, Roy Merrick joined in the alibi defense, expressing contempt for the prosecution's case. "Figure, then," he shot back when Smith asked him where he was in relation to the other defendants. He had told his family that he had been shot through the sleeve by Cooper, but at the trial he said he did not know who fired the shot. He could hardly admit that Cooper had shot at him and also claim that he had been some distance from the murder, unaware of what was happening. Merrick put himself in the ridiculous position of admitting he had been shot, but insisting he had not mentioned it to the people he was standing with at the time.

Merrick displayed little concern about absurdities in his testimony. Smith asked, "How come you didn't tell somebody—what are you laughing at?" Merrick answered, "That fellow there." Smith retorted, "This is a funny occasion to you, is it?" Clearly, Merrick was confident the jury would acquit him.[72]

The first jury acquitted the first group of defendants. Smith asked for a jury from a different county for the second trial and the judge summoned a jury from Crittenden County. But the second of the two trials ended as had the first, with acquittals of all charged. Charlie Merrick said later that the Crittenden County deputy who summoned the jurors was a distant relative of Roy Merrick. Moreover, the Caldwell County sheriff advised the Crittenden deputy to pick only veniremen likely to acquit.[73]

After his fruitless efforts to convict Roy Merrick and the other Night Riders in Lyon County, Smith next turned to the trial of David Amoss in Christian County. Because of Oliver's injuries, Hanbery had rescheduled Amoss's trial, originally set for June 1910, for March 1911. When court convened, a former circuit judge, Thomas Cook, was prominent as a defense attorney. Not trusting Smith to prosecute vigorously, the Law and Order League hired attorneys to assist the Commonwealth attorney. Selden Y. Trimble and John Stites of Hopkinsville and James C. Sims of Bowling Green joined the Commonwealth attorney. Such powerful legal talent suggested at least the possibility of a conviction, and Stites told the governor "we all feel very hopeful indeed."[74]

Out of touch with the reality in the Black Patch, the radical socialist newspaper *Appeal to Reason* hoped to use publicity surrounding the Hopkinsville trial to recruit southerners into the Socialist party. In 1910 the Kansas newspaper dispatched its correspondent to the Black Patch to write a series of ten articles in anticipation of Amoss's trial. The newspaper trumpeted the Night Riders as heroic resisters of "capitalism's invasion of the South."[75] The reporter candidly recorded his admiration for the vigilantes, deploring only the ignorance of some farmers that made violence necessary.[76] In economic hard times, some Black Patchers toyed with socialism, but the Socialists completely misunderstood the tragedy of the Black Patch. Unaware of the profound conservatism of most Night Riders, they did not grasp the masked men's desire to preserve their way of life. Nor did they understand Ewing's desire to participate in the national economy. And they missed the ugly turn the violence took after spinning away from elite control.

Nevertheless, Amoss granted the *Appeal to Reason* reporter an interview, impressing the writer with his cool manner. Hoping the socialists would help him with his expenses, the Night Rider leader claimed to be a reader of the *Appeal to Reason*. Then came the pitch. He "is a poor man, and unless he is given financial assistance this trial will leave him completely stranded," the correspondent reported.[77] Amoss assured the *Appeal to Reason* that he stood ready to go to the gallows for the cause of socialism.

In the expectation that the socialist cause would gain another martyr, the *Appeal to Reason* promised its readers that their correspondent would attend Amoss's trial. But when Hanbery announced the names of veniremen for the trial, Amoss knew he need not fear martyrdom. From the moment Amoss's jury was announced, state prosecutors realized they could not convict the Night Rider general. "VERY few decent citizens" were among those named as jurors, one observer wrote Governor Willson glumly. "The jury wheel was adroitly filled with about the most villainous lot of criminals that night-riding has ever produced."[78]

Despite the hostile jury, Amoss's opponents believed that his Hopkinsville trial ended the Black Patch war. In large part this was because prosecutors revealed the inner workings of the Night Riders, building their case on the testimony of insiders. Black Patch newspapers described Amoss and his activities in great detail, destroying the aura of mystery that had surrounded him. The Amoss trial attracted more attention than the federal trials because the prosecution produced Night Riders willing to testify against their former organization. Five former Riders broke their oaths to testify for the prosecution. Their uncorroborated testimony could not convict Amoss, but they revealed some of the Night Riders' darkest secrets. The witnesses named their former colleagues, described clandestine meetings, and narrated Amoss's involvement in detail. Each day they testified, spectators packed the courthouse. Both of Hopkinsville's newspapers filled their pages with columns of testi-

Dr. David Amoss, the
Night Rider chieftain.
Author's photo, courtesy
of David Porter.

mony, copied almost verbatim by stenographers. Newspapers all across the Black Patch did the same.

Amoss relied on the classic vigilante's defense, an alibi. Although his lawyers described him as "beyond reproach . . . unimpeached and unimpeachable,"[79] few onlookers, even his supporters, thought Amoss told the truth. Prosecutors cleverly asked Amoss the one question he could not possibly answer truthfully. Should the courts convict and punish the men who raided Hopkinsville, they asked, forcing the doctor to declare that lawmen should punish "all violators of the law," repudiating vigilantism. More than guilt or innocence, the Amoss trial was really about authority, and the top Night Rider had endorsed legal authority over vigilantism.

As in the Tennessee prosecution, there was a deeper meaning to the Amoss trial. Anthropologists have found that the ritualized public exposure of criminals can serve as a form of punishment.[80] This was especially true for the intensely secretive Night Riders. The Hopkinsville trial exposed the mysterious leader of the Night Riders to the public in a way the federal trials had not. Amoss was "the object of general attention," a reporter wrote in an understatement. Reporters carefully described his physical appearance. He was, a newspaper reported, "low in stature and stockily built, with ruddy complexion, steel-blue eyes, gray hair and sandy mustache." People all over the Black Patch scrutinized his words and face. In an effort to demonstrate that their client could not have led the Hopkinsville raid, Amoss's lawyers pointed out that the real Night Rider general had been injured and presumably scarred while in Hopkinsville. They asked if he were willing to disrobe to prove his body unmarked. The blushing defendant escaped that indignity (he had been injured in the scalp anyway). But the question made clear the degree of his exposure. Unlike in the federal trials, Black Patch newspapers reported almost every word spoken in the courtroom. The publication of his picture in the newspapers by a technology then not common in the Black Patch allowing reproduction of halftone images diminished the aura of mystery that had surrounded the Night Riders' general. Amoss may have been the first Black Patcher to have his image made common.[81]

In the end the court acquitted Amoss, but the acquittal was clearly a product of law, not Night Rider intimidation. The rules of evidence prohibited a jury from convicting the perpetrator of a conspiracy solely on the evidence of co-conspirators. A legal technicality set Amoss free. The chief Night Rider had been in the hands of the law, at the mercy of a jury and a circuit judge's interpretation of the law. The power of the law had been reasserted, the power of the Night Riders diminished.[82] "Mr. Nightrider," one observer wrote, "is no longer the 'cockey' gentleman of yore and is beginning to look like he is sick of his sins."[83] Although the *Appeal to Reason* had hailed the Night Riders as "revolutionary farmers" and declared Kentucky's "tobacco fields ripe for socialism" before Amoss's trial, after his acquittal they lamely concluded with a single article, dropping their push for new members in the Black Patch.[84]

As if to emphasize the change in Amoss's status, Black Patchers began to spread the rumor that Amoss had dressed like a woman to evade state guards after the Hopkinsville raid. Similar stories gained currency about other Night Riders in hiding.[85] Seventy years after Amoss's trial, Black Patchers repeat the stories without a trace of maliciousness. They were, and still are, a joke on a once-powerful man. In a culture where men were extremely touchy about their masculinity and women were associated with powerlessness, the truth of the story mattered less than the fact that it became a prominent part of Black Patch folklore.

It is possible that Amoss and the other Night Riders acquiesced

in the spread of these stories as a gesture of submission to authorities. In 1982 Roy Merrick's brother Charlie described how his
brother had dressed like a woman to escape arrest. Relating the
story with a look of embarrassed amusement, Charlie invited his
listener to chuckle at a powerful man's discomfiture.[86] It was not
inherently shameful for a southern white male to don a disguise,
even a woman's dress. Men of honor could wear a mask. Their
friends might even admire their cleverness. The dishonor came in
the unmasking, the humiliation of a public challenge to the public
persona. By tolerating such an unmasking, Amoss symbolically surrendered a piece of his prestige and public power to a higher authority, the court system. The stories of his dressing like a woman
marked a loss of power and a denouement for the Night Rider
movement.[87]

After Amoss's acquittal the Commonwealth attorney dismissed
the remaining indictment against him and the five remaining defendants. But no more Night Rider raids or murders occurred after
Amoss's release.[88]

After the trial the already declining Planters' Protective Association degenerated rapidly. Its leaders deserted the sinking ship.
About a year after his trial, the Night Riders' general turned against
the Planters' Protective Association. By the end of 1912 Amoss's
brother—who once operated an Association warehouse—managed
a loose floor in Princeton, meaning he accepted tobacco from individual farmers unpacked in hogsheads and auctioned it off. His
operation represented the antithesis of everything the tightly organized Planters' Protective Association represented.[89] The next year
some farmers made an abortive attempt to organize a new farmers'
organization in opposition to the old PPA. And prominent among
the organizers stood David Amoss.[90] Ewing held on until 1915, but
by that year he was pleading with tobacco growers to place their
tobacco in his dying organization.[91]

Felix Ewing's bid to organize tobacco growers into a trust-like organization failed. The Black Patch proved stubbornly resistant to such modernizing efforts. After the Black Patch war, farmers resumed traditional methods of farming and marketing. Black Patch planters remained at the top of the social structure and their black laborers at the bottom. Tobacco sold for higher and higher prices, reaching the unheard of price of thirty cents a pound in 1919. With prices high, it was no longer necessary to take radical steps to compete with business, and the planters who had once supported Ewing's scheme to centralize control of the Black Patch tobacco crop discarded the Association as quickly as they had picked it up. The traditional ways of growing and marketing tobacco were working just fine. Individual farmers controlled their own crops, unhindered by any regionwide authority.

But Ewing was not the last advocate of cooperation to woo Black Patch tobacco growers. The agricultural depression following World War I prompted Congress to encourage cooperative efforts, and Black Patchers flirted with cooperation again in the 1920s when Louisville newspaper magnate Robert Worth Bingham organized tobacco farmers across the state.[1] In the Great Depression they enthusiastically embraced federal rewards to farmers cutting back on tobacco production.[2] But the New Deal did not challenge traditional Black Patch society: Agricultural Adjustment Administration programs favored the existing social hierarchy, paying benefits to tenants through landlords. Unlike Ewing and Bingham, who had tried to place power in the hands of Association leaders, the federal scheme kept power in the hands of scattered local elites.[3]

The Black Patch tobacco culture continued its timeless seasonal repetition. As always, growers labored over their plant beds in the early spring, in the fields thereafter, and in barns in the fall. These facts of life united Black Patchers of all classes, just as they always had. The forms of community hegemony that had served as a shell for Ewing's scheme outlasted the Association. Black Patchers shared work, found communal comfort when loved ones died, and enjoyed revivalistic religion, just as they had done before the Black Patch war. They remained divided on industrialization, some welcoming the new order, some resisting it. The shared language of nicknames and anecdotes so disorienting to strangers continued to unite Black Patchers after the Black Patch war as it had before. They simply absorbed incidents involving the Night Riders into the local folklore, telling and retelling the same stories until phrases and sentences hardened in their memories. Often the stories analyzed power relationships, chronicling the rise and fall of the Night Riders. Thus, when the Night Riders told Wash Fletcher to run, he ran so fast "you could have played marbles on his coattail."[4] But when Night Rider power ebbed, their enemies loomed larger in Black Patch folklore. The soldiers hunting David Amoss rode "some of the finest horses you ever looked at, had a big rifle strapped on 'em on their horse saddle, a big .38 colt scabbard and just had a warrant for one little man."[5]

But Night Rider vigilantism discredited "politics out-of-doors." All over the Black Patch fathers told sons that while vigilantism might seem appealing, such activity always went astray and should be avoided. Even vigilantes with the best intentions—like the Night Riders—inevitably get off track. An atmosphere of lawlessness tempts vigilantes to settle personal disputes or exact revenge against their neighbors. For that reason, vigilantism is an unsatisfactory remedy for a community's ills. Many Black Patchers remain committed to their communities in the face of industrialization, but they learned a valuable lesson about the limits of community action.

The Black Patch war forever changed the region. Black Patchers learned they lived on a landscape of divided loyalties. Many historians have "discovered" the breakdown of community values in America—at widely differing times—but something far subtler happened when the Black Patch encountered the twentieth century. Communities survived to shelter residents from an impersonal world, but Black Patchers learned not to count on neighbors to stand with them against outsiders—some of their neighbors were allied with those outsiders. Such knowledge makes night riding and vigilantism less likely. People fight for a community ideal only when they can credibly believe there is a community ideal in the first place. Black Patchers still had their communities, but those communities sheltered people with a variety of attachments to the wider world. The "mechanical solidarity" that sociologist Emile Durkheim described as characteristic of primitive communities had long been absent from the Black Patch—and now everyone knew it.[6]

Even so, this knowledge did not immediately end Black Patch violence. For twenty years after Amoss's trial in Hopkinsville vigilantism continued to plague the Black Patch. Some of the persisting intimidation even resembled the original tobacco Night Rider violence. But now local courts refused to knuckle under to coercion. Never again would authorities cave in to mass intimidation as easily as they had in 1905 and 1906. In 1912 tobacco growers in southern Lyon County once more received letters warning them to put their tobacco in the Planters' Protective Association. Whereas previous judges had tolerated such conduct, Judge John Hanbery refused to countenance it, sternly ordering a grand jury to investigate. In 1916 he launched a vigorous investigation of a similar letter-writing campaign in Christian County.[7] In the neighboring judicial district, voters elected Carl Henderson as judge. He had vigorously prosecuted Night Riders in Crittenden County, even leading a contingent of militia into Caldwell County to arrest alleged vigilantes. Now, as judge, he repeatedly ordered grand juries to investigate any hint of night riding.[8]

A byproduct of the legal system's new authority was increased white supervision of black citizens. A few months after Amoss's trial, the Christian County attorney announced that idle blacks would be arrested and made to work for the county. Farmers cutting tobacco begged for hands while some blacks refused to work, the attorney observed. The official announced that he planned to employ a special patrol to round up labor.[9]

During World War I the state judiciary enjoyed unprecedented popular support in their efforts to suppress disorder. In 1916 Judge Henderson still warned grand juries to search out Night Riders, but the next year such instructions were no longer necessary. Instead he declared that all vagrants must either join the army or find work.[10] Princeton's newspaper declared the town freer of loafers than it had ever been before. But in this hour of the nation's greatest crisis, the paper wanted to root out every last vagrant. It was unthinkable for any able-bodied man to live in America without doing his part to make the flag honored and respected. The newspaper published a series of syndicated cartoons urging readers to resist temptations to steal or loaf.[11]

World War I accelerated the movement of blacks out of Kentucky. Increased discipline and loss of freedoms marked by more rigid segregation probably encouraged many to move northward.[12] It seems likely the migration served as a kind of natural selection process. The most recalcitrant blacks departed, leaving behind those most skilled at surviving in a southern white culture. In any case, the departure of so many blacks defused racial tensions and helped those residents remaining in the Black Patch avoid violence.

An episode involving Kentucky's Governor Augustus O. Stanley illustrates the change in official attitudes toward extralegal violence. In 1917 the town of Murray went wild when the local judge granted a continuance to a black defendant charged with murder and sent him to Paducah to be held in the interim. A mob followed the judge to his hotel, stormed the building, and forced him to rescind the continuance and return the prisoner to the local jail. The judge gave in to the mob's demands. Governor Stanley personally countermanded the order, telling Paducah jailers to keep the prisoner safely in their own jail. Going to Murray, he directly confronted the mob, telling them they would have to hang their governor before lynching the defendant. Lynching fever dissipated.[13] The contrast between Stanley and Augustus Willson is striking. After the raid on Hopkinsville, Willson had pondered traveling to the Black Patch and confronting the Night Riders directly. When Willson finally did tour western Kentucky in the fall of 1908 he could only taunt the vigilantes.

After Amoss's trial, Kentuckians accepted the law as supreme. In 1920 Kentucky lawmakers unanimously passed a tough antilynching law. Both Democratic and Republican legislators agreed that the murder of a prisoner by a mob "shall be prima facie evidence of neglect of duty on the part" of the sheriff.[14] After the Black Patch war lawmen began standing up to lynch mobs—something they had previously refused to do. As a result lynching declined sharply. The Ku Klux Klan revival that swept the nation in the 1920s was muted in Kentucky.[15]

The changed attitude affected potential vigilantes as well. The Night Riders had not seen themselves as representing disorder. Like Charles Tyler's fictional Ku Klux Klan, they perceived themselves as reasserting order and even law. They could maintain such a perception because onlookers endorsed it. They embodied the moral authority of their community, and they used it to overawe their opponents. However, with the legal system functioning, vigilantes could act only with the certain knowledge that they represented lawlessness and disorder, not order. They lacked the moral authority to awe their opponents. The mob Governor Stanley faced knew that he symbolized order. Thus confronted, they collapsed.

The Black Patch experienced dramatic change in the twentieth century. The spread of diversified farming in the 1960s challenged the traditional tobacco culture with extensive livestock, wheat, and soybean production. Dark fired tobacco remains labor-intensive, but the use of tractors and other farm machinery has brought mechanization to Kentucky and Tennessee tobacco fields. Northern corporations came to the Black Patch seeking cheaper labor and lower utility bills. As a result, more Black Patchers work in industry today than in agriculture.[16]

In the early 1960s schools in the Kentucky Black Patch reluctantly desegregated—the last in the Commonwealth to do so. The surviving community structure made desegregation a more peaceful process than it otherwise might have been. Confronted late at night by a crowd of angry citizens, the principal of Trigg County High School defused tensions by contacting a community leader, their minister. The willingness of the community hierarchy to stand up to potential vigilantes demonstrated the continued importance of neighborhood leadership and also contrasted with their acquiescence in Night Riding fifty-five years earlier. Perhaps because of the heritage of the Black Patch war, community leaders solved a potentially explosive problem locally, within the community.[17]

But many parts of the Black Patch still resist outside control. Two episodes illustrate this. In 1989 in Princeton, Kentucky, twenty-seven people signing themselves "LeRoi Warehouse Against the Union" voiced traditional resistance to outsiders in a letter published in the local newspaper. The letter warned readers against attempts by the International Ladies Garment Workers' Union to organize employees of a local clothing manufacturer. The writers claimed that the union, which they called the "Fat Rat," "is a little more than upset because so many people at Princeton LeRoi are content to live their life with peace and harmony with each other." The letter stigmatized the union as an outsider; worse, a northern outsider. "The home of the 'Big Fat Rat,'" the letter declared, "is either Missouri, Indiana, Illinois or Pennsylvania." The writers closed by pleading with readers to reject union organization "for the sake of our home town, Princeton, Ky." On May 25, 1989, workers at the LeRoi plant in Princeton and in nearby Cadiz rejected unionization 279 to 94.[18]

In Cadiz, Kentucky, an anonymous letter writer wrote the local newspaper complaining bitterly about local clannishness. The writer was shocked by the close kinship still apparent in Trigg County neighborhoods. "My thought, after I had lived there for awhile is, the people had inter-married so much that their brains had run out," he wrote bitterly. Black Patchers remained biased against non-locals. "No outsider who buys a home there can ever sell it without losing several thousand dollars," he claimed. After recounting episodes where locals resisted development, the writer concluded, "If you are an outsider you are up for grabs, and you can't have anything."[19] It was a complaint that could just as easily have been made before the Black Patch war as after it. Outsiders still never really understand the Black Patch.

The juggernaut of pervasive national commercialism characteristic of American life in the last quarter of the twentieth century represents the most recent challenge to traditional Black Patch community life. In her stories of western Kentucky, novelist and short story writer Bobbie Ann Mason has chronicled the anguish of traditional folk coping with failing farms, shopping malls, and television.[20] Mason shows the persistence of old values in a new age. "He won't set foot off this place," one character says of a Black Patcher. "He's growed to it."[21] The genius of Mason's fiction lies in her ability to contrast telling details of the older culture with the minutiae of modern life. In a story entitled "Residents and Transients," a resident asks if a house has a canning kitchen. A transient laughs, "No, but it has a rec room."[22] Like everyone else, Black Patchers stubbornly hold to traditional ways while accommodating the future.

In the Black Patch, Americans confront an industrialized, competitive, bureaucratic culture. In the end their traditional communities survive but in an altered state. Black Patchers continue to evidence a stubborn attachment—even love—for their enduring neighborhoods and communities. But they understand things have changed. They live in a place of divided loyalties—rec rooms and canning kitchens.

Notes

1. James O. Nall, *The Tobacco Night Riders of Kentucky and Tennessee, 1905–1909* (Louisville, 1939); John G. Miller, *The Black Patch War* (Chapel Hill, 1936); Harry Kroll, *Riders in the Night* (Philadelphia, 1965); Bill Cunningham, *On Bended Knees: The Night Rider Story* (Nashville, 1983). Numerous novelists have used the Black Patch war as a backdrop. The best is Robert Penn Warren, *Night Rider* (Boston, 1939). For the role of planters, see Christopher Waldrep, "Planters and the Planters' Protective Association in Kentucky and Tennessee," *Journal of Southern History* 52 (November 1986): 565–88. The question of antebellum planters' durability after emancipation has been a lively one at least since the publication of C. Vann Woodward's *Origins of the New South, 1877–1913* (Baton Rouge, 1951) and Jonathan Wiener's rebuttal in *Social Origins of the New South: Alabama, 1860–1885* (Baton Rouge, 1978). Scholars have documented the role of landed and aristocratic elements in postbellum farmers' movements. See Waldrep, "Planters and the Planters' Protective Association," n. 4.

2. Daniel Walker Howe, *The Political Culture of the American Whigs* (Chicago, 1979), 29–42, 299.

3. E. P. Thompson, *The Making of the English Working Class* (New York, 1963), 60ff.

4. John Phillip Reid, *In a Defiant Stance: The Conditions of Law in Massachusetts Bay, the Irish Comparison, and the Coming of the American Revolution* (University Park, Penn., 1977); Gordon S. Wood notes that the self-discipline exercised by American mobs was not unique to America. See "A Note on Mobs in the American Revolution," in *William and Mary Quarterly*, 3d series, 23 (October 1966): 635–42; Pauline Maier, "Popular Uprisings and Civil Authority in Eighteenth-Century America," *William and Mary Quarterly*, 3d series, 27 (January 1970): 3–35; Paul A. Gilje, *The Road to Mobocracy: Popular Disorder in New York City, 1763–1834* (Chapel Hill, 1987).

5. Bruce Laurie, "Fire Companies and Gangs in Southwark: The 1840s," in Allen F. Davis and Mark H. Haller, eds., *The Peoples of Philadelphia* (Philadelphia, 1973), 71–87.

6. David Warren Sabean, *Power in the Blood: Popular Culture and Village Discourse in Early Modern Germany* (Cambridge, 1989), 21–30, 29 (quotation). See also Emile Durkheim, *The Division of Labor in Society*, trans. George Simpson (Glencoe, 1947), 69–275; Thomas Bender, *Community and Social Change in America* (New Brunswick, 1978), 17–128. Bender's book, and Sabean's, are particularly useful for pointing out the problems with scholars' traditionally linear approach to community studies. The present work presents a nonlinear analysis: some Black Patchers sought modernization, some sought traditional community life. One paradigm does not neatly follow another.

7. Paul A. Gilje, "The Baltimore Riots of 1812 and the Breakdown of the Anglo-American Mob Tradition," *Journal of Social History* 13 (Summer 1980): 547–64; idem, *The Road to Mobocracy: Popular Disorder in New*

York City, 1763–1834 (Chapel Hill, 1987); Iver Bernstein, *The New York City Draft Riots: Their Significance for American Society and Politics in the Age of the Civil War* (New York, 1990), 4–8; Altina L. Waller, "Community, Class and Race in the Memphis Riot of 1866," *Journal of Social History* 18 (Winter 1984): 233–46.

8. Steven Hahn describes self-sufficient rural Georgians determinedly resistant to the forces of modernization. Hahn, *The Roots of Southern Populism: Yeomen Farmers and the Transformation of the Georgia Upcountry, 1850–1890* (New York, 1983); David Thelen depicts Missourians united in a fight to save their families and traditional communities from capitalist modernizers. Thelen, *Paths of Resistance: Tradition and Dignity in Industrializing Missouri* (New York, 1986); see also Altina L. Waller, *Feud: Hatfields, McCoys, and Social Change in Appalachia, 1860–1900* (Chapel Hill, 1988); Paul Boyer and Stephen Nissenbaum, *Salem Possessed: The Social Origins of Witchcraft* (Cambridge, 1974).

1 The Black Patch

1. Robert Penn Warren, *Night Rider* (Boston, 1939), 14; Daniel Joseph Singal, *The War Within: From Victorian to Modernist Thought in the South, 1919–1945* (Chapel Hill, 1982), 354–55.

2. Thomas Littlepage, report of interview with C. M. Bourne, October 14, 1905, file 3085, Bureau of Corporations, Tobacco Investigation Records, Record Group 122 (National Archives, Washington, D.C.).

3. Including the Kentucky counties of Caldwell, Christian, Logan, Lyon, Simpson, Todd, and Trigg and the Tennessee counties of Cheatham, Davidson, Dickson, Humphreys, Houston, Montgomery, Robertson, Smith, Sumner, Stewart, and Wilson. See James O. Nall, *The Tobacco Night Riders of Kentucky and Tennessee, 1905–1909* (Louisville, 1939), 2; interview with Joe Moore, Sr., February 19, 1983; newspaper clipping (Tennessee State Library and Archives, Nashville, Tenn.).

4. J. D. B. DeBow, comp., *Statistical View of the United States . . . Being a Compendium of the Seventh Census . . .* (Washington, D.C., 1854), 236, 308. The three counties are Montgomery and Robertson in Tennessee and Christian in Kentucky.

5. Sam Bowers Hilliard, comp., *Atlas of Antebellum Southern Agriculture* (Baton Rouge, 1984), 43; Carl Ortwin Sauer, *Geography of the Pennyroyal: A Study of the Influence of Geology and Physiography upon the Industry, Commerce and Life of the People* (Frankfort, Ky., 1927), 157–58.

6. Montgomery, Robertson, Cheatham, Stewart, Dickson, Houston counties, Tennessee, and Logan, Todd, Christian, and parts of Trigg and Caldwell counties, Kentucky.

7. Thomas Littlepage, "Memorandum of Interview with Ed. R. Tandy," November 8, 1905, file 3028, Bureau of Corporations, Tobacco Investigation Records, Record Group 122 (National Archives).

8. Including, in Kentucky, the counties of Livingston, McCracken, Marshall, Calloway, Graves, Ballard, Carlisle, Hickman, and Fulton and the

Tennessee counties of Henry, Weakley, Obion, Carroll, and Benton. See Nall, *The Tobacco Night Riders,* 2.

9. U.S. Census Office, *Twelfth Census of the United States Taken in the Year 1900,* vol. 5, *Agriculture, Part 1, Farmers, Live Stock, and Animal Products* (Washington, D.C., 1902), 84–87, 122–25.

10. James Turner, "Understanding the Populists," *Journal of American History* 67 (September 1980): 365.

11. Charles Fort Account Book with diary entries, box 3, Fort family papers (Tennessee State Library and Archives, Nashville, Tenn.).

12. James A. Thomas, *A Pioneer Tobacco Merchant in the Orient* (Durham, 1928), passim, esp. chap. 1 and pp. 40–43; Jerome E. Brooks, *The Mighty Leaf: Tobacco through the Centuries* (Boston, 1952), 144, 282, 301, 302; Lewis Cecil Gray, *History of Agriculture in the Southern United States to 1860,* 2 vols. (Gloucester, Mass., 1958), 2:760–62.

13. Clarksville Edition of the *National Trade Review* (1895), 36; William Henry Perrin, *County of Christian, Kentucky: Historical and Biographical* (Chicago, 1884), 139.

14. Henry V. Poor, *Poor's Manual of the Railroads of the United States for 1888* (New York, 1888), 692–701; idem, *Poor's Manual for the Railroads of the United States for 1883* (New York, 1883).

15. Boynton Merrill, Jr., *Jefferson's Nephews: A Frontier Tragedy* (Princeton, 1976), 117–18; Sam Steger, "Historical Notebook," Princeton *Leader,* January 2, 1985.

16. Hambleton Tapp and James C. Klotter, *Kentucky: Decades of Discord, 1865–1900* (Frankfort, Ky., 1977), 299–300; Steven Hahn, *The Roots of Southern Populism: Yeoman Farmers and the Transformation of the Georgia Upcountry, 1850–1890* (New York, 1983), 34–40; Edward F. Prichard, Jr., "Popular Political Movements in Kentucky, 1875–1900" (senior thesis, Princeton University, 1935), 20–21; Caldwell County Poll Books, May 30, 1868 (Caldwell County Clerk's Office, Princeton, Ky.); Princeton *Banner,* October 25, 1877.

17. Caldwell County Poll Books, May 30, 1868 (Caldwell County Clerk's Office, Princeton, Ky.); Princeton *Banner,* October 25, 1877; Hahn, *Roots,* 144. For an example of boosters' rhetoric, see Hopkinsville *South Kentuckian,* November 13, 1888.

18. James Brady Foust, "The Eastern Dark-Fired Tobacco Region of Kentucky and Tennessee" (M.S. thesis, University of Tennessee, 1966), passim.

19. Interview with Bernard Jones, June 12, 1982; Harriet A. Byrne, *Child Labor in Representative Tobacco-Growing Areas* (Washington, 1926), 4.

20. William Faulkner, *Go Down Moses* (New York, 1940), 75.

21. James S. Street diary, James S. Street Papers (Department of Library Special Collections, Manuscripts, Western Kentucky University, Bowling Green, Ky.). See also Byrne, *Child Labor,* 5; J. B. Killebrew and Herbert Myrick, *Tobacco Leaf: Its Culture and Cure, Marketing and Manufacture* (New York, 1897, 1918), 151–78; William Scherffius, H. Woosley, and C. A. Mahan, *The Cultivation of Tobacco in Kentucky and Tennessee* (Washington, D.C., 1909), 1–28; J. B. Killebrew, *Tobacco: How to Culti-*

vate, Cure and Prepare for Market (Nashville, n.d.), 1–14; idem, *Tobacco: Its Culture in Tennessee, with Statistics of Its Commercial Importance, etc.* (Nashville, 1876), 17–72; Charles S. Guthrie, "Tobacco: Cash Crop of the Cumberland Valley," *Kentucky Folklore Record* 14 (April–June, 1968): 38–43; Suzanne Marshall Hall, "Breaking Trust: The Black Patch Tobacco Culture of Kentucky and Tennessee, 1900–1940" (Ph.D. diss., Emory University, 1989), 47–70.

22. Interview with Orman Cannon, October 17, 1981; Byrne, *Child Labor,* 6.

23. Interview with Herbert Carney. For a discussion of gang and task systems of labor see Leon F. Litwack, "The Ordeal of Black Freedom," in Walter J. Fraser and Winfred B. Moore, eds., *The Southern Enigma: Essays on Race, Class and Folk Culture* (Westport, Conn., 1983), 46–48. See also William Kaufman Scarborough, *The Overseer: Plantation Management in the Old South* (Athens, 1966), 80–82.

24. Interview with Robert Holt; Byrne, *Child Labor,* 7; Hall, "Breaking Trust," 46–70.

25. Killebrew, *Tobacco: Its Culture in Tennessee,* 56–63; interview with Robert Holt.

26. Interview with Robert Holt.

27. John G. Miller, *The Black Patch War* (Chapel Hill, 1936), 5.

28. Cadiz *Record,* May 8, 1986.

29. Hall, "Breaking Trust," 27–28.

30. Durwood Dunn, *Cades Cove: The Life and Death of a Southern Appalachian Community, 1818–1937* (Knoxville, 1988), 148–49.

31. Interview with Christine Waldrep, transcript, June 11, 1973.

32. Karen Halttunen, *Confidence Men and Painted Women: A Study of Middle-Class Culture in America, 1830–1870* (New Haven, 1982), 146–47.

33. Sue Lynn Stone, " 'Blessed Are They That Mourn': Expressions of Grief in South Central Kentucky, 1870–1910," *Register of the Kentucky Historical Society* 85 (Summer 1987): 213–36; interview with Corinne Wadlington, May 21, 1990; interview with Mary Lou Walton, May 21, 1990.

34. Edward W. Starling and Thomas Sugrue, *Starling of the White House* (New York, 1946), 14–15.

35. T. H. Breen, *Tobacco Culture: The Mentality of the Great Tidewater Planters on the Eve of the Revolution* (Princeton, 1985); Edmund S. Morgan, *American Slavery, American Freedom: The Ordeal of Colonial Virginia* (New York, 1975), 286–87; Jacob M. Price, *France and the Chesapeake: A History of the French Tobacco Monopoly, 1674–1791, and of Its Relationship to the British and American Tobacco Trades* (Ann Arbor, 1973), 1:520–657.

36. This shaming ritual is described by Bertram Wyatt-Brown, in *Southern Honor: Ethics and Behavior in the Old South* (New York, 1982), as characteristic of the South. Durwood Dunn notes that a small, highly motivated group can effectively control a larger, less well organized group. *Cades Cove,* 111.

37. Christopher Waldrep, " 'So Much Sin': The Decline of Religious Discipline and the 'Tidal Wave of Crime," *Journal of Social History* 23 (Spring 1990): 535–52.

38. Harmony Baptist Church Minutes, August 10, 1903.
39. Cadiz Baptist Church Minutes, December 8, 1898.
40. *Minutes of the 76th Bethel Baptist Association, August 1900* (Russellville, n.d.).
41. Hopkinsville *Kentuckian,* February 28, 1907; Minutes, Little River and Bethel Associations.
42. Caldwell County Grand Jury Indictments, Commonwealth Order Books (Circuit Court Clerk's Office, Princeton, Ky.); Waldrep, " 'So Much Sin'," 535–52.
43. Robert Penn Warren, Oral History Memoir, Oral History Collection, Columbia University, 60–62, quoted by Rick Gregory, untitled essay kindly lent by the author.

2 The Tobacco Trust

1. Roland Marchand, *Advertising the American Dream: Making Way for Modernity, 1920–1940* (Berkeley and Los Angeles, 1985), 340–63.
2. Lewis Cecil Gray, *History of Agriculture in the Southern United States to 1860,* 2 vols. (Gloucester, Mass., 1958), 2:754–55, 760–62.
3. Bundle labeled "Depositions 1859, 1860, 1865, 1866, 1867, 1875, 1878, 1882, 1884" (Caldwell County Court Clerk's Office, Princeton, Ky.). Bellsford is sometimes spelled Brelsford.
4. Newspaper advertisement clipped in O'Hara Records (Kentucky Building, Western Kentucky University, Bowling Green, Ky.); Leland Smith, "A History of the Tobacco Industry in Kentucky from 1783 to 1860" (M.A. thesis, University of Kentucky, 1950), 61 and chap. 4. As early as 1830 Clarksville, Tennessee, stemmeries prepared tobacco for shipment to New Orleans. See Ursula Smith Beach, *Along the Warioto; or A History of Montgomery County, Tennessee* (Nashville, 1964), 117–20.
5. O'Hara Records (Western Kentucky University).
6. Kentucky vol. 6, p. 19, R. G. Dun and Co. Collection (Baker Library, Harvard University Graduate School of Business Administration, Boston, Mass.).
7. Tennessee vol. 26, p. 160, R. G. Dun and Co. Collection.
8. Kentucky vol. 6, p. 7, R. G. Dun and Co. Collection.
9. Emma Wilson, *Under One Roof* (New York, 1955), 26–27.
10. See, for example, Jacquelyn Dowd Hall et al., *Like a Family: The Making of a Southern Cotton Mill World* (Chapel Hill, 1987), 12; I. A. Newby, *Plain Folk in the New South: Social Change and Cultural Persistence, 1880–1915* (Baton Rouge, 1989), 38–39; Steven Hahn, *The Roots of Southern Populism: Yeoman Farmers and the Transformation of the Georgia Upcountry, 1850–1890* (New York, 1983), 50–85; Elizabeth Fox-Genovese and Eugene Genovese, *Fruits of Merchant Capital: Slavery and Bourgeois Property in the Rise and Expansion of Capitalism* (Oxford, 1983), 249–64.
11. Smith, "A History of the Tobacco Industry in Kentucky from 1783 to 1860," 48, 103.
12. J. D. B. DeBow, *Statistical View of the United States . . . A Compendium of the Seventh Census . . .* (Washington, 1854), 189; Edward F. Prichard, Jr.,

"Popular Political Movements in Kentucky, 1875–1900" (senior thesis, Princeton University, 1935), 36; Hambleton Tapp and James C. Klotter, *Kentucky: Decades of Discord, 1865–1900* (Frankfort, Ky., 1977), 300.

13. Harold D. Woodman, in *King Cotton and His Retainers: Financing and Marketing the Cotton Crop of the South, 1800–1925* (Lexington, 1968), 269–94, showed how improvements in communication technology revolutionized the cotton trade. The results were similar in the tobacco business.

14. Charles W. McCurdy, "The *Knight* Sugar Decision of 1895 and the Modernization of American Corporate Law, 1869–1903," *Business History Review* 53 (Autumn 1979): 314–23; Martin J. Sklar, *Corporate Reconstruction of American Capitalism, 1890–1916: The Market, the Law, and Politics* (Cambridge, 1988), 49–50.

15. 6 U.S. Stat. 209; Sklar, *The Corporate Reconstruction of American Capitalism,* 114–16.

16. *United States* v. *Trans-Missouri Freight Association,* 166 U.S. 290–374; Alfred D. Chandler, Jr., *The Visible Hand: The Managerial Revolution in American Business* (Cambridge, Mass., 1977), 332–33, 375; Sklar, *Corporate Reconstruction,* 127–45.

17. Robert Wiebe, *The Search for Order, 1877–1920* (New York, 1967), 32; see also Carter Goodrich, *Government Promotion of American Canals and Railroads, 1800–1890* (New York, 1960); Eric Foner, *Reconstruction: America's Unfinished Revolution, 1863–1877* (New York, 1988), 466–68; Wallace D. Farnham, " 'The Weakened Spring of Government': A Study in Nineteenth-Century American History," *American Historical Review* 68 (April 1963): 676.

18. *Report of the Commissioner of Corporations on the Tobacco Industry,* 3 parts (Washington, D.C., 1909), 1:63–93; Robert F. Durden, *The Dukes of Durham, 1865–1929* (Durham, 1975), 17–72; Nannie May Tilley, *The Bright Tobacco Industry: 1860–1929* (Chapel Hill, 1948), 251–62.

19. Glenn Porter and Harold C. Livesay, *Merchants and Manufacturers: Studies in the Changing Structure of Nineteenth-Century Marketing* (Baltimore, 1971), 203–4.

20. House Committee on Ways and Means, Subcommittee on Internal Revenue, *Hearings on the Relief of Tobacco Growers before a Subcommittee on Internal Revenue of the Committee on Ways and Means,* 58th Cong., 2d sess., February 4 and 25, 1904, printed as Senate Document 390, 60th Congress, 1st sess., 19, 21, 40, 62.

21. A. W. Madsen, *The State as Manufacturer and Trader: An Examination Based on the Commercial, Industrial and Fiscal Results Obtained from Government Tobacco Monopolies* (London, 1916), 107–23.

22. Ibid., 12–23.

23. A. M. Tillman to Henry Taft, February 28, 1905, Justice Department Central Files, Record Group 60 (National Archives, Washington, D.C.).

24. "Statement by J. C. Kendrick, Pres. of Clarksville Board of Trade," n.d., file 3087, Bureau of Corporations, Tobacco Investigation Records, Record Group 122 (National Archives). Hereinafter cited as Tobacco Investigation.

25. Thomas Littlepage, "Memorandum interview with Mr. J. H. Smith,

Mayor of Clarksville," n.d., file 3087, Tobacco Investigation; statement by J. C. Kendrick, pres. of Clarksville Board of Trade, n.d., ibid.; Eugene P. Lyle, Jr., "They That Rode by Night," *Hampton's Magazine* 22 (February 1909): 180.

26. Thomas Littlepage, report of interview with E. C. Morrow, November 8, 1905; Littlepage, report of interview with Ed. R. Tandy, November 8, 1905 and October 25, 1905; Herbert Knox Smith, report of interview with Joseph Ferigo, August 1, 1905; "Additional Information from Mr. Ferigo," with handwritten corrections by Ferigo, November 25, 1905; report of interview with Joseph Ferigo, September 29, 1905; Littlepage, report of interview with W. G. Dunnington, October 31, 1905; M. C. Brady to Littlepage, October 22, 1905; Charles S. Moore, "Report on the Information Obtained from the Italian Tobacco Regie, Relative to the Purchase of Leaf Tobacco in the United States by the Italian Government," August 26, 1905; Littlepage, report of interview with C. P. Warfield, October 24, 1905; Littlepage, report of interview with J. H. Smith, n. d., received October 18, 1905, all in file 3087, Tobacco Investigation.

27. Littlepage, report of interview with Dunnington, ibid.

28. W. E. Burghardt Du Bois, "The Negroes of Farmville, Virginia: A Social Study," *Bulletin of the Department of Labor* (January 1898): 4–5, 19.

29. Herbert Clarence Bradshaw, *History of Prince Edward County, Virginia: From Its Earliest Settlements through Its Establishment in 1754 to Its Bicentennial Year* (Richmond, 1955), 300–301, 526–27, 442, 533, 538, 544, 548, 695; Dunnington's obituary, Farmville *Herald*, August 4, 1922; Farmville *Herald*, September 1, 1899 (quotation).

30. Farmville *Herald*, February 23, 1940; The Dunnington Tobacco Company, Inc., "Over 80 Years! Dealers in Fine Tobaccos" (xeroxed pamphlet kindly lent by Dolly Dunnington Orgain); *Today and Yesterday in the Heart of Virginia* (Farmville, 1935), 105–8. The Farmville *Herald* advocated the inflationary monetary policies favored by farmers.

31. Farmville *Herald*, April 11, 1902; Richmond *Dispatch*, quoted in Farmville *Herald*, December 7, 1900.

32. Speech by H. D. Fort, Farmville *Herald*, August 30, 1907.

33. Farmville *Herald*, December 11, 1896. W. P. Gilliam was Dunnington's partner; see ibid., October 6, 1905.

34. Clarksville *Daily Leaf-Chronicle*, February 6, 1902, September 19, 22, 1904.

35. Statement by Polk Prince, Guthrie, Kentucky, file 3028, Tobacco Investigation. See also statements of A. O. Dority, tobacco buyer, and W. H. Hook, Montgomery County, Tennessee tobacco grower in A. O. Stanley Papers (Special Collections, University of Kentucky Libraries, Lexington, Ky.).

36. Report of Littlepage interview with J. D. Ryan, October 20, 1905, file 3088, Tobacco Investigation; report of Littlepage interview with W. E. Corlew, October 16, 1905, file 3085, ibid.

37. Statement of J. W. Jones, Oak Grove, Christian County, Kentucky, ibid.; memorandum of an interview with H. C. Long, farmer, Clarksville, Tennessee, November 5, 1905, ibid.

38. Statement of J. W. Jones, Oak Grove, Christian County, Ky., ibid.
39. "Additional Information from Mr. Ferigo," ibid.; House Committee on Ways and Means, Subcommittee on Internal Revenue, *Hearings on the Relief of Tobacco Growers before a Subcommittee on Internal Revenue of the Committee on Ways and Means,* 58th Cong., 2d sess., Feb. 4 and 25, 1904, printed as Senate Document 390, 60th Congress, 1st sess., 20.
40. Report of Littlepage interview with A. O. Dority, October 18, 1905, file 3088, Tobacco Investigation.
41. Wilson, *Under One Roof,* 13, 27, 131.
42. Littlepage interview with Ed. R. Tandy, November 8, 1905, file 3028, Tobacco Investigation.
43. Testimony of Edwin Hodge, transcript of evidence, vol. 2, transcript of defendant's evidence, *Imperial Tobacco Company, etc.* v. *Commonwealth of Kentucky,* case 43036, Court of Appeals Records (Public Records Division, Kentucky Department for Libraries and Archives, Frankfort, Ky.), 536–43.
44. Wilson, *Under One Roof,* 148, 146; Littlepage, report of interview with J. D. Ryan, October 20, 195, file 3088, Tobacco Investigation.
45. Gavin Wright, in *Old South, New South: Revolutions in the Southern Economy since the Civil War* (New York, 1986), 7–12, 64–70, contrasts regional with national labor markets. Many of his insights can be applied to local tobacco markets—in some ways, they, too, were isolated from the larger market.
46. But in some counties—those with the greatest tobacco production—blacks formed up to a third of the total. I am not including farm managers in these calculations. U.S. Census Office, *Twelfth Census of the United States Taken in the Year 1900,* vol. 5, *Agriculture . . . Part 1* (Washington, D.C., 1902), 84–87, 122–25. The Eastern Dark Fired District includes Simpson, Logan, Todd, Christian, Trigg, Caldwell, and Lyon counties in Kentucky and Smith, Wilson, Sumner, Robertson, Davidson, Cheatham, Dickson, Humphreys, Houston, Stewart, and Montgomery counties in Tennessee. The Black Patch war occurred in the Eastern Dark Fired District. The other districts in western Kentucky include the Henderson Stemming District, the Western Dark Fired District (south of Paducah), and the Bowling Green One-Sucker district. The Black Patch is made up of the Western and Eastern Dark Fired Districts. See James O. Nall, *The Tobacco Night Riders of Kentucky and Tennessee, 1905–1909* (Louisville, 1939), 2.
47. Smith, "A History of the Tobacco Industry in Kentucky from 1783 to 1860," 17.
48. Crandall A. Shifflett, *Patronage and Poverty in the Tobacco South: Louisa County, Virginia, 1860–1900* (Knoxville, 1982), xii–xiii. According to Shifflett patrons in a system of patronage capitalism had little need to morally justify their system by extending kindnesses to labor.
49. A key difference between paternalism and patronage lies in the extension of medical care to laborers. Slaveowners undoubtedly did provide medicines to their slaves more readily than patrons did to their clients. But some postbellum employers of black labor did care for their clients.

In 1870 a Black Patch diarist recorded a relative's sadness over the sickness of one of her servants. The relative went to work "liberally & energetically to supply his wants. She is very much attached to her family servants." Richard L. Troutman, ed., *The Heavens Are Weeping: The Diaries of George Richard Browder, 1852–1886* (Grand Rapids, Mich., 1987), 227.

50. Interview with Clyde Quisenberry, August 6, 1982.
51. Troutman, ed., *The Heavens Are Weeping: The Diaries of George Richard Browder,* 324. Another, less favored, worker only got a loan.
52. Interview with Clyde Quisenberry. White planters also displayed paternalistic feelings when they mourned the death of trusted blacks. When one diarist's tenant died, he grieved, "This is a sad day for black and white." Another diarist noted the loss of "Malinda our oldest family servant" in 1898. "Owing to our attachment to her the funeral was held in our house." The white patrons of one Kentucky black man paid their friend the ultimate compliment in 1904: "His skin was dark but his soul was white." R. H. McGaughey, *Life with Grandfather* [diary of Robert McGaughey], (Hopkinsville, 1981), 140; Charles Fort, account book with diary entries, folder 2, box 3, Fort Family Papers (Manuscript Section, Tennessee State Library and Archives, Nashville, Tenn.); Tombstone of Keg Opeland, October 18, 1904, River View Cemetery, recorded in Lyon County Historical Society, *Cemeteries of Lyon County, Kentucky* (n.p., 1989), 278.
53. House Committee on Ways and Means, Subcommittee on Internal Revenue, *Hearings on the Relief of Tobacco Growers before a Subcommittee on Internal Revenue of the Committee on Ways and Means,* 58th Cong., 2d sess., February 4 and 25, 1904, printed as Senate Document 390, 60th Congress, 1st sess., 38–39.
54. Theodore Rosengarten, *All God's Dangers: The Life of Nate Shaw* (New York, 1974), 27, 28, 28–35, 50–53. "Nate Shaw" described his father as shattered by white paternalism.
55. Interview with Clyde Quisenberry.
56. *The Town* (New York, 1957), 312.
57. Report of Littlepage interview with Washington Anderson, Charles Barker, Dick Hampton, Henry Priestly, Henry Dinwiddie, October 23, 1905, file 3085, Tobacco Investigation.
58. Report of Littlepage interview with Washington Anderson, October 23, 1905, ibid.
59. Report of Littlepage interview with Anderson, Barker, Hampton, Priestly, Dinwiddie, ibid.
60. Report of Littlepage interview with Dave Cowherd, n.d., received by Bureau of Corporations October 25, 1905, file 3084, Tobacco Investigation; Littlepage interview with Anderson, Barker, Hampton, Priestly, Dinwiddie, October 23, 1905, file 3085, Tobacco Investigation.
61. Wilson, *Under One Roof,* 27–28; for the decline of paternalism in the 1890s, see George M. Fredrickson, *The Black Image in the White Mind: The Debate on Afro-American Character and Destiny, 1817–1914* (New York, 1971), chap. 9.

3 Farmers Respond

1. Ted Ownby, "The Defeated Generation at Work: White Farmers in the Deep South, 1865–1890," *Southern Studies* 23 (Winter 1984): 325–347 (quotation is on 325).

2. Farmville (Virginia) *Herald,* August 10, 1906.

3. Jonathan Periam, *The Groundswell: A History of the Origin, Aims, and Progress of the Farmers' Movement . . .* (Cincinnati, 1874), 112–13.

4. Richard Hofstadter, *The Age of Reform from Bryan to F.D.R.* (New York, 1955), 126; David Thelen, *Paths of Resistance: Tradition and Dignity in Industrializing Missouri* (New York, 1986), passim, but esp. chap. 5; see also Samuel P. Hays, *The Response to Industrialism, 1877–1920* (Chicago, 1957).

5. Robert C. McMath, Jr., "Sandy Land and Hogs in the Timber (Agri)cultural Origins of the Farmers' Alliance in Texas," in Steven Hahn and Jonathan Prude, eds., *The Countryside in the Age of Capitalistic Transformation: Essays in the Social History of Rural America* (Chapel Hill, 1985), 205–6; McMath, *Populist Vanguard: A History of the Southern Farmers' Alliance* (New York, 1975), esp. chap. 10; Lawrence Goodwyn, *Democratic Promise: The Populist Moment in America* (New York, 1976).

6. For a brief biography of the founder of the Grange, see Theodore Saloutos, "Founder of the Grange: Oliver Hudson Kelley," in Joseph G. Knapp, ed., *Great American Cooperators* (Washington, D.C., 1967), 7–9.

7. Periam, *The Groundswell,* 38–40.

8. Ibid.

9. J. A. Everitt, *The Third Power: Farmers to the Front* (Indianapolis, 1905), 71.

10. Ibid., 85–86.

11. Periam, *The Groundswell,* 38–40.

12. Everitt, *The Third Power,* 71.

13. See Periam, *Groundswell,* 104, 112–14; Steven Hahn, *The Roots of Southern Populism: Yeoman Farmers and the Transformation of the Georgia Upcountry, 1850–1890* (New York, 1983), 15–133.

14. Periam, *Groundswell,* 111–12; Joseph G. Knapp, *The Rise of American Cooperative Enterprise, 1620–1920* (Danville, Ill., 1969), 49.

15. James D. Bennett, "Some Notes on Christian County, Kentucky, Grange Activities," *Register of the Kentucky Historical Society* 64 (July 1966): 232. Grangers also opposed a law requiring fences and attacked gambling and racing at the county fair. Hopkinsville *Semi-Weekly South Kentuckian,* February 8, 1884, December 4, 1885.

16. McMath, *Populist Vanguard,* 18–19; see also Knapp, *American Cooperative Enterprise,* 57–68.

17. Nashville *Weekly Toiler,* August 21, October 2, 1889.

18. Goodwyn, *Democratic Promise,* 126.

19. Nashville *Weekly Toiler,* June 4, 1890.

20. "Jno. M. Foster and the Robertson County Association," *Black Patch Journal* 1 (August 1907): no pagination.

21. Tennessee, volume 26, p. 124, R. G. Dun and Company Credit Ledgers

(unpublished Dun archives, Baker Library, Harvard University, Boston, Mass.). Most research on planter persistence has been in the cotton South. For an exception, see John Burdick, "From Virtue to Fitness: The Accommodation of a Planter Family to Postbellum Virginia," *Virginia Magazine of History and Biography* 93 (January 1985): 14–35. Although Burdick's research concerns only one family, the Hubards, it suggests that persistence may have been more difficult for tobacco planters than for cotton planters. For tobacco growers, access to labor, not land, is the pivotal determinant of wealth.

22. Fort Family Papers (Manuscript Section, Tennessee State Library and Archives, Nashville, Tenn.; hereinafter TSLA).

23. Robertson County Tax List, 1904 (microfilm, TSLA).

24. "Jno. M. Foster and the Robertson County Association," *Black Patch Journal* 1 (August 1907): no pagination.

25. Ibid.; see Robert H. Wiebe, *The Search for Order, 1877–1920* (New York, 1967), 17.

26. Reports that Ferigo was touring the markets preparatory to buy directly from farmers were published in the Clarksville *Daily Leaf-Chronicle,* September 6, 1901, and in the Hopkinsville *Kentuckian,* September 6, 1901; Clarksville *Leaf-Chronicle,* October 17, 1901.

27. Charles Fort, "A Radical Corpuscle," *Tom Watson's Magazine* 4 (March 1906): 73–76.

28. Clarksville *Daily Leaf-Chronicle,* October 5, 21, 22, 23, 1901; Paducah *Sun,* October 17, 1901.

29. Clarksville *Daily Leaf-Chronicle,* December 10, 1901.

30. Hopkinsville *Kentuckian,* January 22 and February 2, 1904; Clarksville *Leaf-Chronicle,* February 8, 1904.

31. Clarksville *Leaf-Chronicle,* September 7, 1904.

32. *Western Tobacco Journal,* August 15, 1904.

33. Nashville *Banner,* July 30, 1904. Rick S. Gregory credits the PPA with promoting such Progressive innovations as better roads, county agents, an agricultural experiment station in the Black Patch, and consistent tobacco grading. The PPA also secured government help in combating insect pests. See Gregory, "Desperate Farmers: The Dark Tobacco District Planters' Protective Association of Kentucky and Tennessee, 1904–1914" (Ph.D. diss., Vanderbilt, 1989), 232–55.

34. Clarksville *Daily Leaf-Chronicle,* February 6, 1902, September 19 and 22, 1904.

35. Clarksville *Leaf-Chronicle,* September 7, 1904.

36. Nashville *Banner,* March 2, 1904.

37. Hopkinsville *Kentuckian,* September 2, 1905.

38. Clarksville *Leaf-Chronicle,* June 24, 1905.

39. Trenton *News,* quoted in the Hopkinsville *Kentuckian,* March 11, 1904.

40. Hopkinsville *Kentuckian,* February 23, 1904.

41. Littlepage, report of interview with C. M. Bourne, October 14, 1905, Bureau of Corporations, Tobacco Investigation Records, Record Group 122 (National Archives, Washington, D.C.).

42. U.S. Census Office, *Twelfth Census of the United States . . . 1900,* vol. 5,

Agriculture . . . Part I (Washington, D.C., 1902), 84–87; Bureau of Census, *Thirteenth Census of the United States . . . 1910,* vol. 7, *Agriculture, 1909 and 1910* (Washington, 1913), 582–90, 634–45.

43. Littlepage interview with J. H. Gerhart, October 23, 1905, file 3084, Tobacco Investigation Records.

44. Littlepage interview with John B. Ferguson, October 28, 1905, file 3085, Tobacco Investigation Records.

45. Springfield, Tenn., *Black Patch Journal* 2 (December 1908): 3. Bertram Wyatt-Brown has argued effectively that southern men often acted out of a fear of being shamed by women. See *Southern Honor: Ethics and Behavior in the Old South* (New York, 1982), 52–55.

46. "The Glorious Women of the Black Patch," *Black Patch Journal* 1 (May 1907): no pagination; "Stand by Your Guns" is in the same place.

47. Drew Gilpen Faust, "Altars of Sacrifice: Confederate Women and the Narratives of War," *Journal of American History* 76 (March 1990): 1200–28; Wyatt-Brown, *Southern Honor: Ethics and Behavior in the Old South,* 35, 39–40, 52–54. In Association propaganda, Ewing's secretary emerged as the ideal of heroic southern womanhood. Made independent by the death of her husband, she had raised and educated her small children and worked as a school teacher. Like women all over the Black Patch, she had stood up to fight the trust. "A Preposterous Charge," *Black Patch Journal* 2 (December 1908): 29; ibid., 2 (August 1908): no pagination.

48. Hopkinsville *Kentuckian,* October 31, 1902.

49. Louisville *Courier-Journal,* September 25, 1904; Clarksville *Leaf-Chronicle,* September 26, 1904; Nashville *Banner,* September 26, 1904 (quotation); Hopkinsville *Kentuckian,* September 24, 1904.

50. Clarksville *Leaf-Chronicle,* September 26, 1907.

51. Clarksville *Leaf-Chronicle,* September 27, 1904.

52. Ibid., October 8, 1904; Mayfield *Daily Messenger,* October 18, 1904; *Western Tobacco Journal,* October 17, 1904. But money problems continued. Ewing journeyed to New York hoping to win more money for the Association, only to be rebuffed. As late as February 18, 1905, Association supporters still worried that there was "still a hitch in the money arrangements." *Farmers' Home Journal,* February 18, 1905.

53. Account book of Charles Henry Fort, Fort Family Papers (TSLA); Mayfield *Daily Messenger,* December 28, 1904.

54. Bank of Elkton Records, Box 1, Todd County Circuit Court Records (Kentucky Department for Libraries and Archives; hereinafter cited as KDLA).

55. Clarksville *Leaf-Chronicle,* March 15, 1906.

56. Clarksville *Leaf-Chronicle,* March 2, 1909.

57. Interview with Robert Holt, September 1, 1984.

58. C. Vann Woodward, *Origins of the New South, 1877–1913* (Baton Rouge, 1951), 386. Dewey W. Grantham, *Southern Progressivism: The Reconciliation of Progress and Tradition* (Knoxville, 1983), 324, puts the number at 35,000. Eugene P. Lyle, Jr., in "Night Riding—A Reign of Fear," *Hampton's*

Magazine 22 (April 1909): 472, estimated that "of possibly fifty thousand growers, Ewing's Association is handling the crop of around forty thousand." Figures on the proportion of the crop the Association controlled are more reliable. Association leaders claimed to control 24,999 hogsheads of tobacco out of 100,000 produced in 1904. In 1905 the Association sold 35,638 of 90,000 produced. In 1906 the Association sold 39,369 hogsheads of 80,000 produced. In 1907 the Association claimed to control 50,000 of 60,000 hogsheads grown. See N. E. Greene to A. O. Stanley, August 17, 1907, Augustus O. Stanley Papers, Special Collections (University of Kentucky Library, Lexington, Ky.) and *The Tobacco Planters' Yearbook, 1908* (Guthrie, 1908), 6–7. Ewing himself presented slightly different statistics.

59. *Farmers' Home Journal,* February 18, April 15, 1905.
60. Interview with Mrs. A. V. Hall, July 29, 1982.
61. Transcript of evidence, *Menees* v. *Matthews,* 123, Record Group 21 (Federal Records Center, East Point, Ga.).
62. John M. Gresham, comp., *Biographical Cyclopedia of the Commonwealth of Kentucky* (Chicago, 1896), 225–26; Christian County, Kentucky, Will Book "O," 575–78 (Christian County Court Clerk's Office, Hopkinsville, Ky.).
63. Manuscript Census Returns, Twelfth Census of the United States, 1900, Robertson County, Tennessee, Schedule 1—Population; Manuscript Census Returns, Eighth Census of the United States, 1860, Robertson County, Tennessee, Schedule 1—Free Population (microfilm, TSLA); 1904 Tax list for Robertson County (ibid.); Thomas Littlepage interview with Polk Prince, October 20, 1905, Tobacco Investigation Records; 1892 Logan County Tax List (microfilm, KDLA); George Locke and R. C. Hunt, *Atlas of Logan County, Kentucky* (Dayton, Ohio, 1877, 1980), 12.
64. Association leaders can be identified in *The Tobacco Planters' Yearbook, 1908* (Guthrie, Ky., 1908). Real estate holdings are from tax lists (microfilm, TSLA) and Trigg County, Kentucky, Tax List for 1904 (microfilm, KDLA).
65. Stewart County Historical Society, *Stewart County Heritage, Dover, Tennessee* (n.p., 1980), 269.
66. Cadiz *Record,* November 16, 1905, and G. B. Bingham to President Theodore Roosevelt, November 15, 1905, 60-20-2, Department of Justice Central Files, Record Group 60 (National Archives, Washington, D.C.); Manuscript Census Returns, Twelfth Census of the United States, 1900, Trigg County, Kentucky, Schedule 1—Population (microfilm, KDLA).
67. James McGready, "A Short Narrative of the Revival of Religion in Logan County," *New York Missionary Magazine and Repository of Religious Intelligence* (February, April, May, June, 1803): 74–75, 151–55, 192–99, 234–36; John Andrews, "Sketch of the Character of the Rev. James McGready," in James McGready, *The Posthumous Works of the Reverend and Pious James M'Gready, Late Minister of the Gospel, in Henderson, Kentucky,* 2 vols. (Louisville, Nashville, 1831, 1833), 1:vi–vii.
68. McMath, *Populist Vanguard,* 64, 75, 81; Nashville *Weekly Toiler,* Decem-

ber 18, 1889, July 9, 1890; Samuel S. Hill, Jr., "The South's Two Cultures," in Hill, ed., *Religion and the Solid South* (Nashville, 1972), 51–54; Clarksville *Leaf-Chronicle,* May 21, March 6, 1906.

69. *Farmers' Home Journal,* September 30, 1905.

4 Local Problems, Federal Help

1. 83 U.S. (Wall.) 36 (1873); Lawrence M. Friedman, *A History of American Law* (2d ed.; New York, 1985), 342–45.
2. Harold M. Hyman, *A More Perfect Union: The Impact of the Civil War and Reconstruction on the Constitution* (New York, 1973), 67–68; Steven Hahn, "Class and State in Postemancipation Societies: Southern Planters in Comparative Perspective," *American Historical Review* 95 (February 1990): 75–98.
3. Harry August Volz III, "Party, State, and Nation: Kentucky and the Coming of the American Civil War" (Ph.D. diss., University of Virginia, 1982), 16; James E. Copeland, "Where Were the Kentucky Unionists and Secessionists?" *Register of the Kentucky Historical Society* 71 (October 1973): 344–63.
4. James M. McPherson, *Battle Cry of Freedom: The Civil War Era* (New York, 1988), 392–405.
5. R. M. Hall to W. H. Sidell, October 31 [1863], letterbook, Provost Marshal Records, Record Group 110 (National Archives, Washington, D.C.; hereinafter cited as NA). See also Stephen V. Ash, *Middle Tennessee Society Transformed, 1860–1870: War and Peace in the Upper South* (Baton Rouge, 1988), 64–174.
6. R. M. Hall to Col. James B. Fry, January 21, [186]4, Hall to Major W. H. Sidell, February 8, [186]4, Provost Marshal Records (NA).
7. Hall to Sidell, March 7, [186]4, ibid.
8. John H. Morgan, to Sidell, October 31 [186]4, ibid.
9. *Records of the Union and Confederate Navies,* series 1, vol. 22 (Washington, D.C., 1894–1922), 186–87. Such actions characterized the Civil War in the Black Patch. See, for example, *The War of the Rebellion: A Compilation of the Official Records of the Union and Confederate Armies* (Washington, D.C., 1880–1901), series 4, vol. 44, pt. 1, 514; ibid., series 1, vol. 45, pt. 1, 791–806; ibid., series 1, vol. 39, pt. 1, 876; ibid., series 1, vol. 22, 371, 378; ibid., series 1, vol. 4, 215–19; ibid., series 1, vol. 4, 218–19; ibid., series 1, vol. 39, pt. 1, 876; *The Papers of Ulysses S. Grant* (Carbondale, 1970, 1972), 3:392–93, 4:341.
10. Lon Carter Barton, "The Reign of Terror in Graves County," *Register of the Kentucky Historical Society* 46 (April 1948): 491.
11. Barton, "The Reign of Terror in Graves County," 485–95; E. Merton Coulter, *The Civil War and Readjustment in Kentucky* (Chapel Hill, 1926), 173–288; Benny F. Craig, "Northern Conquerors and Southern Deliverers: The Civil War Comes to the Jackson Purchase," *Register of the Kentucky Historical Society* 75 (January 1975): 17–30.
12. John Morgan to General James Fry, September 10, 1865, letter book 2, First District of Kentucky, Provost Marshal Records, Record Group 393

(NA); George C. Wright, *Racial Violence in Kentucky, 1865–1940: Lynchings, Mob Rule, and "Legal Lynchings"* (Baton Rouge, 1990), chap. 1.

13. John H. Donovan to Levi F. Burnett, June 2, 1866, letterbook 176, Owensboro office, Freedmen's Bureau, Records of the Bureau of Refugees, Freedmen, and Abandoned Lands, Kentucky, Record Group 105 (NA). This suggests a decisive shift in the personnel controlling Black Patch courts. The antebellum planter elite would not have harassed their former slaves to the same extent as lower class whites. See Ash, *Middle Tennessee Society Transformed,* 196–97. For the Freedmen's Bureau, see Donald G. Nieman, *To Set the Law in Motion: The Freedmen's Bureau and the Legal Rights of Blacks, 1865–1868* (Millwood, N.Y., 1979); Jonathan M. Wiener, *Social Origins of the New South: Alabama, 1860–1885* (Baton Rouge, 1978), 43–58.

14. A. Benson Brown to Ben P. Runkle, August 31, 1868, letterbook 177, Freedmen's Bureau Records (NA).

15. Ibid.

16. W. James Kay to Col. Ben P. Runkle, December 16, 1867, letterbook 176, ibid.

17. A. Benson Brown to Ben P. Runkle, September 24, 1868, letterbook 178, ibid.; Brown to Runkle, September 30, 1868, ibid.

18. S. A. Clayden to William Lindsay, January 1, 1868, William Lindsay Papers (Special Collections, University of Kentucky Libraries, Lexington, Ky.).

19. *Commonwealth* v. *Johnson,* 78 Kentucky 509–13.

20. Caldwell County Order Book 4, entry for November 8, 1880, p. 511 (Caldwell Circuit Court Clerk's Office, Princeton, Ky.); Wright, *Racial Violence in Kentucky,* chap. 7.

21. Hahn, "Class and State in Postemancipation Societies: Southern Planters in Comparative Perspective," 83–98.

22. 26 U.S. Stat. 619.

23. 26 U.S. Stat. 618–19; 28 U.S. Stat. 568–69; 30 U.S. Stat. 449–51; House Committee on Ways and Means, Subcommittee on Internal Revenue, *Hearings on the Relief of Tobacco Growers before a Subcommittee on Internal Revenue of the Committee on Ways and Means,* 58th Cong., 2d sess., February 4 and 25, 1904, 18–63; E. M. Flack to A. O. Stanley, February 19, 1904, Flack to Stanley, February 12, 1904, file 3054, Bureau of Corporations, Tobacco Investigation, Record Group 122 (NA); Nashville *Banner,* April 3, 1905; Clarksville *Leaf-Chronicle,* January 6, 19, February 23, March 2, April 1, 6, 19, 28, May 4, 1904; *Western Tobacco Journal,* August 1, 1904; *Tobacco World,* February 7, 1888.

24. *International Harvester Co. of America* v. *Commonwealth* 124 Kentucky 548–49; for state police power, see Morton Keller, *Affairs of State: Public Life in Late Nineteenth Century America* (Cambridge, Mass., 1977), 409–38.

25. Robert M. Ireland, *Little Kingdoms: The Counties of Kentucky, 1850–1891* (Lexington, 1977).

26. *Commonwealth* v. *Chattanooga Im'p. & M'f'g. Co.* 126 Kentucky 637.

27. *Official Report of the Proceedings and Debates of the Convention Assem-*

bled at Frankfort, on the Eighth Day of September, 1890, to Adopt, Amend, or Change the Constitution of the State of Kentucky (Frankfort, Ky., 1890), 3659–60; Augustus E. Willson to Kentucky Senate and House of Representatives, February 26, 1908, *Journal of the House of Representatives* (Louisville, 1908), 531–32; *International Harvester Co. of America v. Commonwealth,* 124 Kentucky 544.

28. Tillman to Attorney General, December 17, 1905; Attorney General to A. E. Garner, December 20, 1904; Tillman to Attorney General, December 23, 1904; Tillman to Attorney General, January 20, 1905, all in files 60 20 0, 60-20-1, Department of Justice Central Files (NA).

29. Tillman to Attorney General, March 2, 1905, ibid.

30. James C. McReynolds to Attorney General, January 19, 1909, ibid.

31. Clarksville *Leaf-Chronicle,* June 24, July 13, 1905.

32. Nashville *Banner,* October 3, 1905. The meeting between Ferigo and the Association men occurred in the midst of an investigation of the Italian Regie by the United States government's Bureau of Corporations. In August 1905 Bureau of Corporations agents interviewed Ferigo and some of his associates and would again question them not long after their negotiations with Ewing. Agents questioned Ferigo as to exactly what transpired at his meeting in the Hotel Latham. His account is the only record we have of it. See "Interview with Mr. Ferigo, Italian Regie, Relative to his Method of Purchasing Tobacco in Kentucky and Tennessee" and "Memorandum of Interview with W. G. Dunnington," file 3028, Tobacco Investigation.

33. Hopkinsville *Kentuckian,* September 7, 12, 1905.

34. Clarksville *Leaf-Chronicle,* October 18, 1905.

35. Gaines to Victor H. Metcalf, September 5, 1905, file 3039, Tobacco Investigation; James R. Garfield to Littlepage, October 24, 1905, file 891, part 2, ibid.

36. Hans B. Thorelli, *Federal Antitrust Policy: Organization of an American Tradition* (Baltimore, 1955), 553.

37. Martin J. Sklar, *The Corporate Reconstruction of American Capitalism, 1890–1916: The Market, the Law, and Politics* (Cambridge, England, 1988), 184–203.

38. William Letwin, *Law and Economic Policy in America: The Evolution of the Sherman Antitrust Act* (New York, 1965), 240–45; James Madison Russell, "Business and the Sherman Act, 1890–1914," (Ph.D. diss., University of Iowa, 1966), 190–94.

39. Muhse to Herbert Knox Smith, August 13, 1905, file 3174, part 3, Tobacco Investigation.

40. Smith to Muhse, August 15, 1905, ibid.

41. Muhse to Smith, August 18, 1905, ibid.

42. Clarksville *Leaf-Chronicle,* July 13, 1906; Littlepage to Commissioner of Corporations, October 9, 1905, file 891, part 2, Tobacco Investigation.

43. Littlepage to Commissioner of Corporations, October 9, 1905, file 891, part 2, ibid.

44. Ibid.; Littlepage interview with W. H. Simmons, November 9, 1905, file 3056(31), Tobacco Investigation.

45. John H. Nelson interview with Luther A. Graham, November 27, 1905, file 3852, part 8, Tobacco Investigation; Littlepage interviews with Washington Anderson, Dick Hampton, Henry Priestly, and Henry Dinwiddie, of Woodlawn, Tennessee, October 23, 1905, file 3085, part 9, ibid.

46. Littlepage to Commissioner of Corporations, October 9, 1905, file 891, part 2, ibid.

47. Littlepage to Commissioner of Corporations, n.d., answered October 31, 1905, ibid.

48. Littlepage to Commissioner of Corporations, November 12, 1905, ibid.

5 *"Hillbillies" and "Possum Hunters"*

1. Minutes Dark Tobacco Growers Protective Association, Clarksville, Tennessee, box 3, Robertson Yeatman Johnson Collection (Tennessee State Library and Archives, Nashville, Tenn.); Clarksville *Leaf-Chronicle,* June 6, 1911. Tracy Campbell, in "The Politics of Despair: The Tobacco Wars of Kentucky and Tennessee" (Ph.D. diss., Duke University, 1988), 231–32, argues that even at its height in 1907 the Association controlled "barely over half the estimated acreage of the Black Patch." This depends on where the boundaries are drawn. If the Black Patch is defined as the Paducah and Hopkinsville-Clarksville districts, then the total output was around 120 million pounds. If other districts are added, such as the Henderson Stemming district, then the total goes up. The Association always focused its efforts in the Hopkinsville-Clarksville district. In that region some counties were almost solid for the Association.

2. "History of the Planters' Protective Association: Some Reasons Why It Was Organized," *Black Patch Journal* 2 (August 1908): no pagination.

3. Victoria Alice Saker, "Benevolent Monopoly: The Legal Transformation of Agricultural Cooperation, 1890–1943" (Ph.D. diss., University of California, Berkeley, 1990), 59–97; Edwin G. Nourse, *The Legal Status of Agricultural Co-Operation* (New York, 1927), 241–46. Not until the Clayton Act (1914) were farm cooperatives exempted from prosecutions. Kentucky also had an anti-trust law, passed in 1890. Kentucky's law forbade any "association of persons . . . in any way interested in any pool, trust, combine, agreement, confederation or understanding . . . for the purpose of regulating or controlling or fixing the price of any merchandise, manufactured articles or property of any kind." John D. Carroll, *The Kentucky Statutes* (Louisville, 1909), chap. 101, sections 3915–21.

4. Martin J. Sklar, *The Corporate Reconstruction of American Capitalism, 1890–1916: The Market, the Law, and Politics* (Cambridge, 1988), 223–27. The Supreme Court's decision in *Loewe* v. *Lawlor,* extending the Sherman Act to unions, was unanimous. Few trust cases involving business resulted in unanimous decisions. See also Melvin I. Urofsky, *A March of Liberty: A Constitutional History of the United States* (New York, 1988), 562–65.

5. 26 U.S. Stat. 209.

6. Richard L. Troutman, ed., *The Heavens Are Weeping: The Diaries of George Richard Browder, 1852–1886* (Grand Rapids, Mich., 1987), 400.

7. Caldwell County Circuit Court Commonwealth Order Book 3, 230 (Caldwell Circuit Court Clerk's Office, Princeton, Ky.); *Commonwealth v. Hodges* 137 Kentucky 246; *Owen County Burley Tobacco Society v. Brumback* 128 Kentucky 152.

8. Saker, "Benevolent Monopoly," 117–18.

9. *Imperial Tobacco Company, etc. v. Commonwealth of Kentucky* case 13036, Court of Appeals records (Public Records Division, Kentucky Department for Libraries and Archives, Frankfort, Ky.).

10. Ibid., April 29, 1905.

11. *Farmers' Home Journal,* July 9, 1905. The same was true the following year. Ibid., April 7, 1906.

12. Deposition of J. G. Moore, 9 May 1906, *Dark Tobacco District Planters Protective Association v. S. N. Morrow,* case 2969, Robertson County Chancery Court Records, Springfield, Tenn.

13. Deposition of Charles Williams, n.d., ibid; see also deposition of W. F. Williams, May 9, 1906, ibid.

14. Hopkinsville *Kentuckian,* December 20, 1904.

15. Clarksville *Leaf-Chronicle,* October 18, 1905.

16. *Farmers' Home Journal,* February 18, 1905.

17. Ibid., June 24, 1905.

18. Ibid., October 1, 1907.

19. Ibid., July 8, 1907.

20. Ibid., July 23, 1907.

21. Cadiz *Record,* March 16, 1905.

22. Ibid., April 5, 1905.

23. Clarksville *Leaf-Chronicle* quoted in Hopkinsville *Kentuckian,* January 19, 1905.

24. E. P. Thompson, "Time, Work-Discipline and Industrial Capitalism," *Past and Present* 38 (December 1967): 56–97; David Montgomery, "Workers' Control of Machine Production in the Nineteenth Century," *Labor History* 17 (Fall 1976): 485–509; Herbert G. Gutman, "Work, Culture, and Society in Industrializing America, 1815–1919," *American Historical Review* 78 (June 1973): 531–87; Alan Dawley, *Class and Community: The Industrial Revolution in Lynn* (Cambridge, Mass., 1976).

25. E. P. Thompson, *The Making of the English Working Class* (New York, 1963), 201, 231.

26. *Acts of the State of Tennessee Passed by the Fifty-Fifth General Assembly, 1907* (Nashville, 1907), chap. 155, pp. 460–61; Carroll, *The Kentucky Statutes,* chap. 103a, pp. 1579–80.

27. *Laws of the State of Mississippi, Passed at a Regular Session of the Mississippi Legislature, Held in the City of Jackson, October, November and December 1865* (Jackson, 1866), 84–85; R. H. Clark, T. R. R. Cobb, and David Irwin, *The Code of the State of Georgia* (Atlanta, 1967), 869–70; A. J. Walker, *The Revised Code of Alabama* (Montgomery, 1967), 703; Edward I. Bullock and William Johnson, comps., *The General Statutes of the*

Commonwealth of Kentucky . . . (Frankfort, Ky., 1873), 655. See William Cohen, "Negro Involuntary Servitude in the South, 1865–1940: A Preliminary Analysis," *Journal of Southern History* 42 (February 1976): 31–60.

28. *Acts of the State of Tennessee Passed by the Fifty-Fifth General Assembly, 1907* (Nashville, 1907), chap. 154, p. 459; Carroll, *The Kentucky Statutes,* chap. 103a, pp. 1579–80. See also A. L. Dorsey, "System Out of Chaos," *Black Patch Journal* 1 (May 1907): no pagination.

29. Eugene P. Lyle, Jr., "The Night Riders," *Hampton's Magazine* 22 (March 1909): 344.

30. Ibid., 346; Clarksville *Leaf-Chronicle,* August 28, 1905.

31. The text of the Stainback Resolves was mailed to President Theodore Roosevelt. See G. B. Bingham, Secretary PPA, Trigg County, to Roosevelt, November 5, 1905, Department of Justice Central Files, Record Group 60 (National Archives, Washington, D.C.).

32. Thompson, *The Making of the English Working Class,* 64.

33. John Phillip Reid, *In a Defiant Stance* (University Park, Penn., 1977), 122–23; Paul A. Gilje, *The Road to Mobocracy* (Chapel Hill, 1987), 37–68; Iver Bernstein, *The New York City Draft Riots* (New York, 1990), 5; Dirk Hoerder, *People and Mobs: Crowd Action in Massachusetts during the American Revolution, 1765–1780* (Berlin, 1971), passim; Pauline Maier, "The Charleston Mob and the Evolution of Popular Politics in Revolutionary South Carolina, 1765–1784," *Perspectives in American History* 4 (1970): 173–96.

34. W. D. Blanks, "Corrective Church Discipline in the Presbyterian Churches of the Nineteenth Century South," *Journal of Presbyterian History* 44 (June 1966): 89–105; William W. Sweet, "The Churches as Moral Courts of the Frontier," *Church History* 2 (March 1933): 3–21; Cortland Victor Smith, "Church Organization as an Agency of Social Control: Church Discipline in North Carolina, 1800–1860" (Ph.D. diss., University of North Carolina, 1966); Donald G. Mathews, *Religion in the Old South* (Chicago, 1977), 39–46; Anne C. Loveland, *Southern Evangelicals and the Social Order, 1800–1860* (Baton Rouge, 1980), 38, 97; Richard M. Cameron, *Methodism and Society in Historical Perspective* (New York, Nashville, 1961), 128–31, 271.

35. Clarksville *Leaf-Chronicle,* November 2, 1905.

36. Jim Long, Jim Morris, Jim Draughon, Jack Carter, and Tom Lattimer were the five appointed. Testimony of T. L. Polk in transcript of evidence, *Menees* v. *Matthews, et al.;* Clarksville *Leaf-Chronicle,* November 7, 1905; the minutes of the meeting are extant: Dark Tobacco Growers Protective Association-Clarksville, Tennessee, Robertson Yeatman Johnson Collection, box 3 (TSLA).

37. Dark Tobacco Growers Protective Association-Clarksville, Tennessee, Robertson Yeatman Johnson Collection, box 3 (TSLA).

38. Hopkinsville *Kentuckian,* November 23, 1905.

39. Cadiz *Record,* November 16, 1905; G. B. Bingham to Roosevelt, November 15, 1905, Department of Justice Central Files (National Archives); Trigg County Tax List, 1904 (microfilm, KDLA).

40. Interview with John F. White, December 31, 1985.

41. Cadiz *Record,* November 18, 1905.
42. W. C. White testimony, Change of Venue Hearing, *Commonwealth* v. *Kelly* (Trigg County Circuit Clerk's Office, Cadiz, Ky.)
43. White testimony, *Commonwealth* v. *Kelly.*
44. Testimony of James H. Lackey, ibid.
45. Testimony of Robert Warfield, *Menees* v. *Matthews, et al.,* U.S. Circuit Court for the Middle District of Tennessee Records (Federal Records Center, East Point, Ga.); Emilus Champion to William Crumbaugh, October 5, 1909, A. E. Willson Papers (Filson Club, Louisville, Ky.); interview with Mack S. Linebaugh, August 19, 1984.
46. Clarksville *Leaf-Chronicle,* November 23, 1906.
47. Ibid., August 21, October 28, 1907.
48. Ibid., October 29, 1907.
49. Ibid., November 25, 1907.
50. Hopkinsville *Kentuckian,* December 20, 1904 and May 24, 1906.
51. T. L. Polk testimony in Transcript of Evidence, *Menees* v. *Matthews, et al.*
52. Thomas Menees testimony in *Menees* v. *Matthews, et al.* transcript.

6 Night Riders

1. James O. Nall, *The Tobacco Night Riders of Kentucky and Tennessee, 1905–1909* (Louisville, 1939), 50. Printed copies of Stanley's speech do not contain such a reference, but Stanley often did not deliver his speeches exactly as published. Stanley's speech is in A. O. Stanley Papers (Special Collections, University of Kentucky Libraries, Lexington, Ky.).
2. Interview with Edward Martin, June 11, 1982.
3. *Farmers' Home Journal,* January 27, 1906.
4. Minutes, Wallonia Christian Church (microfilm, Mormon Genealogical Society, Latter-Day Saints Library, Salt Lake City, Utah); Hopkinsville *Kentuckian,* November 6, 1915.
5. Kentucky, vol. 6, p. 29, R. G. Dun and Co. Collection (Baker Library, Harvard University Graduate School of Business Administration, Boston, Mass.).

   David Amoss was born October 19, 1857. E. N. Amoss sent his son first to Wallonia Institute, a small school that still stands a few miles down the road from Cobb, and then to James O. Ferrell's Military High School in Hopkinsville. Ferrell's high school offered courses not only in English but also Greek, Latin, and "higher mathematics." A Baptist Sunday School teacher, Ferrell assured parents that strict discipline would be maintained at his school. The local newspaper described his discipline as "rigid" and said that in the Civil War his stern sense of duty on one occasion led him to report himself for neglect of duty. Hopkinsville *Semi-Weekly South Kentuckian,* July 27, 1886.

   Amoss attended Ferrell's school in 1875 and 1876, becoming a lieutenant and graduating eighteenth in a class of seventy-seven. After he left that school he earned a degree in medicine in Cleveland, Ohio, in 1880. Better educated than most country doctors, Amoss tried practicing in a bigger city, and from 1897 to 1902 lived in Paducah. Dissatisfied with city life, he returned to Cobb. Hopkinsville *Kentuckian,* July 27, 1907.

6. Girard, Kansas *Appeal to Reason,* October 15, 1910.

7. Interview with George Cortner, April 8, 1982. The defendants were indicted for violation of Kentucky's Reconstruction-era Ku Klux Klan Law. Amoss and another defendant pled guilty to breach of peace and were each fined $50, an unusually stiff penalty for breach of peace in Caldwell County at that time. The Commonwealth attorney declined to prosecute the other defendants. Caldwell County Circuit Court Commonwealth Orders Book 1, 515, 541–42; Commonwealth Orders book 2, 15, 64.

8. Girard, Kansas, *Appeal to Reason,* October 15, 1910.

9. Watson, however, opposed socialism and sharply criticized socialists. See, for example, "The Cow and the Socialist," *Tom Watson's Magazine* 5 (August 1906): 161–69; see also Charles Q. De France, "Populism," ibid. 3 (May 1905): 305–7. Watson's chief complaint against socialism is that it would confiscate farmers' property.

10. Tom Watson, "Lynch Law," *Tom Watson's Magazine* 3 (December 1905): 153.

11. Ibid., 154.

12. See Charles Fort, "A Radical Corpuscle," *Tom Watson's Magazine* 4 (March 1906): 73–76; idem, "How Sentiment was Discouraged in Sim," ibid. 3 (January 1906): 297–98; idem, "Ructions," ibid. 4 (May 1906): 363–75; idem, "Those That Are Joined Together," ibid. 4 (April 1906): 228–38; idem, "The Fat Lady Who Climbed Fences," ibid. 5 (August 1906): 228–32; idem, "Mrs. Bonticue and Another Landlord," ibid. 4 (June 1906): 542–54; idem, "A Great Human Principle," ibid. 5 (October 1906): 549–58.

13. Clarksville *Leaf-Chronicle,* December 5, 1906; Paducah *Sun,* December 6, 1906; *Western Tobacco Journal,* December 10, 1906; State Department File 2976, frame 20 (microfilm, National Archives, Washington, D.C.; hereinafter cited as NA).

14. Interview with Clyde Quisenberry, August 6, 1982.

15. Mark C. Carnes, *Secret Ritual and Manhood in Victorian America* (New Haven, 1989); interview with Mabel Martin, June 11, 1982.

16. Interview with Jim Lawrence, July 30, 1983; Henry Bennett's Petition, *Bennett* v. *D. A. Amoss, et al.,* case #1901, in the Circuit Court of the United States, Sixth Circuit Western District of Kentucky (Federal Records Center, Chicago, Illinois); interview with Joe Ellis Scott, April 5, 1985.

The Night Rider oath: "I—— ——, in the presence of almighty God, and these witnesses, take upon myself these solemn pledges and obligations: that I will never reveal any of the secrets, signs, or pass-words of this order, either by word or writing, to any person or persons who are not entitled to the same in accordance with the rules and regulations of this order. I furthermore promise and swear that I will never reveal or cause to be revealed by word or act to any person or persons any of the transactions of this order in lodge room or out of the lodge room unless, after due trial and examination, I find them or him just and legally entitled to the same, and not then unless I believe the business and welfare of the order will be benefited by such information given. I furthermore promise and swear that I will obey all orders or summons coming from my lodge, either day or night, unless prevented by sickness of self or family.

"I furthermore promise and swear that I will not use this order, or under cover of this order, to do anything as a personal enemy for personal revenge. To all of this I most solemnly promise and swear, putting myself under no less penalty than may be put upon me by order of this lodge."

17. Interview with Joe Ellis Scott.

18. G. W. Long to R. D. Hill, January 16, 1906, Department of Justice Central Files, Record Group 60 (NA); Mayfield *Daily Messenger,* December 12, 1905; Hopkinsville *Kentuckian,* December 12, 14, 1905; Clarksville *Leaf-Chronicle,* December 9, 12, 14, 1905; Marion Williams, *Story of Todd County, Kentucky, 1820–1970* (Nashville, 1972), 58–61.

19. Menees testimony in *Menees* v. *Matthews, et al.,* U.S. Circuit Court for the Middle District of Tennessee Records (Federal Records Center, East Point, Ga.).

20. John Johnson testimony, ibid.

21. Sanborn Insurance Map, Eddyville, November 1905.

22. Interview with Tom Cash, January 15, 1982; Clarksville *Leaf-Chronicle,* November 12, 1906; Paducah *Sun,* November 12, 1906; Crittenden *Press,* November 15, 1906.

23. Eugene P. Lyle, Jr., "The Night Riders," *Hampton's Magazine* 22 (March 1909): 348.

24. J. W. Street diary, p. 181 (entry for February 15, 1908), J. W. Street Papers (Kentucky Museum and Library, Western Kentucky University, Bowling Green, Ky.).

25. Interview with Tom Cash; interview with John Parrent, Oct. 16, 1982.

26. Paducah *Evening Sun,* November 12, 1906.

27. Sanborn Insurance Map, Princeton, December 1906.

28. Interview with Edward Martin and his wife, Mabel, June 11, 1982; Clarksville *Leaf-Chronicle,* December 6, 1906; deposition of Mrs. Johnson Crider [Annie Roche], March 4, 1910, *Imperial Tobacco Company* v. *Spring Garden Insurance Company,* bundle 506 (Caldwell County Circuit Clerk's Office, Princeton, Ky.); Paducah *Evening Sun,* December 1, 1906; Hopkinsville *Kentuckian,* December 4, 1906.

29. The losses of tobacco at the John G. Orr factory are described in proof of loss statements filed in *Imperial Tobacco Company* v. *The Pennsylvania Fire Insurance Company, idem* v. *Connecticut Fire Insurance Company, idem* v. *Hanover Insurance Company, idem* v. *Calendonian Insurance Company, idem* v. *Spring Garden Insurance Company* bundle 506 (Caldwell County Circuit Court Clerk's Office, Princeton, Ky.); Nall, *The Tobacco Night Riders,* 67, gives the losses at the Stegar and Dollar tobacco fac-

tory. Hopkinsville *Kentuckian,* December 6, 1906, and Clarksville *Leaf-Chronicle,* December 3, 1906. For Gallaher's statement, see ibid., December 27, 1906.

30. Night Riders identified in *Menees* v. *Matthews, et al.* Occupations and property holdings are from manuscript census schedules for 1900, Montgomery and Robertson counties, Tennessee, and Robertson County tax rolls, 1904 (microfilm, Tennessee State Library and Archives, Nashville, Tenn.; hereinafter cited as TSLA).

31. *Hollowell* v. *Hollowell, et al.,* Case #1877, Record Group 21 (Federal Records Center, Chicago). According to local folklore, some defendants outsmarted the Hollowells by putting all their property in their wives' names.

32. *Farmers' Home Journal,* March 13, 1909.

33. Eugene P. Lyle, Jr., "The Night Riders," *Hampton's Magazine* 22 (March 1909): 350.

34. Manuscript Census Returns, Twelfth Census of the United States, 1900, Caldwell County, Schedule 1—Population (microfilm, Kentucky Department for Libraries and Archives; hereinafter cited as KDLA); Caldwell County mortgage records (Caldwell County Court Clerk's Office, Princeton, Ky.); Paducah *Evening Sun,* May 23, 1908, describes assets of the defendants.

　　Some Masons joined the Night Riders, and it seems likely that the inspiration for some of the Riders' rites came from that organization. The Night Riders in Wallonia met on the second floor of the Christian Church, where the Masons also met. Other fraternal organizations probably played a role in the Night Rider organization as well. At least one man Amoss hired to organize Night Rider lodges was also an organizer for Woodsmen of the World, a fraternal organization similar to the Masons. Testimony of Arthur Cooper, *Commonwealth* v. *Amoss;* interview with George Cortner; Richard Maxwell Brown, *Strain of Violence: Historical Studies of American Violence and Vigilantism* (New York, 1975), 106, notes that the "relationship between Freemasonry and vigilantism was frequently an intimate one." Lynn Dumenil, *Freemasonry and American Culture, 1880–1930* (Princeton, 1984), chap. one, describes a period of increased popularity for the Masons after 1880 that closely corresponds to a period of intensified vigilantism. Eugene P. Lyle, Jr., in "Night Riding—A Reign of Fear," *Hampton's Magazine* 22 (April 1909), reported that Amoss visited Nashville "and studied carefully the records of the Ku-Klux-Klan." But only Lyle claims that Amoss used the Klan as a model and one wonders if such a trip was necessary to an ex-whitecapper.

35. Richard Maxwell Brown, "Legal and Behavioral Perspectives on American Vigilantism," *Perspectives in American History* 5 (1971): 121; Princeton *Twice-a-Week Leader,* December 2, 1919; Cadiz *Record,* May 4, 1911.

36. One of Governor Willson's spies singled out Wright as a particularly "warm" Night Rider. See Stites to Willson, May 27, 1910, Willson Papers. Interview with Durwood Wright, April 4, 1985; interviews with Clyde Quisenberry, February 18, 1984, July 3, 1984, and August 6, 1982; cer-

tificate of death, J. T. Wright, February 21, 1945 (Registrar of Vital Statistics, Commonwealth of Kentucky, Frankfort, Ky.); Trigg County Will Book K, 267–68, December 26, 1941 (Trigg County Court Clerk's Office, Cadiz, Ky.); Wright's inventory, March 9, 1945, Inventory, Appraisements and Sale Bills, Book 7, 121–22 (ibid.). Marriage presented mulattoes with a delicate problem in a racist culture. Choice of a mate required that they declare their allegiance to either the white or black communities. See Florence Mars, *Witness in Philadelphia* (Baton Rouge, 1977), 44–52.

37. Tracy Alan Campbell, "The Politics of Despair: The Tobacco Wars of Kentucky and Tennessee" (Ph.D. diss., Duke University, 1988), 132–36, 182–84. Campbell also surveyed Night Rider victims in Todd and Trigg counties, Kentucky. But whereas I found fourteen victims in Trigg alone, he found only twelve in both counties. Nevertheless, his conclusions are consistent with his own findings in Montgomery and mine in Trigg County.

38. Interview with Orman Cannon.

39. Paducah *Evening Sun,* April 16, 1907.

40. Arthur Krock, *Memoirs: Sixty Years on the Firing Line* (New York, 1968), 49. As a reporter for the Louisville *Herald,* Krock covered the Night Riders. He later became treasurer of the Kentucky Tobacco Growers' Cooperative Association.

41. Cadiz *Record,* June 6, 1907.

42. Interview with Clyde Quisenberry.

43. Clarksville *Leaf-Chronicle,* February 9, 1907; interview with H. W. Smith, April 1, 1985.

44. See, for example, Bill Cunningham, *On Bended Knees: The Night Rider Story* (Nashville, 1983); Campbell, "The Politics of Despair."

45. Clarksville *Leaf-Chronicle,* March 7, 1907. Ewing claimed the membership of the PPA to be 27,000 in 1907. Ibid., November 25, 1907. For PPA estimates of its membership, see chapter 5.

46. Pete Daniel, *Breaking the Land: The Transformation of Cotton, Tobacco, and Rice Cultures since 1880* (Urbana, Chicago, 1985), chap. 6; George T. Blakey, *Hard Times and New Deal in Kentucky, 1929–1939* (Lexington, 1986), chap. 5.

47. Clarksville *Leaf-Chronicle,* May 3, 1906.

48. Copy of Ewing to Joseph E. Washington, October 19, 1908, Washington Family Papers, box 19, folder 23 (TSLA).

49. Clarksville *Leaf-Chronicle,* February 21, March 6, 7, 20, and May 3, 1906.

50. For complaints about the continued scarcity of labor, see *Farmers' Home Journal,* June 9, August 25, 1906.

51. Clarksville *Leaf-Chronicle,* January 1, 1906; Minutes of the Planters' Protective Association of Montgomery County, Tenn., Robertson Johnson Yeatman Papers (TSLA).

52. *Farmers' Home Journal,* May 20, 27, 1905.

53. Ibid., November 4, 1905.

54. Ibid., February 19, 1909.

55. Clarksville *Leaf-Chronicle,* February 21, March 6, 7, 20, and May 3, 1906.

56. Ibid., December 14, 1906.

57. Ibid., January 1, 1906.

58. Much as New York rioters made "a bid to gain sway over an entire city" in 1863. Iver Bernstein, *The New York City Draft Riots*, 6.

59. Information on the various lodges is from a report by detective "John Smith" enclosed in John Stites (of Hopkinsville) to Willson, May 27, 1910, Willson Papers; interview with Joe Ellis Scott.

60. Interview with Durwood Wright. The New York *Times* estimated the Night Rider force at four hundred. Most press accounts put their number at five hundred. New York *Times*, December 8, 1907; Paducah *Sun*, December 7, 1908; Atlanta *Constitution*, December 8, 1907; Los Angeles *Times*, December 8, 1907; Memphis *Commercial-Appeal*, December 8, 1907.

61. Descriptions of the warehouses destroyed by the Night Riders are contained in petitions of their owners in their suits against insurance companies refusing to pay claims because of the riot clause in the policies. See *W. T. Cooper* v. *Glen Falls Insurance Company*, case 6034; *idem* v. *City of New York Insurance Company*, case 6033; *idem* v. *Rochester German Insurance Company*, case 6035; *Tandy and Fairleigh Tobacco Company* v. *Firemen's Fund Insurance Company*, case 6032; *W. T. Tandy* v. *The Glen Falls Insurance Company*, case 5060; *idem* v. *The Rochester German Insurance Company*, case 5060; *idem* v. *Williamsburg Fire Insurance Company*, case 5059; *R. M. Wooldridge and Company* v. *Hamburg-Breman Fire Insurance Company*, case 5044; *idem* v. *The Georgia Home Insurance Company*, case 5045; *W. G. Dunnington and Company* v. *Atlas Assurance Company, Limited*, case 5025; *idem* v. *German-American Insurance Company*, case 5024; *idem* v. *Hamburg-Bremen Fire Insurance Company*, case 5022; *idem* v. *Hanover Fire Insurance Company*, case 5019; *idem* v. *Royal Insurance Company*, case 5020; *idem* v. *American Central Insurance Company*, case 5023; *idem* v. *Firemen's Fund Insurance Company* case 5021, box 45, Christian Circuit Court Common Law Cases (Public Records Division, KDLA).

62. Hopkinsville *Kentuckian*, December 10, 1907; Hopkinsville *Weekly New Era*, December 13, 1907.

63. Testimony of Arthur Cooper, transcript of Evidence, *Commonwealth* v. *Amoss;* interview with Joe Ellis Scott.

64. Hopkinsville *Weekly New Era*, December 13, 1907.

65. Interview with Mrs. Harvey White, August 18, 1982; Erskine Birch Bassett Scrapbook; Hopkinsville *Kentuckian*, August 19, 1909; Lyle, "The Night Riders," 351.

66. Testimony of Bob Fairleigh, *Commonwealth* v. *Amoss*. Fairleigh was a member of the posse.

67. Ibid.; Bassett Scrapbook; Lyle, "The Night Riders," 351.

68. Interview with anonymous. Rumors circulated that Bassett's posse injured as many as fifteen raiders. John Stites to Willson, February 27, 1911, Willson Papers.

69. Interview with anonymous; testimony of Arthur N. Cooper, *Commonwealth* v. *Amoss*.

70. New York *Times,* December 8, 1908; Chicago Sunday *Tribune,* December 8, 1907; Memphis *Commercial-Appeal,* December 8, 12, 1907; Los Angeles *Times,* December 8, 1907; Atlanta *Constitution,* December 8, 12, 1907.

7 Local Law

1. Paul A. Gilje, "The Baltimore Riots of 1812 and the Breakdown of the Anglo-American Mob Tradition," *Journal of Social History* 13 (Summer 1980): 549.
2. Ursula Smith Beach, *Along the Warioto: A History of Montgomery County, Tennessee* (Nashville, 1964), 87, 89; interview with Billy Daniel, April 1, 1985; W. P. Titus, *Picturesque Clarksville, Past and Present: A History of the City of Hills* (1887), 285–86.
3. Charles Waller Tyler, *The K.K.K.* (1902; rpt., Freeport, N.Y., 1972).
4. Ibid., 52, 53.
5. Ibid., 82–83.
6. Ibid., 281–84.
7. Ibid., 290.
8. Ibid., 294–95.
9. Paducah *Evening Sun,* April 22, 1908.
10. Interview with Mrs. Enoch Kem, June 13, 1983.
11. Ibid.; Clarksville *Leaf-Chronicle,* April 23, 1908, summarizes Robert's account of the incident as does the Paducah *Evening Sun,* April 23, 1907, May 11, 1908.
12. Hopkinsville *Kentuckian,* December 15, 1906.
13. Eugene P. Lyle, Jr., "The Night Riders," *Hampton's Magazine* 22 (March 1909): 348.
14. Interview with Fairrie Cook, April 1, 1985; *Tennessee* v. *Sam Hornberger, et al.,* case 3718, June term, 1906, Robertson County Circuit Court; Robertson County Circuit Court Minute Book, 470–71; Nashville *Banner,* n.d., dateline June 14, clipping in Ralph Winters Papers, Sam Winters Collection, Clarksville, Tennessee.
15. Clarksville *Leaf-Chronicle,* September 30, 1907, and March 16, 1908; Eugene P. Lyle, Jr., "Night Riding—A Reign of Fear," *Hampton's Magazine* 22 (April 1909): 463–65.
16. Bennett's name is frequently spelled "Vaughn," but his tombstone gives the spelling as "Voyn." Clarksville *Leaf-Chronicle,* August 14, December 19, 20, 23, 1907, and January 14, 1908.
17. Interview with Will "Jack" Wills, July 30, 1983.
18. Testimony of Captain E. C. Walker, transcript of Kelly Venue Hearing.
19. Ernest Burgess to Ralph Winters, April 30, 1969, unidentified newspaper clipping, Jo Ella Warren to Ralph Winters, March 20, 1969, Ralph Winters Papers (Sam Winters Collection, Clarksville, Tenn.); interview with Henry Taylor, August 18, 1984; interview with Mrs. Polk Fletcher; interview with George Izor Stainback.
20. Dancey Fort, diary, January 6, 1908 (H. W. Smith Collection, Clarksville, Tenn.).

21. This account is based on testimony at the so-called Gardner-Hunt trial. No transcript has yet been found of this trial, but the Clarksville *Leaf-Chronicle* published lengthy notes on the testimony of witnesses. H. M. Caldwell testimony, Clarksville *Leaf-Chronicle,* September 26, 1908; B. H. Sory testimony, September 22, 1908; C. P. Warfield testimony, September 26, 1908; Dr. T. H. Marble testimony, September 25, 1908. Mayor Northington did not testify. C. W. Tyler did not testify but published a letter in the *Leaf-Chronicle,* October 5, saying he had arranged for the county to pay half the money needed to hire six extra policemen. Police Chief Robinson testified, September 16, that Sory had the same authority over the guards he did. Hereinafter dates following the names of witnesses will indicate the issues of the *Leaf-Chronicle* carrying the account of that witness's testimony.

22. Dancey Fort diary, March 9, 1908.

23. The Night Riders whipped James Welch. Opponents of the Night Riders claimed Welch was a spy. Interview with Robert Holt; [A. L. Dorsey?], "The Bennett Boys," *Black Patch Journal* 2 (May 1908): no pagination; Lyle, "Reign of Fear," 464. Lyle's article reproduces a letter the Night Riders sent to the Welches.

24. Testimony of Will Crouch, September 24; testimony of C. R. Crouch, September 16; testimony of Robert Morrison, September 24.

25. Sam Moore, John Gardner, Joe Gerhart, Walter Hunt, and a constable, Henry Cook, accompanied Sory. All later testified that it was their intent to capture and arrest the masked men, not shoot them. Testimony of Henry Cooke, September 23; testimony of Sam Moore, September 24; testimony of Joe Gerhart, September 25; testimony of John Gardner, September 19 and 21; testimony of Walter Hunt, September 18; testimony of B. H. Sory, September 22; Lyle, "Reign of Fear," 462.

26. Testimony of Squire A. L. Davis, September 15; Lyle, "Reign of Fear," 463.

27. M. C. Rinehart to Sam Winters, October 1, 1982, Sam Winters Papers, Clarksville. Rinehart's account is suspect. He claims to have participated in the raid on Hopkinsville and to have entered the city by commandeering a train. No such incident was reported in the press at the time.

28. Interview with Carney Holt, June 9, 1985.

29. Testimony of Will Crouch, September 24.

30. Testimony of John Gardner and Walter Hunt, September 19 and 21; testimony of Ben Story, September 22; testimony of Sam Moore, September 24; testimony of Joe Gerhart, September 25.

31. Interview with Robert Holt; Clarksville *Leaf-Chronicle,* October 22, 1906.

32. Clarksville *Leaf-Chronicle,* May 28, 1908; Lyle, "Reign of Fear," 463.

33. Albrecht to A. E. Willson, March 23, 1908, Willson Papers (Filson Club, Louisville, Ky.).

34. Interview with Billy Daniel, April 1, 1985; Lyle, "The Night Riders," 339. The farm where the Night Riders destroyed the mules was operated by Lige Nicholson and his mother, Caroline.

35. Interview with Collier Goodlett, Jr., April 1, 1985; interview with H. W. Smith. For a history of the Pinkertons and an account of their pro-

cedures, see James D. Horan, *The Pinkertons: The Detective Dynasty That Made History* (New York, 1967).

36. Dancey Fort diary, September 8, 1908.

37. Clarksville *Leaf-Chronicle,* September 11, 1908.

38. Ibid., October 2, 1908.

39. Ibid., October 3, 1908. The defendants were granted a new trial in Nashville in 1911. At this second trial they were acquitted. Nashville *Banner,* December 5, 1911; Clarksville *Leaf-Chronicle,* December 5, 1911; *State* v. *John Gardner and Walter Hunt,* minutes of the Court (Davidson County Criminal Court Clerk's Office, Nashville, Tenn.).

40. Tracy Alan Campbell, "The Politics of Despair: The Tobacco Wars of Kentucky and Tennessee" (Ph.D. diss., Duke University, 1988), 4.

8 State Law

1. Minutes, Dark Tobacco Growers Protective Association, Clarksville, Tennessee, box 3, Robertson Yeatman Johnson Collection (Tennessee State Library and Archives, Nashville, Tenn.).

2. Patricia Watlington, *The Partisan Spirit: Kentucky Politics, 1779–1792* (New York, 1972), 35–78.

3. *Official Report of the Proceedings and Debates in the Convention . . . to Adopt, Amend, or Change the Constitution of the State of Kentucky* (Frankfort, 1890), 5014 (quotation); Arthur Krock, *The Editorials of Henry Watterson* (Louisville, 1923), 105, 106, 110, 113, and passim; Edward F. Prichard, Jr., "Popular Political Movements in Kentucky, 1875–1900" (senior thesis, Princeton University, 1935), 1–31.

4. Humbleton Tapp and James C. Klotter, *Kentucky: Decades of Discord, 1865–1900* (Frankfort, Ky., 1977), 310.

5. George C. Wright, *Racial Violence in Kentucky, 1865–1940: Lynchings, Mob Rule, and "Legal Lynchings"* (Baton Rouge, 1990), 174. Tapp and Klotter, *Kentucky: Decades of Discord,* 19–59; Prichard, "Popular Political Movements in Kentucky," 1–31.

6. Wright, *Racial Violence in Kentucky,* 50.

7. Ibid., chap. 1, Appendix A; Tapp and Klotter, *Decades of Discord,* 40–47.

8. As late as 1894 one agnostic could declare, "I would think of turning Christian when Kentucky goes Republican." Nicholas C. Burckel, "From Beckham to McCreary: The Progressive Record of Kentucky Governors," *Register of the Kentucky Historical Society* 76 (October 1978): 285.

9. Prichard, "Popular Political Movements in Kentucky," 200–201, 233–34, 236; Wright, *Racial Violence in Kentucky;* James C. Klotter, "William O'Connell Bradley," in Lowell H. Harrison, ed., *Kentucky's Governors, 1792–1985* (Lexington, 1985), 107–10; John E. Wilz, "The 1895 Election: A Watershed in Kentucky Politics," *Filson Club History Quarterly* 37 (April 1963): 117–36.

10. James C. Klotter, *William Goebel: The Politics of Wrath* (Lexington, 1977), 100–108.

11. Burckel, "From Beckham to McCreary," 286–94.

12. Louisville *Courier-Journal,* October 22, 1907; A. E. Willson, Scrapbook,

August 1907–January 1908, "Will Kentuckians Vote to Place a Trust Lawyer in the Governor's Chair This Year?" campaign booklet in Willson Scrapbook, May 1907–October 1907, Willson Papers; Robert K. Foster, "Augustus E. Willson and the Republican Party of Kentucky, 1895–1911" (M.A. thesis, University of Louisville, 1956), 61–68. Willson's enemies revived the "trust lawyer" charge in 1914 when he waged a losing campaign for the U.S. Senate. Louisville *Herald,* November 2, 1914, October 17 and 21, 1907; Paducah *Evening Sun,* October 22, 1907.

13. Christopher Waldrep, ed., "A 'Trust Lawyer' Tries to Help Kentucky Farmers: Augustus E. Willson's 1907 Letter to George B. Cortelyou," *Register of the Kentucky Historical Society* 83 (Autumn 1985): 347–55. Historians generally credit Willson with little sympathy for farmers. See, for example, Burckel, "From Beckham to McCreary," 296.

14. Louisville *Herald,* October 9, 11, 12, 1907; Paducah *Sun,* October 4, 5, 1907; Kentucky *State Journal,* quoted in Louisville *Courier-Journal,* November 11, 1907; Foster, "Augustus E. Willson and the Republican Party," 67.

15. Louisville *Post,* July 30, 1907; Paducah *Sun,* October 5, 1907; Thomas H. Appleton, Jr., "Augustus Everett Willson," in Harrison, ed., *Kentucky's Governors, 1792–1985.* Willson's only potential rival for the Republican nomination was John W. Yerkes, commissioner of internal revenue under Roosevelt. In a letter to Yerkes, Willson pledged not to oppose Yerkes if he chose to run again. "Your former strong campaign for Governor gives you just ground for consideration by the party." Although Yerkes did not run, citing ill health, he refused to endorse Willson. Willson to Yerkes, March 21, and Yerkes to Willson, March 30, 1907, folder 27, Willson Papers.

16. Louisville *Herald,* December 11, 1907; Kentucky *State Journal,* December 11, 1907.

17. Klotter, "William O'Connell Bradley," in Harrison, ed., *Kentucky's Governors, 1792–1985,* 107–9; idem., *William Goebel: The Politics of Wrath* (1977); Prichard, "Popular Political Movements in Kentucky," 161–83, 204–13.

18. Louisville *Evening Post,* December 7, 1907; Louisville *Herald,* December 8, 1907.

19. Willson Scrapbook, December 1907–January 1908, Willson Papers.

20. Louisville *Courier-Journal,* December 12, 1907; Louisville *Herald,* December 12, 1907.

21. Even so, Democrats bitterly criticized him for his alleged unconstitutional deployment of troops. Burckel, "From Beckham to McCreary," 296.

22. Eric Foner, *Reconstruction: America's Unfinished Revolution, 1863–1877* (New York, 1988), 440–41.

23. G. W. Long to Willson, December 12, 1907, Willson Papers; M. H. Thatcher to Willson, December 12, 1907; ibid.; A. R. Burnam to Willson, December 13, 1907; ibid.; John Stites to Willson, December 10, 1907, ibid.

24. John Stites to Willson, December 14, 1907, folder 70; "Governor Will-

son's Administration" (typewritten manuscript, folders 123a, 124, n.d.), 9-a; Long to Willson, December 21, 1907, Willson Papers.

25. John Stites to Willson, December 14, 1907, folder 70, Willson Papers; "Governor Willson's Administration," 9-a, ibid.; Harlan to Willson, December 13, 1907, folder 69, ibid.

26. Louisville *Courier-Journal,* December 16, 19, 1907; Willson to Philip Preston Johnston, December 15, 1907, folder 71, Willson Papers.

27. Louisville *Times,* December 20, 1907; Louisville *Courier-Journal,* December 21, 1907; Ewing to Willson, December 19, 1907, folder 73, Willson Papers. The press took a positive view of the conference. The Kentucky *State Journal,* December 21, 1907, reported that the conference was so successful that a Willson for vice president boom and an O'Rear for senator boom were starting.

28. Hopkinsville *Kentuckian,* January 4, 7, 1908; New York *Times,* January 4, 1908; Clarksville *Leaf-Chronicle,* January 3, 1908.

29. Albrecht to Willson, April 2, 1908, Willson Papers.

30. G. B. Starling to Charles McCarroll, March 3, 1908, McCarroll Papers (Kentucky Museum and Library, Western Kentucky University, Bowling Green, Ky.).

31. Interview with Ira D. Smith. In 1903 Cook's political opponents charged that he "packed" juries. Hopkinsville *Kentuckian,* April 28, 1903.

32. Cook to Willson December 26, 1907, folder 74 and December 28, 1907, folder 75, Willson Papers; E. M. Flack to Willson, December 29, 1907, folder 75, ibid.

33. Earlington *Bee,* January 9, 1908; Hopkinsville *Kentuckian,* August 10 and January 2, 1908; *Commonwealth* v. *G. B. Powell,* case 2973, Christian County Circuit Court bundles, box 5 (Public Records Division, Kentucky Department for Libraries and Archives, Frankfort, Ky.); *Commonwealth* v. *H. R. Crenshaw,* case 3022, ibid.; Clarksville *Leaf-Chronicle,* June 5, 1908.

34. Albrecht to Willson, February 25, 1908, Willson Papers.

35. Cadiz *Record,* January 9, 16, June 11, 1908; *Commonwealth* v. *J. M. Weaver,* case 3037, box 6, Christian County Court Papers (Public Records Division, Kentucky Department for Libraries and Archives); *Commonwealth* v. *Gano Warder,* case 3058, ibid.; Hopkinsville *Kentuckian,* March 26, 28, 1908. Luther Gray may have been a Night Rider himself. He was indicted in Crittenden County Court and named in four different federal lawsuits by Night Rider victims. Crittenden County Commonwealth Orders, book 7, 228–29 (Crittenden County Circuit Clerk's Office). He was named as a reluctant witness against Amoss. Hopkinsville *Kentuckian,* June 14, 1910; Bassett to Willson, June 17, 1910, Willson Papers. There were rumors that the Night Riders planned to storm the Hopkinsville jail and rescue Warder. Arthur Miles to Willson, July 28, 1908, ibid.; Cadiz *Record,* November 5, 1908. The chief witness against Warder was Hopkinsville night policeman Booth Morris.

36. Starling to McCarroll, March 3, 1908, McCarroll Papers.

37. John Stites to Willson, December 10, 1907, folder 69, Willson Papers.

38. Willson to Robert Peters, March 27, 1908, folder 80, Willson Papers.

39. Kentucky State Guard Special Order Number 8, February 4, 1908 (Boone

National Guard Center, Frankfort, Ky.).

40. Root to Willson, January 24, 1908, Willson Papers; Stites of Louisville to Willson, March 24, 1908, ibid.; Z. O. King to Willson, June 1, 1908, ibid.; Stites of Louisville to Willson, March 29, 1911, ibid.; Brown to Willson, March 20, 1911, ibid.

41. Albrecht to Willson, February 27, 1908, ibid.

42. Anna Imogene Bennett West, "The Night Riders," 1977 (unpublished manuscript kindly lent by Geneva Dycus, Dycusburg, Ky.).

43. West, "The Night Riders," 2; Crittenden *Record-Press,* February 13, 1908; interview with Joe Ellis Scott.

44. Bennett wrote an account of the raid, published in the Crittenden *Record-Press,* February 13, 1908.

45. Crittenden *Record-Press,* February 13, 1908.

46. Ibid.; James O. Nall, *The Tobacco Night Riders of Kentucky and Tennessee, 1905–1909* (Louisville, 1939), 103–5.

47. West, "The Night Riders," 5.

48. Nall, *Tobacco Night Riders of Kentucky and Tennessee,* 105.

49. W. P. Black to Willson, May 18, 1908, Willson Papers; Charles Ratliff to Willson, August 11, 1911, ibid. Bennett's daughter identified Nabb as the leader of the Night Riders that whipped her father. West, "The Night Riders," 3.

9 *Federal Law, Local Order*

1. Susan Jones interview with Kerby Jennings, November 19, 1973 (Forrest C. Pogue Oral History Institute, Department of History, College of Humanistic Studies, Murray State University, Murray, Ky.).

2. Murray *Ledger,* April 9, 1908.

3. Willson Scrapbook (microfilm, Pogue Library, Murray State University, Murray, Ky.).

4. Murray *Ledger,* April 16, 1908.

5. Ibid., August 6, 1908; Willson Scrapbook, Murray; Paducah *Sun,* April 3, 1908.

6. Paducah *Sun,* April 3, 1908.

7. Murray *Ledger,* April 16, 1908; Willson Scrapbook, Murray.

8. Willson Scrapbook, Murray.

9. Augustus E. Willson scrapbook (microfilm, Pogue Library, Murray State University, Murray, Ky.).

10. John L. Lee to Milton D. Purdy, December 28, 1905, Department of Justice Central Files (National Archives, Washington, D.C.; hereinafter cited as NA).

11. A. G. Morton to John L. Lee, January 10, 1906, Department of Justice Central Files; the letter signed "The Game 65" is on file in ibid.; J. W. Scott to W. G. Dunnington and Company, January 6, 1906, ibid.

12. Bruner to G. W. Long, January 19, 1906, ibid.

13. Acting Attorney General to R. D. Hill, January 26, 1906, ibid.; Bruner to Long, February 1, 1906, ibid.

14. Thatcher to Attorney General, February 3, 1906, ibid.

15. Acting Attorney General to Long, February 6, 1906, ibid.

16. Acting Attorney General to R. D. Hill, January 26, 1906; Ben L. Bruner to G. W. Long, February 1, 1906, ibid.

17. G. W. Long to Secretary of State, December 21, 1907. The secretary of state told aides he was "particularly desirous of pleasing the Government of Italy." Illegible to Solicitor, December 20, 1907. At one point the secretary told his assistant to "inject some smiles, in the form of a regret" to the Italian ambassador. R. B[acon] to Mr. Adee, December 20, 1907. A notation at the bottom of Bacon's memorandum, though, says, "I would not like to say anything that the Italian Government might disingenuously twist into an admission of federal responsibility for the situation in Kentucky." File 2976, State Department Numerical Files (NA).

18. John Pickrell to Judge Malcolm Yeaman, December 12, 1906, file 60-20-6, Record Group 60, Justice Department Central files (NA).

19. 26 U.S. Stat. 209 (1890).

20. DuRelle to Attorney General, December 26, 1906, file 60-20-5, Justice Department Central Files, Record Group 60 (NA); Hans B. Thorelli, *Federal Antitrust Policy: Organization of American Tradition* (Baltimore, 1955), 389–94.

21. Intrastate commerce was considered to be within the purview of the states. Charles W. McCurdy, "The *Knight* Decision of 1895 and the Modernization of American Corporation Law, 1869–1903," *Business History Review* 53 (Autumn 1979): 304–42.

22. See, for example, *United States* v. *Debs et al.* 64 F. 724 (1894); *United States* v. *Elliott et al.* 64 F.27 (1894); *United States* v. *Workingmen's Amalgamated Council of New Orleans et al.* 54 F. 994 (1893).

23. Eric Foner, *Free Soil, Free Labor, Free Men: The Ideology of the Republican Party before the Civil War* (London, 1970), 38.

24. Roosevelt to Liberty Hyde Bailey, August 10, 1908, in Elting E. Morison, ed., *The Letters of Theodore Roosevelt*, 8 vols. (Cambridge, 1952), 6:4841. There is no reason to believe Roosevelt necessarily disapproved of their vigilantism. Roosevelt himself tried to join a vigilante movement in 1884—only to be rejected as too impetuous. As late as 1915 he wrote approvingly of vigilantism. Richard Maxwell Brown, "Legal and Behavioral Perspectives on American Vigilantism," *Perspectives in American History* 5 (1971): 121, 138n.

25. *United States* v. *Elliott et al.* 64 F at 34.

26. Roosevelt to Winthrop Murray Crane, October 22, 1902 in *Letters,* 3:362.

27. Roosevelt to Robert Bacon, October 5, 1902, and Roosevelt to Winthrop Murray Crane, October 22, 1902, in *Letters,* 3:339–41, 359–66. Kentucky Governor Willson's correspondents referred to the anthracite coal strike and urged him to emulate Roosevelt's actions. Management and labor also urged Roosevelt to intervene in a strike by Colorado miners in 1903–4. Although state militia proved unable to subdue rioters, Roosevelt refused to intervene. *Letters,* 3:632, 656.

28. John G. Miller, *The Black Patch War* (Chapel Hill, 1936), 29.

29. Ibid., 31.

30. Petition, *Robert H. Hollowell* v. *John E. Hollowell et al.,* file 1877, Circuit

Court of the United States for the Western District of Kentucky (Federal Archives and Records Center, Chicago).

31. *Proceedings of the 23d Annual Meeting of the Kentucky State Bar Association . . . 1924* (Louisville, [1924]), 207–10; James E. Copeland, "Where Were the Kentucky Unionists and Secessionists?" *Register of the Kentucky Historical Society* 71 (October 1973): 344–63; Ralph A. Wooster, *The Secession Conventions of the South* (Princeton, 1962), 207–22; James R. Robertson, "Sectionalism in Kentucky from 1855 to 1865," *Mississippi Valley Historical Review* 4 (June 1917): 49–63.

32. Miller, *Black Patch War*, 52.

33. Paducah *Evening Sun*, April 22, 1908; Clarksville *Leaf-Chronicle*, April 23, 1908.

34. Paducah *Evening Sun*, April 23, 1908.

35. Mary M. Stolberg, "The Evolution of Frontier Justice: The Case of Judge Isaac Parker," *Prologue* 20 (Spring 1988): 7–23; Lawrence M. Friedman, *A History of American Law* (2d ed.; New York, 1985), 371–84.

36. Cadiz *Record*, April 30, 1908.

37. Clarksville *Leaf-Chronicle*, May 13, 1908.

38. Cadiz *Record*, May 14, 1908.

39. Miller, *Black Patch War*, 84.

40. Clarksville *Leaf-Chronicle*, May 13, 1908.

41. Cadiz *Record*, May 14, 1908.

42. Miller, *Black Patch War*, 77.

43. Louisville *Herald*, October 13, 1908; New York *Times*, October 4, 1908.

44. Eugene P. Lyle, Jr., "They That Rode by Night: The Story of Kentucky's Tobacco War," *Hampton's Magazine* 22 (February 1909): 175–87. See, for example, New York *Times*, September 30, October 29, 1909.

45. *Hampton's Magazine* 22 (March 1909): 352; see also Eugene P. Lyle, Jr., "Night Riding—A Reign of Fear," *Hampton's Magazine* 22 (April 1909): 461–74.

46. Girard, Kansas, *Appeal to Reason*, September 3, 1910.

47. Miller, *Black Patch War*, 75.

48. Ibid., 84–85.

10   "Shirt-tail" Night Riders

1. Interview with Elizabeth Durrett, June 18, 1983.

2. Joel Williamson, *The Crucible of Race: Black-White Relations in the American South since Emancipation* (New York, 1984), chap. 9, disparages the "grit thesis" which placed blame for racial violence on lower-class whites. All classes shared the same racial attitudes toward blacks. Differences existed in tone, not substance. George Wright, in *Racial Violence in Kentucky, 1865–1940: Lynchings, Mob Rule, and "Legal Lynchings"* (Baton Rouge, 1990), adopts this notion wholesale, presenting white society as an undifferentiated monolith. For confirmation that lynch mobs could include the "better sort," see Leonard Dinnerstein, *The Leo Frank Case* (Athens, 1966), 139, and James R. McGovern, *Anatomy of a Lynching: The Killing of Claude Neal* (Baton Rouge, 1982), 67ff.

But for a perceptive corrective of Williamson's anti-grit thesis, see Barbara J. Fields, "Ideology and Race in American History," in J. Morgan Kousser and James M. McPherson, *Region, Race, and Reconstruction: Essays in Honor of C. Vann Woodward* (New York, 1982), 143–77.

3. Kelly Testimony, transcript of Kelly Venue Hearing, 264–65 (Trigg County Circuit Clerk's Office, Cadiz, Ky.); interview with Will "Jack" Wills.

4. Clement Eaton, *The Growth of Southern Civilization, 1790–1860* (New York, 1961), 232–33; John G. Miller, unpublished reminiscences, Miller Papers (Department of Library Special Collections, Manuscripts Division, Western Kentucky University, Bowling Green, Ky.); Cadiz *Record,* May 4, 1905; Paducah *Sun,* October 11, 13, 24, November 16, 1905; J. Winston Coleman, "Old Kentucky Iron Furnaces," *Filson Club History Quarterly* 31 (July 1957): 227–42; David Sullivan interview with Genella Bogard, August 6, 1976 (Land Between the Lakes Series, College of Humanistic Studies, Forrest C. Pogue Oral History Institute, Department of History, Murray State University, Murray, Ky.); Manuscript Census Returns, Twelfth Census of the United States, 1900, Lyon and Trigg counties, Kentucky, Schedule 1—Population (microfilm).

5. Manuscript Census Returns, Thirteenth Census of the United States, 1910, Lyon and Trigg counties, Kentucky, Schedule 1—Population (microfilm).

6. Interview with John F. White, December 31, 1985; Manuscript Census Returns, Thirteenth Census of the United States, 1910, Lyon and Trigg counties, Kentucky, Schedule 1—Population (microfilm).

7. Interview with Boyd Hudson, January 15, 1982.

8. Interview with Boyd Hudson; Eugene P. Lyle, Jr., "Night Riding—A Reign of Fear," *Hampton's Magazine* 22 (April 1909): 468.

9. Anna Imogene Bennett West, "The Night Riders," 1977 (unpublished manuscript kindly lent by Geneva Dycus).

10. *Nat Frizzell* v. *E. Champion, et al.* case 1897, filed August 22, 1908; *G. W. Gordon* v. *D. A. Amoss, et al.* case 1938, filed February 2, 1909; *Maggie Scruggs* v. *E. Champion, et al.* case 1895, filed July 7, 1908 (all in the United States District Court for the Sixth Circuit, Western District of Kentucky at Paducah); Manuscript Census Returns, Twelfth Census of the United States, 1900, Marshall and Lyon counties, Kentucky, Schedule 1—Population.

11. Tandy W. Ferguson testimony, Trigg County Circuit Court Grand Jury Minutes, May 1908 (Trigg County Circuit Court Clerk's Office, Cadiz, Ky.).

12. John Collins testimony, ibid.

13. Robert L. Collins testimony, ibid.; John Kelly testimony in *Commonwealth* v. *Kelly,* transcript of change of venue hearing (Trigg County Circuit Court Clerk's Office, Cadiz, Ky.).

14. Kelly Testimony, Kelly Venue Hearing transcript, 261ff.

15. Ibid.; Bertram Wyatt-Brown, "Community, Class, and Snopesian Crime: Local Justice in the Old South," in Orville Vernon Burton and Robert C. McMath, eds., *Class, Conflict, and Consensus: Antebellum Southern Com-*

munity Studies (Westport, 1982), 173–206; Douglas Hay, "Property, Authority, and the Criminal Law," in Douglas Hay et al., eds., *Albion's Fatal Tree: Crime and Society in Eighteenth-Century England* (New York, 1975), 17–64.

16. Lyon County Tax List for 1863 (microfilm, Kentucky Department for Libraries and Archives, Frankfort, Ky.); manuscript census returns, Eighth Census of the United States, 1860, Lyon County, Kentucky, Schedule 1—Population (microfilm).

17. *Memorial Record of Western Kentucky* (Chicago, 1904), 13–14; Paducah *Evening Sun,* March 21, 1925.

18. Robert M. Ireland, *Little Kingdoms: The Counties of Kentucky, 1850–1891* (Lexington, 1977), 144, 147, and chap. 5; Lyon County Order Book "f," 46–48, 107–8 (Lyon County Circuit Court Clerk's Office, Eddyville, Ky.).

19. W. L. Crumbaugh to Willson, February 19, 1908, Willson Papers.

20. Ibid.

21. Ibid.

22. Interview with Tom Cash, January 15, 1982.

23. Ibid.

24. Clarksville *Leaf-Chronicle,* February 17, 1908. Newspapers generally had trouble explaining the Eddyville raid. The Earlington *Bee* noted that "the raid was not altogether in the interest of the tobacco association, as only one of the men [the operator of the pool room] had any connection with tobacco business" and his relations with the PPA were good. A Hopkinsville lawyer wrote that the Eddyville raid was "a little worse than anything yet done in the matter of whipping men. They whipped ten—not one of whom, it is said, had any sort of connection with the tobacco business." Joe McCarroll to Willson, February 18, 1908, Willson Papers.

25. Owensboro *Daily Messenger,* February 18, 1908.

26. J. W. Street diary, March 7, 1908, James W. Street Papers (Kentucky Library and Museum, Western Kentucky University, Bowling Green, Ky.).

27. Earlington *Bee,* February 20, 1908; Crittenden *Record-Press,* February 20, 1908; Eugene P. Lyle, Jr., "The Night Riders," *Hampton's Magazine* 22 (March 1909): 347.

28. J. W. Street diary, February 15, 1908.

29. Joe McCarroll to Charles McCarroll, February 18, 1908, McCarroll Papers (Kentucky Library, Manuscript Division, Western Kentucky University, Bowling Green, Ky.). For the comments of other puzzled observers after the Eddyville raid, see Clarksville *Leaf-Chronicle,* February 17, 1908; Earlington *Bee,* February 20, 1908; Paducah *News-Democrat,* February 17, 1908; Street Diary, February 15, 1908.

30. Crumbaugh to Willson, February 19, 1908, Willson Papers. Crumbaugh corresponded with Governor Willson but, in a way, even his friend in Frankfort had let him down. If troops had been sent to Eddyville when they were sent to Hopkinsville, the law could have prevailed in Lyon County and all would have been at peace.

31. Crumbaugh to Willson, February 21, 1908, Willson Papers.

32. Crumbaugh to Willson, February 21, 1908; Opal McCollum to John S.

Cooper, June 25, 1957, Cooper Papers (Special Collections, University of Kentucky Libraries, Lexington, Ky.).

33. Crumbaugh to Willson, February 21, 1908, Willson to Crumbaugh, February 22, 1908, Willson Papers.

34. Crumbaugh to Willson, February 29, 1908, ibid.

35. Albrecht to Willson, February 26, 1908, ibid.

36. Crumbaugh to Willson, February 29, 1908, ibid.

37. Crumbaugh to Willson, March 12, 1908, and February 29, 1908, ibid.

38. Owensboro *Daily Messenger,* March 11, 1908; Clarksville *Leaf-Chronicle,* March 13, 1908; New York *Times,* April 21, 1909.

39. Earlington *Bee,* August 6, 1908. Rumors spread that miners planned to take advantage of the same climate of violence by carrying out Night Rider-like raids on mines and mine property. Z. O. King to Willson, June 1, 1908, Willson Papers.

40. Wright, *Racial Violence in Kentucky,* 138.

41. The two defendants acquitted were tried by local jurors. After their trials, the judge obtained a jury from McCracken County. Cadiz *Record,* July 9, 1908.

42. Hopkinsville *Kentuckian,* April 5, 2, 1910; Commonwealth Orders Book 7, 605 (Crittenden Circuit Clerk's Office, Marion, Ky.).

43. Lyon County Commonwealth Order Book B, 594–98 (Lyon County Circuit Court Clerk's Office, Eddyville, Ky.); Paducah *News-Democrat,* May 7, 1908; Hopkinsville *Kentuckian,* August 22, 1908.

44. Hopkinsville *Kentuckian,* August 18, 1908.

45. Ziba O. King to Willson, August 20, 1908, Willson Papers.

46. Paducah *Evening Sun,* August 19, 1908; Hopkinsville *Kentuckian,* August 25, 1908.

47. Ibid.

48. Paducah *Evening Sun,* August 21, 1908; Krone interview in Louisville *Herald,* n.d., in Willson Scrapbook (Filson Club, Louisville, Ky.). Smith, in an interview in the Clarksville *Leaf-Chronicle,* August 25, 1908, denied all Krone's charges.

49. Hopkinsville *Kentuckian,* August 25, 1908.

50. J. Barbour and John D. Carroll, *Kentucky Statutes . . .* (Louisville, 1894), 277–78.

51. Transcript of Change of Venue Hearing, *Commonwealth* v. *Kelly,* Trigg County bundles (Trigg County Circuit Clerk's Office, Cadiz, Ky.).

52. New York *Times,* July 23, 1908.

53. Bassett to Willson, September 24, 1908; Nall, *Night Riders,* 170n.

54. Nall, *Tobacco Night Riders,* 170.

55. Louisville *Times* quoted in the Cadiz *Record,* October 8, 1908.

56. Bassett to Willson, June 17, 1910, Willson Papers.

57. Interview with Clyde Quisenberry, August 6, 1982.

58. Interview with Charlie Merrick, August 6, 1982.

59. Interview with Clyde Quisenberry; interview with Charlie Merrick, August 6, 1982.

60. Interview with Bernard Jones, June 12, 1982.

61. Interview with David Porter, October 16, 1982.

62. Interview with W. O. Ferguson, July 7, 1984.

63. Interview with Bernard Jones.

64. Ibid.; Hopkinsville *Kentuckian,* June 14, 1910.

65. Interview with Bernard Jones; interview with Charlie Merrick.

66. Interview with Bernard Jones; Hopkinsville *Kentuckian,* June 14, 1910.

67. Interview with Bernard Jones.

68. Lyle, "The Night Riders," 339; Clarksville *Leaf-Chronicle,* June 8, 1908.

11   *"No Longer the Cockey Gentleman of Yore"*

1. [A. L. Dorsey?], "The Night Rider," *Black Patch Journal* 1 (February 1908): no pagination.

2. Cadiz *Record,* October 29, 1908; Louisville *Herald,* October 28, 1908.

3. Cadiz *Record,* October 29, 1908.

4. Krone to Willson, December 7, 1908, Willson Papers (Filson Club, Louisville, Ky.).

5. Clarksville *Leaf-Chronicle,* November 12, 1908.

6. Ibid.

7. Ibid., September 20, 1909.

8. Paducah *Sun,* November 16, 1908; Louisville *Courier-Journal,* November 17, 1908.

9. Princeton *Twice-A-Week Leader,* January 29, 1909.

10. Hopkinsville *Kentuckian,* February 9, 1909.

11. Ibid.

12. Ibid., February 13, 1909.

13. Princeton *Twice-A-Week Leader,* February 19, 1909.

14. John D. Carroll, *Kentucky Statutes* (Louisville, 1909), 1579–80.

15. Hopkinsville *Kentuckian,* January 28, 30, February 9, 11, 13, 18, March 6, 11, 13, 1909. Prosecutions of persons selling and buying pledged tobacco are in *Commonwealth* v. *Imperial Tobacco Company,* case 4080; *Commonwealth* v. *John Redd,* case 4081; *Commonwealth* v. *Imperial Tobacco Company,* case 4083; *Commonwealth* v. *J. B. Ramsey,* case 4084; *Commonwealth* v. *J. R. Berry,* case 4085; *Commonwealth* v. *G. W. English,* case 4086; *Commonwealth* v. *Gilbert Hooks,* case 4087, all in Christian County indictments, box 7 (Public Records Division, Kentucky Department for Libraries and Archives, Frankfort, Ky.; hereinafter cited as KDLA). The county attorney ultimately asked that all these prosecutions be dismissed.

16. Clarksville *Leaf-Chronicle,* July 6, 1911.

17. Ibid., August 4, 1911.

18. Testimony of A. L. Peay, Dancey Fort, Michael Savage, M. G. Lyle, in Clarksville *Leaf-Chronicle,* July 1, 1909; testimony of Edmond Hunter, ibid., June 30, 1909.

19. Clarksville *Leaf-Chronicle,* March 13, 1909.

20. Rinehart to Sam Winters, October 1, 1982 (Winters Papers, Clarksville, Tenn.).

21. Interview with Robert Holt, April 1, 1985; R. T. Shannon, *Public and Permanent Statutes of a General Nature, Being an Annotated Code of Tennessee . . .* (Nashville, 1896), section 6429.

22. Clarksville *Leaf-Chronicle,* June 29, 1909.

23. Ibid., June 30, July 3, 1909.

24. Hopkinsville *Kentuckian,* August 26, 1909, April 5, 1910; Clarksville *Leaf-Chronicle,* July 17, 1909.

25. C. W. Tyler to Governor Malcolm R. Patterson, June 17, 1910, Patterson Papers (Tennessee State Library and Archives, Nashville, Tenn.).

26. Governor Peay, Commutation of Marcellus Rinehart, December 24, 1924, ibid.; Rinehart to Winters, October 1, 1982, Winters Papers.

27. Clarksville *Leaf-Chronicle,* August 6, 1908; Louisville *Herald,* October 11, 1908; Paducah *Sun,* October 22, 1909.

28. Crittenden *Record-Press,* November 4, 1909; W. L. Crumbaugh to Willson, November 3, 1909, June 19, 1910, Willson Papers.

29. *L. A. Baker* v. *Dr. E. Champion, et al.,* case 1894; *Maggie Scruggs* v. *Dr. E. Champion, et al.,* case 1895; *Nat Frizzell* v. *E. Champion,* case 1897 (Federal Archives and Records Center, Chicago, Ill.).

30. Clarksville *Leaf-Chronicle,* September 8, 1909. Lee Baker won her suit, but court records do not indicate any effort to enforce the judgment. Maggie Scruggs dropped her suit, probably because she reached an out-of-court settlement with the defendants.

31. Paducah *News-Democrat,* April 19, 1911; Paducah *Evening Sun,* April 18, 1911.

32. Hopkinsville *Kentuckian,* November 24, 1910.

33. *Paducah Evening Sun,* April 18, 1911; Paducah *News-Democrat,* April 18, 1911; *Laura Toomey* v. *D. A. Amoss et al.,* case 1934.

34. Crumbaugh to Willson, October 6, 1909, Willson Papers; Champion to Willson, October 5, 1909, ibid.

35. Champion to Willson, December 1, 1909, ibid.

36. Willson to Crumbaugh, December 4, 1909, ibid.

37. E. M. Flack to Willson, February 10, 1910, ibid.

38. Interview with Ira Dorman Smith, August 7, 1982, ibid.

39. Hopkinsville *Kentuckian,* March 1, 1910.

40. Summons, March 7, 1910, box 6, Christian County Circuit Court Papers (KDLA).

41. *C. W. Rucker* v. *D. A. Amoss, et al.,* case 1933, Records of the District Court of the United States (Federal Archives and Records Center, Chicago); *Henry Bennett* v. *D. A. Amoss et al.,* case 1901, ibid.

42. Warrant, March 15, 1910, box 6, Christian County Circuit Court Papers (KDLA).

43. Bill of Indictment, *Commonwealth* v. *D. A. Amoss, et al., ibid.* Jurors also listed Hugh Lyon as a witness against Amoss.

44. J. B. Malone, Guy Dunning, Newton Nichols, John Robinson, and Irvin Glass.

45. John D. Carroll, ed., *The Kentucky Statutes* (Louisville, 1903), section

1223. This revised a statute passed April 11, 1873. Edward Bullock et al., comps., *The General Statutes of Kentucky* (Frankfort, Ky., 1881), 366–67.

46. Kenneth S. Greenberg, "The Nose, the Lie, and the Duel in the Antebellum South," *American Historical Review* 95 (February 1990): 57–74.

47. Interview with Bernard Jones, June 12, 1982; warrant, box 6, Christian County Circuit Court Papers (KDLA).

48. Crumbaugh to Willson, June 6, 1910, Willson Papers (Filson Club, Louisville, Ky.).

49. Crumbaugh to Willson, June 6, 1910, Willson Papers (Filson Club, Louisville, Ky.).

50. Oliver testimony, transcript of evidence, *Commonwealth* v. *Amoss.*

51. Ibid.

52. Crumbaugh to Willson, June 6, 1910, Willson Papers (Filson Club, Louisville, Ky.).

53. Ibid.

54. Interview with Charlie Merrick, August 5, 1982.

55. Caldwell County Deed Box 26, 528–29 (Caldwell County Court Clerk's Office, Princeton, Ky.).

56. Hopkinsville *Kentuckian,* May 31, 1910.

57. Christopher Waldrep, "'Human Wolves': The Night Riders and the Killing of Axiom Cooper," *Register of the Kentucky Historical Society* 81 (Autumn 1983): 414–15.

58. Interview with Charlie Merrick; testimony of Noah Oliver, E. B. Bassett, Mrs. Tom Litchfield, "Evidence Brought Forth at the Coroner's Inquest Held in the South Eastern Part of Lyon County at the Scene of the Killing of Axiom Cooper," August 3, 1910, stenographic report (Lyon County Circuit Court Clerk's Office). Hereinafter cited as "Coroner's Inquest."

59. Testimony of Tom Litchfield, "Coroner's Inquest." Cooper's statement is on file at the Lyon County Circuit Clerk's Office. It reads, "I hereby certify that on this day July 30th 1910 near Rinaldo, Lyon County, Ky that Alonzo Gray and Vilas (or Silas) Mitchell encountered me and knocked me down, and that Bart Critmore and Spunk Critmore were implicated in the affair; and furthermore that Roy Merrick did shoot me. To all this I solemnly swear. Axiom X (his mark) Cooper."

60. Interview with Charlie Merrick.

61. Bassett to Willson, December 7, 1911, Willson Papers (Filson Club, Louisville, Ky.).

62. Interview with Charlie Merrick.

63. Ibid.; Owensboro *Twice-A-Week Messenger,* August 6, 1910; Mayfield *Daily Messenger,* August 10, 1910.

64. Gray to Willson, July 21, 1910, Willson Papers (Filson Club, Louisville, Ky.); Bassett to Willson August 1, 1910, ibid.; P. P. Johnson to Bassett, August 1, 1910, ibid.; Paducah *Sun,* August 4, 1910.

65. John Stites to Willson, August 2, 1910, Willson Papers (Filson Club, Louisville, Ky.).

66. Willson to Stites, August 4, 1910, ibid.; Paducah *News-Democrat,* August 4, 1910.

67. Crumbaugh to Willson, August 3, 1910, Willson Papers (Filson Club, Louisville, Ky.); "Coroner's Inquest."

68. Hopkinsville *Kentuckian,* August 27, 1910.

69. Bassett to Willson, December 8, 1910, Willson Papers (Filson Club, Louisville, Ky.).

70. Paducah *News-Democrat,* December 10, 1910.

71. Crittenden *Record-Press,* December 22, 1910; Hopkinsville *Kentuckian,* December 10, 20, 22, 1910; Paducah *News-Democrat,* December 7, 9, 10, 11, 15, 17, 21, 22, 1910; Paducah *Evening Sun,* December 9, 13, 17, 21, 1910; stenographic report of testimony, *Commonwealth* v. *Alonzo Gray, et al.,* 5, 13 (Lyon County Circuit Court Clerk's Office, Eddyville, Ky.).

72. *Commonwealth* v. *Gray, et al.,* stenographic report, 24, 27.

73. Interview with Charlie Merrick.

74. John Stites of Hopkinsville to Willson, January 31, 1911, Willson Papers (Filson Club, Louisville, Ky.).

75. Girard, Kansas, *Appeal to Reason,* September 3, 1910.

76. Ibid., September 10, 1910.

77. Ibid., October 15, 1910.

78. E. B. Bassett to Willson, March 7, 1911, Willson Papers.

79. Hopkinsville *Daily Kentucky New Era,* March 16, 1911; Hopkinsville *Kentuckian,* March 18, 1911.

80. Gernet, "Sur l'execution Capitale," in *Anthropologie de la Grece Antique* (Paris, 1968), 289–90, quoted in René Girard, *Violence and the Sacred,* 298–99.

81. *Daily Kentucky New Era,* March 7, 1911.

82. On boundary maintaining, see Kai T. Erikson, *Wayward Puritans: A Study in the Sociology of Deviance* (New York, 1966), 9–27; see also Harold Garfinkel, "Successful Degradation Ceremonies," *American Journal of Sociology* 61 (January 1956): 420–24.

83. E. B. Bassett to Willson, March 14, 1911, Willson Papers.

84. Girard, Kansas, *Appeal to Reason,* September 3, 10, 17, 24, October 1, 8, 15, 29, November 5, 12, 1910, April 1, 1911.

85. Many of the persons interviewed for this dissertation repeated this story. See above for Merrick's feminine disguise.

86. There is a parallel here with slave honor. See Bertram Wyatt-Brown, "The Mask of Obedience: Male Slave Psychology in the Old South," *American Historical Review* 93 (December 1988): 1228–52.

87. Greenberg, "The Nose, the Lie, and the Duel in the Antebellum South," 57–74.

88. Notation on indictments, *Commonwealth* v. *Dr. D. A. Amoss et al.* (KDLA).

89. Princeton *Twice-A-Week Leader,* December 17, 1912.

90. Ibid., June 19, 1913.

91. Princeton *Twice-A-Week Leader,* October 22, 1915; Rick S. Gregory, "Desperate Farmers: The Dark Tobacco District Planters' Protective Association of Kentucky and Tennessee, 1904–1914" (Ph.D. diss., Vanderbilt University, 1989), 258.

Epilogue

1. Victoria Alice Saker, "Benevolent Monopoly: The Legal Transformation of Agricultural Cooperation, 1890–1943" (Ph.D. diss., University of California, Berkeley, 1990), chap. 3; William E. Ellis, "Robert Worth Bingham and the Crisis of Cooperative Marketing in the Twenties," *Agricultural History* 56 (January 1982): 99–116; Carlos Clifton Erwin, "Economic Analysis of the Dark Tobacco Growers Cooperative Association of Western Kentucky and Tennessee" (M.S. thesis, University of Kentucky, 1948); S. E. Wrather, "Tobacco Marketing Organizations in Western Kentucky and Tennessee with Special Emphasis on Early Organization" (M.S. thesis, University of Kentucky, 1933).

2. George T. Blakey, *Hard Times and New Deal in Kentucky, 1929–1939* (Lexington, 1986), 113–21.

3. Ibid., 121; Pete Daniel, *Breaking the Land: The Transformation of Cotton, Tobacco, and Rice Cultures since 1880* (Urbana and Chicago, 1985), 117–22.

4. Interview with George Izor Stainback, August 17, 1984.

5. Interview with Clyde Quisenberry, August 6, 1982.

6. Emile Durkheim, *The Division of Labor in Society,* trans. George Simpson, (Glencoe, 1947), 69–275.

7. Princeton *Twice-A-Week Leader,* August 23, 1912, March 3, 1916.

8. Ibid., March 2, June 6, October 24, 1916.

9. Ibid., September 15, 1911.

10. Ibid., June 5, 1917.

11. Ibid., June 19, 1917. For the cartoons, "If We Only Could Resist," see ibid., for example, August 31, September 4, 18, 21, November 27, 1917.

12. The thesis that segregation intensified during this period is still most persuasively argued by C. Vann Woodward, *The Strange Career of Jim Crow* (3d ed.; New York, 1974). Woodward's book has proven controversial. For an analysis, see John Herbert Roper, *C. Vann Woodward, Southerner* (Athens, 1987), chap. 7; C. Vann Woodward, *Thinking Back: The Perils of Writing History* (Baton Rouge, 1986), chap. 5. Recent evidence tends to support Woodward's original argument. See John William Graves, "Jim Crow in Arkansas: A Reconsideration of Urban Race Relations in the Post-Reconstruction South," *Journal of Southern History* 55 (August 1989): 421–48.

13. Princeton *Twice-a-Week Leader,* January 12, 1917; New York *Herald,* quoted in ibid., February 2, 1917; George C. Wright, *Racial Violence in Kentucky, 1865–1940: Lynchings, Mob Rule, and "Legal Lynching"* (Baton Rouge, 1990), 190–94.

14. George C. Wright, *Racial Violence in Kentucky,* chap. 6

15. Ibid.; David M. Chalmers, *Hooded Americanism: The History of the Ku Klux Klan* (New York, 1981), 154–56.

16. Gregory, "Desperate Farmers" (Ph.D. diss., Vanderbilt, 1989), 267–82.

17. Comments by John D. Minton, Ohio Valley History Conference, Western Kentucky University, October 4–5, 1985.

18. Princeton *Leader,* May 17, 1989. LeRoi manufactures socks and tights, as well as infants' wear. Princeton *Leader,* May 31, 1989.

19. Cadiz *Record,* March 2, 1988.

20. Bobbie Ann Mason, *Shiloh and Other Stories* (New York, 1982); idem, *In Country* (New York, 1985); idem, *Spence + Lila* (New York, 1988); idem, *Love Life: Stories* (New York, 1989).

21. Mason, "The Ocean," in *Shiloh and Other Stories,* 149.

22. Mason, "Residents and Transients," in ibid., 125.

Primary Sources

MANUSCRIPT COLLECTIONS

Bibliography

John S. Cooper Collection. Special Collections. University of Kentucky Libraries, Lexington, Kentucky.

Dark Tobacco Growers Protective Association of Clarksville, Tennessee. Minutes. Robertson Yeatman Johnson Collection. Tennessee State Library and Archives, Nashville, Tennessee.

Dancey Fort Diary. H. W. Smith Collection. Clarksville, Tennessee.

R. G. Dun and Company Collection. Baker Library, Harvard University Graduate School of Business Administration, Boston, Massachusetts.

Fort Family Papers. Tennessee State Library and Archives, Nashville, Tennessee.

Lyon-O'Hara Families Papers. Manuscripts Department. Kentucky Museum and Library, Western Kentucky University, Bowling Green, Kentucky.

William McCarroll Papers. Manuscripts Department. Kentucky Museum and Library, Western Kentucky University, Bowling Green, Kentucky.

John Goodrum Miller Papers. Manuscripts Department. Kentucky Museum and Library, Western Kentucky University, Bowling Green, Kentucky.

O'Hara Records. Manuscripts Department. Kentucky Museum and Library, Western Kentucky University, Bowling Green, Kentucky.

A. O. Stanley Papers. Special Collections. University of Kentucky Libraries, Lexington, Kentucky.

James W. Street Papers. Kentucky Library and Museum, Western Kentucky University, Bowling Green, Kentucky.

T. O. Turner Papers. Special Collections. University of Kentucky Libraries, Lexington, Kentucky.

Washington Family Papers. Tennessee State Library and Archives, Nashville, Tennessee.

Augustus E. Willson Papers. Filson Club, Louisville, Kentucky.

Ralph Winters Papers. Private Collection. Clarksville, Tennessee.

NEWSPAPERS

Black Patch Journal
Cadiz *Record*
Clarksville *Leaf-Chronicle*
Farmville [Virginia] *Herald*
Girard [Kansas] *Appeal to Reason*
Henderson *Gleaner*
Hickman *Courier*
Hopkinsville *Kentuckian*
Hopkinsville *New-Era*
Louisville *Herald*
Mayfield *Daily Messenger*
Murray *Ledger*
Nashville *Banner*
New York *Times*

Paducah *News-Democrat*
Paducah *Sun*
Princeton *Twice-A-Week Leader*
Watson's Jeffersonian Magazine
Western Tobacco Journal

GOVERNMENT DOCUMENTS

Kentucky

Annual Report of the State Fire Marshal of Kentucky 1906. Louisville: n.d.
Caldwell County Court Clerk's Office. Bundle labeled "Depositions 1859, 1860, 1865, 1866, 1867, 1875, 1878, 1882, 1884."
Office of the Insurance Commissioner. Correspondence to the Insurance Department, 1902–1912, Division of Archives and Records, Department for Libraries and Archives, Frankfort.
Office of the Insurance Commissioner. Letterbooks 455, 456, 457, 458, 459, 1906–1908. Division of Archives and Records, Department for Libraries and Archives, Frankfort.
Official Report of the Proceedings and Debates of the Convention Assembled at Frankfort on the Eighth Day of September, 1890, to Adopt, Amend or Change the Constitution of the State of Kentucky. Frankfort, 1890.
Proceedings of the State Board of Equalization of Kentucky. 1902–1911.

United States

House Committee on Ways and Means, Subcommittee on Internal Revenue. *Hearings on the Relief of Tobacco Growers before a Subcommittee on Internal Revenue of the Committee on Ways and Means.* 58th Cong., 2d sess., February 4 and 25, 1904. Printed as Senate Document 390, 60th Cong., 1st sess.
Justice Department Central Files. Record Group 60, National Archives, Washington, D.C.
Provost Marshal Records, Kentucky. Record Group 110, National Archives, Washington, D.C.
Records of the Bureau of Refugees, Freedmen, and Abandoned Lands, Kentucky. Record Group 105, National Archives, Washington, D.C.
Report of the Commissioner of Corporations on the Tobacco Industry. 3 parts. Washington, D.C.: United States Government Printing Office, 1909.
Tobacco Investigation Records. Bureau of Corporations. Department of Commerce and Labor. Record Group 122, National Archives, Washington, D.C.
United States v. *American Tobacco Company* 221 U.S. L. ed.
Yearbook of the United States Department of Agriculture. 1904–1920.

INTERVIEWS WITH THE AUTHOR

Bagwell, Noel. Clarksville, Tennessee, April 8, 1985.
Cannon, Orman. Lyon County, Kentucky, October 17, 1981.

Carney, Herbert. Port Royal, Tennessee, September 1, 1984.

Caroland, Ernest. Adams, Tennessee, March 30, 1985.

Cash, Tom. Eddyville, Kentucky, January 15, 1982.

Cook, Mrs. Fairy. Clarksville, Tennessee, April 1, 1985.

Cortner, George. Cobb, Kentucky, April 8, 1982.

Daniel, William M. Clarksville, Tennessee, April 1, 1985.

Davidson, Eugene. Robertson County, Tennessee, February 19, 1983.

Durrett, Elizabeth. Clarksville, Tennessee, June 18, 1983.

Dycus, Geneva. Dycusburg, Kentucky, August 2, 1989.

Edmunds, William F. Hopkinsville, April 6, 1982.

Ferguson, W. O. Caldwell County, Kentucky, April 5, 1985.

Fletcher, Mrs. Polk. Adams, Tennessee, July 28, 1983; May 26, 1984.

Fowler, Daniel E. Lexington, Kentucky, July 28, 1983.

Goodlett, Collier. Clarksville, Tennessee, April 1, 1985.

Goyert, J. Herbert. Metropolis, Illinois, April 8, 1982.

Hall, Mrs. A. V. Lexington, Kentucky, July 29, 1982.

Hall, Hewlett. Caldwell County, Kentucky, August 5, 1982.

Helm, Milton. Metropolis, Illinois, April 8, 1982.

Holt, Carney. Montgomery County, Tennessee, June 9, 1985.

Holt, Robert. Robertson County, Tennessee, September 1, 1984; April 1, 1985.

Hudson, Boyd. Eddyville, Kentucky, January 15, 1982.

Jones, Bernard. Princeton, Kentucky, June 12, 1982.

Kem, Mrs. Enoch. Princeton, Kentucky, June 13, 1983.

Lawrence, Jim. Trigg County, Kentucky, July 30, 1983.

Linebaugh, Mack S. Guthrie, Kentucky, August 19, 1984.

Martin, Edward. Trigg County, Kentucky, June 11, 1982.

Martin, Mabel. Trigg County, Kentucky, June 11, 1982.

Merrick, Charlie. Caldwell County, Kentucky, August 5, 1982; August 6, 1982.

Moore, Joe, Sr. Springfield, Tennessee, February 19, 1983.

Northington, Thad. Guthrie, Kentucky, August 18, 1984.

Parrent, John. Lyon County, Kentucky, October 16, 1982.

Payne, Ruby. Adams, Tennessee, March 31, 1985.

Pope, Myra Lynn. Adams, Tennessee, August 18, 1984.

Porter, David. Cobb, Kentucky, October 16, 1982; February 20, 1983.

Quisenberry, Clyde. Cobb, Kentucky, August 6, 1982; July 3, 1984; February 18, 1984.

Scott, Joe Ellis. Lyon County, Kentucky, April 5, 1985.

Smith, Carol. Metropolis, Illinois, April 8, 1982.

Smith, H. W. Clarksville, Tennessee, April 1, 1985.

Smith, Ira Dorman. Hopkinsville, Kentucky, August 7, 1982.

Stainback, George Izor. July 28, 1983; May 26, 1984.

Steger, Sam. Princeton, Kentucky, June 12, 1982; December 30, 1985.

Strange, John. Adams, Tennessee, February 19, 1983.

Taylor, Henry. Springfield, Tennessee, September 1, 1984.

Trimble, Selden Y. Hopkinsville, Kentucky, August 19, 1982.

Trotter, Shelly. September 1, 1984.

Wadlington, P. C., Jr. Trigg County, Kentucky, July 30, 1983.

Walls, Mose. Keysburg, Kentucky, August 21, 1984.

White, Mrs. Harvey. Hopkinsville, Kentucky, August 18, 1982.

White, John F. Cadiz, Kentucky, December 31, 1985.

Williams, Louise. Adams, Tennessee, August 18, 1984.

Wills, Will J. Cadiz, Kentucky, July 30, 1983; February 19, 1984.

Wilson, Emma P. Hopkinsville, Kentucky, February 19, 1983.

Winters, Bill. Hopkinsville, Kentucky, March 22, 1985.

Wright, Durwood. Cadiz, Kentucky, October 22, 1983; April 4, 1985.

UNPUBLISHED COURT CASES

Lee Baker v. *E. Champion, et al.* case 1894, filed July 7, 1908 in the United States District Court for the Sixth Circuit, Western District of Kentucky at Paducah.

Henry Bennett v. *D. A. Amoss, et al.* Case 1901, filed October 29, 1908, in the United States District Court for the Sixth Circuit, Western District of Kentucky at Paducah.

A. H. Cardin v. *William Neel, et al.* Case 1929, filed January 12, 1909 in the United States District Court for the Sixth Circuit, Western District of Kentucky at Paducah.

Commonwealth v. *James Aldridge and others.* Minutes of examining court. Trigg Quarterly Court. Trigg Circuit Court Clerk's Office, Cadiz, Ky.

Commonwealth v. *John W. Kelly.* Transcript of change of venue hearing. Trigg Circuit Court Clerk's Office, Cadiz, Ky.

Commonwealth v. *Hugh Wallace, etc.* Transcript of evidence. Trigg Quarterly Court. Trigg Circuit Court Clerk's Office, Cadiz, Ky.

Commonwealth of Kentucky v. *David Amoss.* Hopkinsville, Kentucky.

Commonwealth of Kentucky v. *Alonzo Gray, et al.* Stenographic report. Lyon Circuit Court Clerk's Office, Eddyville, Ky.

W. T. Cooper v. *City of New York Insurance Company.* Case 6033. Box 45. Christian Circuit Court Common Law Cases. Public Records Division, Department for Libraries and Archives, Frankfort, Ky.

W. T. Cooper v. *Glenn Falls Insurance Company.* Case 6034. Box 45. Christian Circuit Court Common Law Cases. Public Records Division, Department for Libraries and Archives, Frankfort, Ky.

W. T. Cooper v. *Rochester German Insurance Company.* Case 6035. Box 45. Christian Circuit Court Common Law Cases. Public Records Division, Department for Libraries and Archives, Frankfort, Ky.

W. G. Dunnington and Company v. *American Central Insurance Company.* Case 5023. Box 45. Christian Circuit Court Common Law Cases. Public Records Division, Department for Libraries and Archives, Frankfort, Ky.

W. G. Dunnington and Company v. *Atlas Assurance Company, Limited.* Case 5025. Box 45. Christian Circuit Court Common Law Cases. Public Records Division, Department for Libraries and Archives, Frankfort, Ky.

W. G. Dunnington and Company v. *Firemen's Fund Insurance Company.* Case 5021. Box 45. Christian Circuit Court Common Law Cases. Public Records Division, Department for Libraries and Archives, Frankfort, Ky.

W. G. Dunnington and Company v. *German-American Insurance Company.*

Case 5024. Box 45. Christian Circuit Court Common Law Cases. Public Records Division, Department for Libraries and Archives, Frankfort, Ky.

W. G. Dunnington and Company v. *Hamburg-Bremen Fire Insurance Company.* Case 5022. Box 45. Christian Circuit Court Common Law Cases. Public Records Division, Department for Libraries and Archives, Frankfort, Ky.

W. G. Dunnington and Company v. *Hanover Fire Insurance Company.* Case 5019. Box 45. Christian Circuit Court Common Law Cases. Public Records Division, Department for Libraries and Archives, Frankfort, Ky.

W. G. Dunnington and Company v. *Royal Insurance Company.* Case 5020. Box 45. Christian Circuit Court Common Law Cases. Public Records Division, Department for Libraries and Archives, Frankfort, Ky.

Nat Frizzell v. *E. Champion, et al.* Case 1897, filed August 22, 1908 in the United States District Court for the Sixth Circuit, Western District of Kentucky at Paducah.

G. W. Gordon v. *D. A. Amoss, et al.* Case 1938, filed February 2, 1909, in the United States District Court for the Sixth Circuit, Western District of Kentucky at Paducah.

Robert Hollowell v. *John Hollowell, et al.* Case 1877, filed March 2, 1908 in the United States District Court for the Sixth Circuit, Western District of Kentucky at Paducah.

Imperial Tobacco Company v. *Calendonian Insurance Company.* Bundle 506. Caldwell County Circuit Court Clerk's Office, Princeton, Ky.

Imperial Tobacco Company v. *Commonwealth of Kentucky.* Case 43036. Court of Appeals Records, Public Records Division, Kentucky Department for Libraries and Archives, Frankfort, Ky.

Imperial Tobacco Company v. *Connecticut Fire Insurance Company.* Bundle 506. Caldwell County Circuit Court Clerk's Office, Princeton, Ky.

Imperial Tobacco Company v. *Hanover Insurance Company.* Bundle 506. Caldwell County Circuit Court Clerk's Office, Princeton, Ky.

Imperial Tobacco Company v. *The Pennsylvania Fire Insurance Company.* Bundle 506. Caldwell County Circuit Court Clerk's Office, Princeton, Ky.

Imperial Tobacco Company v. *Spring Garden Insurance Company.* Bundle 506. Caldwell County Circuit Court Clerk's Office, Princeton, Ky.

Mrs. Elise Latham v. *D. A. Amoss, et al.* Case 260 filed November 16, 1911 in the United States District Court for the Sixth Circuit, Western District of Kentucky at Owensboro.

Thomas Menees v. *J. T. Matthews, et al.* Case 3639, in the United States District Court for the Sixth Circuit, Middle District of Tennessee at Nashville.

Milt Oliver v. *D. A. Amoss, et al.* Case 2091, filed May 23, 1911 in the United States District Court for the Sixth Circuit, Western District of Kentucky at Paducah.

C. W. Rucker v. *D. A. Amoss, et al.* Case 1933, filed January 18, 1909, in the United States District Court for the Sixth Circuit, Western District of Kentucky at Paducah.

Maggie Scruggs v. *E. Champion, et al.* Case 1895, filed July 7, 1908, in the

United States District Court for the Sixth Circuit, Western District of Kentucky at Paducah.

Tom Stephens v. *Alonzo Gray, et al.* Case 1970, filed July 3, 1909, in the United States District Court for the Sixth Circuit, Western District of Kentucky at Paducah.

W. T. Tandy v. *The Glen Falls Insurance Company.* Case 5060. Box 45. Christian Circuit Court Common Law Cases. Public Records Division, Department for Libraries and Archives, Frankfort, Ky.

W. T. Tandy v. *The Rochester German Insurance Company.* Case 5060. Box 45. Christian Circuit Court Common Law Cases. Public Records Division, Department for Libraries and Archives, Frankfort, Ky.

W. T. Tandy v. *Williamsburg Fire Insurance Company.* Case 5059. Box 45. Christian Circuit Court Common Law Cases. Public Records Division, Department for Libraries and Archives, Frankfort, Ky.

Tandy and Fairleigh Tobacco Company v. *Firemen's Fund Insurance Company.* Case 6032. Box 45. Christian Circuit Court Common Law Cases. Public Records Division, Department for Libraries and Archives, Frankfort, Ky.

Laura Toomey v. *D. A. Amoss, et al.* case 1934, filed January 18, 1909 in the United States District Court for the Sixth Circuit, Western District of Kentucky at Paducah.

R. M. Woolridge and Company v. *The Georgia Home Insurance Company.* Case 5045. Box 45. Christian Circuit Court Common Law Cases. Public Records Division, Department for Libraries and Archives, Frankfort, Ky.

R. M. Wooldridge and Company v. *Hamburg-Bremen Fire Insurance Company.* Case 5044. Box 45. Christian Circuit Court Common Law Cases. Public Records Division, Department for Libraries and Archives, Frankfort, Ky.

United States v. *Sam Cash.* Case 2085, filed May 15, 1911, in the United States District Court for the Sixth Circuit, Western District of Kentucky at Owensboro.

United States v. *Bart Gray.* Case 2089, filed May 15, 1911, in the United States District Court for the Sixth Circuit, Western District of Kentucky at Owensboro.

United States v. *Ed Gray.* Case 2087, filed May 15, 1911, in the United States District Court for the Sixth Circuit, Western District of Kentucky at Owensboro.

United States v. *A. L. Mitchell.* Case 2086, filed May 15, 1911, in the United States District Court for the Sixth Circuit, Western District of Kentucky at Owensboro.

United States v. *W. J. Mitchell.* Case 2088, filed May 15, 1911, in the United States District Court for the Sixth Circuit, Western District of Kentucky at Owensboro.

United States v. *J. B. Wadlington.* Case 2090, filed May 15, 1911, in the United States District Court for the Sixth Circuit, Western District of Kentucky at Owensboro.

J. F. Van Hooser v. *A. A. Robinson, et al.* Case 239, filed December 17, 1909, in the United States District Court for the Sixth Circuit, Western District of Kentucky at Owensboro.

L. L. Wood v. *D. A. Amoss, et al.* Case 1935, filed February 13, 1909, in the United States District Court for the Sixth Circuit, Western District of Kentucky at Paducah.

CHURCH MINUTE BOOKS

Kentucky

Cadiz Baptist, Trigg County
Donaldson Creek Baptist, Trigg County
Dry Creek Baptist, Trigg County
First Baptist, McCracken County
Hopewell Baptist, Graves County
Locust Grove Baptist, Calloway County
Mt. Zion Baptist, Todd County
Presbyterian Baptist Church of Jesus Christ on Cases Creek
Sinking Spring Baptist, Calloway County
Spring Creek Christian, Graves County
Sulphur Spring Baptist, Simpson County
Trace Creek Baptist, Graves County
Trenton Baptist, Todd County
Wallonia Christian, Trigg County

Tennessee

Crocket's Creek Baptist, Stewart County
Cross Creek Baptist, Stewart County
Gallatin Presbyterian, Sumner County
Harmony Baptist, Robertson County
McMinville Baptist, Warren County
Nevils Creek Baptist, Stewart County
New Hope Baptist, Davidson County
Riddleton Baptist, Smith County
Rushing Creek Baptist, Stewart County
Turnbull Primitive Baptist, Dickson County
Walnut Fork Church, Henry County
Walnut Fork Old School Baptist, Cook County
Walnut Grove Baptist, Stewart County

Secondary Sources

BOOKS

Ash, Stephen V. *Middle Tennessee Society Transformed, 1860–1870: War and Peace in the Upper South.* Baton Rouge: Louisiana State University Press, 1988.
Austin, Aleine. *Matthew Lyon: "New Man" of the Democratic Revolution, 1749–1822.* University Park: Pennsylvania State University Press, 1981.
Ayers, Edward L. *Vengeance and Justice: Crime and Punishment in the Nine-*

teenth-Century American South. New York: Oxford University Press, 1984.

Axton, W. F. Tobacco and Kentucky. Lexington: University Press of Kentucky, 1975.

Bailey, Fred Arthur. Class and Tennessee's Confederate Generation. Chapel Hill: University of North Carolina Press, 1987.

Baker, Clauscine R. First History of Caldwell County, Kentucky. Madisonville, Ky.: Commercial Printers, 1936.

Battle, J. H., W. H. Perrin, and G. C. Kniffin. Kentucky: A History of the State . . . Louisville: F. A. Battey Publishing Co., 1885.

Beach, Ursula Smith. Along the Warioto: A History of Montgomery County, Tennessee. Nashville: McQuiddy Press, 1964.

Beeman, Richard R. The Evolution of the Southern Backcountry: A Case Study of Lunenburg County, Virginia, 1746–1832. Philadelphia: University of Pennsylvania Press, 1984.

Bender, Thomas. Community and Social Change in America. New Brunswick: Rutgers University Press, 1978.

Bensel, Richard Franklin. Yankee Leviathan: The Origins of Central State Authority in America, 1859–1877. Cambridge: Cambridge University Press, 1990.

Bernstein, Iver. The New York City Draft Riots: Their Significance for American Society and Politics in the Age of the Civil War. New York: Oxford University Press, 1990.

Blakey, George T. Hard Times and New Deal in Kentucky, 1929–1939. Lexington: University Press of Kentucky, 1986.

Blassingame, John W. The Slave Community: Plantation Life in the Antebellum South. New York: Oxford University Press, 1972.

Bodenhamer, David J., and James W. Ely, Jr., eds. Ambivalent Legacy: A Legal History of the South. Jackson: University Press of Mississippi, 1984.

Boles, John B. The Great Revival, 1787–1805. Lexington: University Press of Kentucky, 1972.

Bradshaw, Herbert Clarence. History of Prince Edward County, Virginia: From Its Earliest Settlements through Its Establishment in 1754 to Its Bicentennial Year. Richmond: Dietz Press, 1955.

Breen, T. H. Tobacco Culture: The Mentality of the Great Tidewater Planters on the Eve of the Revolution. Princeton: Princeton University Press, 1985.

Brown, Richard Maxwell. Strain of Violence: Historical Studies of American Violence and Vigilantism. New York: Oxford University Press, 1975.

Burton, Orville Vernon. In My Father's House Are Many Mansions: Family and Community in Edgefield, South Carolina. Chapel Hill: University of North Carolina Press, 1985.

Calhoun, Craig. The Question of Class Struggle: Social Foundations of Popular Radicalism during the Industrial Revolution. Chicago: University of Chicago Press, 1982.

Carnes, Mark C. Secret Ritual and Manhood in Victorian America. New Haven: Yale University Press, 1989.

Carpenter, Jesse T. The South as a Conscious Minority, 1789–1861: A Study in Political Thought. New York: New York University, 1930.

Carter, Dan T. *Scottsboro: A Tragedy of the American South.* London: Oxford University Press, 1969.

Cartwright, Joseph H. *The Triumph of Jim Crow: Tennessee Race Relations in the 1880s.* Knoxville: University of Tennessee Press, 1976.

Chalmers, David M. *Hooded Americanism: The History of the Ku Klux Klan.* New York: Franklin Watts, 1981.

Chandler, Alfred D., Jr. *The Visible Hand: The Managerial Revolution in American Business.* Cambridge: Harvard University Press, 1977.

Coffman, Edward. *The Story of Logan County.* Nashville: Parthenon Press, 1962.

Collins, Lewis, and Richard H. Collins. *History of Kentucky: By the Late Lewis Collins, Revised, Enlarged Four-Fold and Brought Down to the Year 1874 by his Son, Richard H. Collins.* 2 vols. Covington, Ky.: Collins and Co., 1878.

Cortner, Richard C. *A "Scottsboro" Case in Mississippi: The Supreme Court and Brown v. Mississippi.* Jackson: University Press of Mississippi, 1986.

Coulter, E. Merton. *The Civil War and Readjustment in Kentucky.* Chapel Hill: University of North Carolina Press, 1926.

Cunningham, Bill. *On Bended Knees: The Night Rider Story.* Nashville: Mc-Clanahan Publishing House, 1983.

Daniel, Pete. *Breaking the Land: The Transformation of Cotton, Tobacco, and Rice Cultures since 1880.* Urbana: University of Illinois Press, 1985.

——. *Standing at the Crossroads: Southern Life in the Twentieth Century.* New York: Hill and Wang, 1986.

Degler, Carl N. *The Other South: Southern Dissenters in the Nineteenth Century.* New York: Harper and Row, 1974.

DeWitt, Benjamin Parke. *The Progressive Movement: A Non-Partisan, Comprehensive Discussion of Current Tendencies in American Politics.* New York: Macmillan, 1915.

Dinnerstein, Leonard. *The Leo Frank Case.* Athens: University of Georgia Press, 1966.

Douglas, Byrd. *Steamboatin' on the Cumberland.* Nashville: Tennessee Book Company, 1961.

Dubom, David B. *The Resisted Revolution: Urban America and the Industrialization of Agriculture, 1900–1930.* Ames: Iowa State University Press, 1979.

Dunn, Durwood. *Cades Cove: The Life and Death of a Southern Appalachian Community, 1818–1937.* Knoxville: University of Tennessee Press, 1988.

Durden, Robert F. *The Dukes of Durham, 1865–1929.* Durham: Duke University Press, 1975.

Eighmy, John Lee. *Churches in Cultural Captivity: A History of the Social Attitudes of Southern Baptists.* Knoxville: University of Tennessee Press, 1972.

Everitt, J. A. *The Third Power: Farmers to the Front.* Indianapolis: published by author, 1905.

Fink, Leon. *Workingmen's Democracy: The Knights of Labor and American Politics.* Urbana: University of Illinois Press, 1983.

Ford, Lacy K., Jr. *Origins of Southern Radicalism: The South Carolina Upcountry, 1800–1860*. New York: Oxford University Press, 1988.

Foner, Eric. *Reconstruction: America's Unfinished Revolution, 1863–1877*. New York: Harper and Row, 1988.

Forgie, George B. *Patricide in the House Divided: A Psychological Interpretation of Lincoln and His Age*. New York: Norton, 1979.

Fox-Genovese, Elizabeth, and Eugene D. Genovese. *Fruits of Merchant Capital: Slavery and Bourgeois Property in the Rise and Expansion of Capitalism*. New York: Oxford University Press, 1983.

Fredrickson, George M. *The Black Image in the White Mind: The Debate on Afro-American Character and Destiny, 1817–1914*. New York: Harper and Row, 1971.

Frese, Joseph R., and Jacob Judd, eds. *American Industrialization, Economic Expansion, and the Law*. Tarrytown, N.Y.: Sleepy Hollow Press, 1981.

Friedman, Lawrence M., and Robert V. Percival. *The Roots of Justice: Crime and Punishment in Alameda County, California, 1870–1910*. Chapel Hill: University of North Carolina Press, 1981.

———. *A History of American Law*. New York: Simon and Schuster, 1985.

Genovese, Eugene D. *Roll, Jordan, Roll: The World the Slaves Made*. New York: Random House, 1974.

Gilje, Paul A. *The Road to Mobocracy: Popular Disorder in New York City, 1763–1834*. Chapel Hill: University of North Carolina Press, 1987.

Gilmore, William J. *Reading Becomes a Necessity of Life: Material and Cultural Life in Rural New England, 1780–1835*. Knoxville: University of Tennessee Press, 1989.

Girard, René. *Violence and the Sacred*. Baltimore: Johns Hopkins University Press, 1972.

Goodwyn, Lawrence. *Democratic Promise: The Populist Moment in America*. New York: Oxford University Press, 1976.

Graham, Hugh Davis, and Ted Robert Gurr, eds., *Violence in America: Historical and Comparative Perspectives*. 2 vols. Washington: United States Government Printing Office, 1969.

Grantham, Dewey W. *Southern Progressivism: The Reconciliation of Progress and Tradition*. Knoxville: University of Tennessee Press, 1983.

Gray, Lewis Cecil. *History of Agriculture in the Southern United States to 1860*. 2 vols. Washington: Carnegie Institution, 1933.

Gresham, John M., comp. *Biographical Cyclopedia of the Commonwealth of Kentucky*. Chicago: John M. Gresham Company, 1896.

Gutman, Herbert G. *Work, Culture, and Society in Industrializing America: Essays in American Working-Class and Social History*. New York: Random House, 1976.

Haber, Samuel. *Efficiency and Uplift: Scientific Management in the Progressive Era, 1890–1920*. Chicago: University of Chicago Press, 1964.

Hahn, Steven. *The Roots of Southern Populism: Yeoman Farmers and the Transformation of the Georgia Upcountry, 1850–1890*. New York: Oxford University Press, 1983.

——— and Jonathan Prude, eds. *The Countryside in the Age of Capitalist Trans-*

formation: *Essays in the Social History of Rural America*. Chapel Hill: University of North Carolina Press, 1985.

Halttunen, Karen. *Confidence Men and Painted Women: A Study of Middle-Class Culture in America, 1830–1870*. New Haven: Yale University Press, 1982.

Harrison, Lowell H., ed. *Kentucky's Governors, 1792–1985*. Lexington: University Press of Kentucky, 1985.

Hart, Roger L. *Redeemers, Bourbons, and Populists: Tennessee, 1870–1896*. Baton Rouge: Louisiana State University Press, 1975.

Hays, Samuel P. *The Response to Industrialism, 1885–1914*. Chicago: University of Chicago Press, 1957.

Hicks, John D. *The Populist Revolt: A History of the Farmers' Alliance and the People's Party*. Minneapolis: University of Minnesota Press, 1972.

Hill, Samuel S., Jr. *Southern Churches in Crisis*. New York: Holt, Rinehart, and Winston, 1966.

——, ed. *Religion and the Solid South*. Nashville: Abingdon Press, 1972.

——, ed. *Religion in the Southern States*. Macon: Mercer University Press, 1983.

Hilliard, Sam Bowers. *Atlas of Antebellum Southern Agriculture*. Baton Rouge: Louisiana State University Press, 1984.

Hindus, Michael Stephen. *Prison and Plantation: Crime, Justice, and Authority in Massachusetts and South Carolina, 1767–1878*. Chapel Hill: University of North Carolina Press, 1980.

History of Tennessee . . . Together with an Historical and a Biographical Sketch of Montgomery, Robertson, Humphreys, Stewart, Dickson, Cheatham, and Houston Counties. . . . Nashville: Goodspeed, 1886.

Hofstadter, Richard. *The Age of Reform, from Bryan to F.D.R.* New York: Alfred A. Knopf, 1974.

Holmes, William F. *The White Chief, James Kimble Vardaman*. Baton Rouge: Louisiana State University Press, 1970.

Howe, Daniel Walker. *The Political Culture of the American Whigs*. Chicago: University of Chicago Press, 1979.

Hyman, Harold. *A More Perfect Union: The Impact of the Civil War and Reconstruction on the Constitution*. New York: Alfred A. Knopf, 1973.

Ireland, Robert M. *The County Courts in Antebellum Kentucky*. Lexington: University Press of Kentucky, 1972.

——. *Little Kingdoms: The Counties of Kentucky, 1850–1891*. Lexington: University Press of Kentucky, 1977.

Jeffreys-Jones, Rhodri. *Violence and Reform in American History*. New York: New Viewpoints, 1978.

Keller, Morton. *Affairs of State: Public Life in Late Nineteenth Century America*. Cambridge, Mass.: Belknap Press, 1977.

Kenzer, Robert C. *Kinship and Neighborhood in a Southern Community: Orange County, North Carolina, 1849–1881*. Knoxville: University of Tennessee Press, 1987.

Kerr, Charles, ed. *History of Kentucky*. Chicago: American Historical Society, 1922.

Killebrew, J. B. *Tobacco: Its Culture in Tennessee with Statistics of Its Commercial Importance.* Nashville: Tavel, Eastman, and Howell, 1876.

————, and Herbert Myrick. *Tobacco Leaf, Its Culture and Cure, Marketing and Manufacture.* New York: Orange Judd Co., 1897.

————. *Tobacco: How to Cultivate, Cure and Prepare for Market.* Nashville: Fertilizer Manufacturers' Assn., n.d.

Kirby, Jack Temple. *Darkness at the Dawning: Race and Reform in the Progressive South.* Philadelphia: University of Pennsylvania Press, 1972.

Klein, Rachel N. *Unification of a Slave State: The Rise of the Planter Class in the South Carolina Backcountry, 1760–1808.* Chapel Hill: University of North Carolina Press, 1990.

Kleppner, Paul. *The Third Electoral System, 1853–1892: Parties, Voters, and Political Cultures.* Chapel Hill: University of North Carolina Press, 1979.

Klotter, James C. *William Goebel: The Politics of Wrath.* Lexington: University Press of Kentucky, 1977.

Knapp, Joseph G. *The Rise of American Cooperative Enterprise, 1620–1920.* Danville, Ill.: Interstate Printing and Publishing Co., 1969.

————, ed. *Great American Cooperators.* Washington, D.C.: American Institute of Cooperation, 1967.

Kolko, Gabriel. *The Triumph of Conservatism: A Reinterpretation of American History.* New York: Free Press, 1963.

Konig, David Thomas. *Law and Society in Puritan Massachusetts: Essex County, 1629–1692.* Chapel Hill: University of North Carolina Press, 1979.

Krock, Arthur. *Memoirs: Sixty Years on the Firing Line.* New York: Funk and Wagnalls, 1968.

————, comp. *The Editorials of Henry Watterson.* Louisville: Courier-Journal Company, 1923.

Kroll, Harry Harrison. *Riders in the Night.* Philadelphia: University of Pennsylvania Press, 1965.

Kulikoff, Allan. *Tobacco and Slaves: The Development of Southern Cultures in the Chesapeake, 1680–1800.* Chapel Hill: University of North Carolina Press, 1986.

Lamoreaux, Naomi R. *The Great Merger Movement in American Business, 1895–1904.* New York: Cambridge University Press, 1985.

Lears, Jackson. *No Place of Grace: Antimodernism and the Transformation of American Culture, 1880–1920.* New York: Pantheon Books, 1981.

Letwin, William. *Law and Economic Policy in America: The Evolution of the Sherman Antitrust Act.* New York: Random House, 1965.

Lieberson, Stanley. *Making It Count: The Improvement of Social Research and Theory.* Berkeley: University of California Press, 1985.

McCloskey, Donald N. *The Rhetoric of Economics.* Madison: University of Wisconsin Press, 1985.

McGovern, James R. *Anatomy of a Lynching: The Killing of Claude Neal.* Baton Rouge: Louisiana State University Press, 1982.

McMath, Robert C., Jr. *Populist Vanguard: A History of the Southern Farmers' Alliance.* New York: Norton, 1975.

McWhiney, Grady. *Cracker Culture: Celtic Ways in the Old South.* Tuscaloosa: University of Alabama Press, 1988.

Madsen, A. W. *The State as Manufacturer and Trader: An Examination Based on the Commercial, Industrial, and Fiscal Results Obtained from Government Tobacco Monopolies.* London: T. Fisher Unwin, Ltd., 1916.

Marchand, Roland. *Advertising the American Dream: Making Way for Modernity, 1920–1940.* Berkeley and Los Angeles: University of California Press, 1985.

Mars, Florence. *Witness in Philadelphia.* Baton Rouge: Louisiana State University Press, 1977.

Mason, Bobbie Ann. *Shiloh and Other Stories.* New York: Harper and Row, 1982.

——. *In Country.* New York: Harper and Row, 1985.

——. *Spence + Lila.* New York: Harper and Row, 1988.

——. *Love Life: Stories.* New York: Harper and Row, 1989.

Matthews, Elmora M. *Neighbor and Kin: Life in a Tennessee Ridge Community.* Nashville: Vanderbilt University Press, 1965.

Meacham, Charles Mayfield. *A History of Christian County, Kentucky: From Oxcart to Airplane.* Nashville: Marshall and Bruce Co., 1930.

Memorial Record of Western Kentucky. Chicago: Lewis Publishing Company, 1904.

Merrill, Boynton, Jr. *Jefferson's Nephews: A Frontier Tragedy.* Princeton: Princeton University Press, 1976.

Miller, John G. *The Black Patch War.* Chapel Hill: University of North Carolina Press, 1936.

Mitchell, Theodore. *Political Education in the Southern Farmers' Alliance, 1887–1900.* Madison: University of Wisconsin Press, 1987.

Montell, William Lynwood. *Killings: Folk Justice in the Upper South.* Lexington: University Press of Kentucky, 1986.

Montgomery, David. *Beyond Equality: Labor and the Radical Republicans, 1862–1872.* New York: Alfred A. Knopf, 1967.

Morgan, Edmund. *American Slavery, American Freedom: The Ordeal of Colonial Virginia.* New York: Norton, 1975.

Mowry, George E. *Theodore Roosevelt and the Progressive Movement.* Madison: University of Wisconsin Press, 1946.

Nall, James O. *The Tobacco Night Riders of Kentucky and Tennessee, 1905–1909.* Louisville, Ky.: Standard Press, 1939.

Nelson, Ralph L. *Merger Movements in American Industry, 1895–1956.* Princeton: Princeton University Press, 1959.

Nelson, William E. *Dispute and Conflict Resolution in Plymouth County, Massachusetts, 1725–1825.* Chapel Hill: University of North Carolina Press, 1981.

Nissenbaum, Stephen. *Salem Possessed: The Social Origins of Witchcraft.* Cambridge: Cambridge University Press, 1974.

Noble, David F. *America by Design: Science, Technology, and the Rise of Corporate Capitalism.* New York: Alfred A. Knopf, 1977.

One Century of Lyon County History. Eddyville, Ky.: Lyon County Historical Society, 1964, 1985.

Paludan, Phillip Shaw. *Victims: A True Story of the Civil War.* Knoxville: University of Tennessee Press, 1981.

Papashvily, Helen Waite. *All the Happy Endings: A Study of the Domestic Novel in America, the Women Who Wrote it, the Women Who Read it, in the Nineteenth Century.* New York: Harper, 1956.

Parsons, Stanley. *The Populist Context: Rural versus Urban Power on a Great Plains Frontier.* Westport, Conn.: Greenwood Press, 1973.

Perlam, Jonathan. *The Groundswell: A History of the Origins, Aims, and Progress of the Farmers' Movement.* . . . Cincinnati: E. Hannaford and Company, 1874.

Perrin, William Henry. *County of Christian, Kentucky: Historical and Biographical.* Chicago: F. A. Battey Publishing Co., 1884.

———. *County of Trigg, Kentucky: Historical and Biographical.* Chicago: F. A. Battey Publishing Co., 1884.

Phillips, Ulrich B. *Life and Labor in the Old South.* Boston: Little, Brown and Co., 1929.

Pitts, John A. *Personal and Professional Reminiscences of an Old Lawyer.* Kingsport, Tenn.: Southern Publishers, 1930.

Poor, Henry V. *Poor's Manual of the Railroads of the United States for 1883.* New York: H. V. Poor, 1883.

———. *Poor's Manual of the Railroads of the United States for 1888.* New York: H. V. Poor, 1888.

Porter, Glenn, and Harold C. Livesay. *Merchants and Manufacturers: Studies in the Changing Structure of Nineteenth-Century Marketing.* Baltimore: Johns Hopkins University Press, 1971.

Price, Jacob M. *France and the Chesapeake: A History of the French Tobacco Monopoly, 1674–1791, and of Its Relationship to the British and French Tobacco Trades.* 2 vols. Ann Arbor: University of Michigan Press, 1973.

Reid, John Phillip. *In a Defiant Stance: The Conditions of Law in Massachusetts Bay, the Irish Comparison, and the Coming of the American Revolution.* University Park: Pennsylvania State University Press, 1977.

Rodgers, Daniel T. *The Work Ethic in Industrial America: 1850–1920.* Chicago: University of Chicago Press, 1974.

Rogers, William Warren. *The One-Gallused Rebellion: Agrarianism in Alabama, 1865–1896.* Baton Rouge: Louisiana State University Press, 1970.

Rohrer, Wayne C., and Louis H. Douglas. *The Agrarian Transition in America: Dualism and Change.* New York: Bobbs-Merrill, 1969.

Roper, John Herbert. *C. Vann Woodward, Southerner.* Athens: University of Georgia Press, 1987.

Rosenhaum, H. Jon, and Peter C. Sederberg, eds. *Vigilante Politics.* Philadelphia: University of Pennsylvania Press, 1976.

Roth, Randolph A. *The Democratic Dilemma: Religion, Reform, and the Social Order in the Connecticut River Valley of Vermont, 1791–1850.* Cambridge: Cambridge University Press, 1987.

Rothert, Otto A. *The Outlaws of Cave-in-Rock: Historical Accounts of the Famous Highwaymen and River Pirates Who Operated in Pioneer Days upon the Ohio and Mississippi Rivers and over the Old Natchez Trace.* Cleveland: Arthur H. Clark Co., 1924.

Royle, Edward, and James Walvin. *English Radicals and Reformers, 1760–1848.* Lexington: University Press of Kentucky, 1982.

Rutman, Darrett B., and Anita H. Rutman. *A Place in Time: Middlesex County, Virginia, 1650–1750*. New York: W. W. Norton, 1984.

Sabean, David Warren. *Power in the Blood: Popular Culture and Village Discourse in Early Modern Germany*. Cambridge: Cambridge University Press, 1989.

Saloutos, Theodore. *Farmer Movements in the South, 1865–1933*. Lincoln: University of Nebraska Press, 1960.

Sauer, Carl Ortwin. *Geography of the Pennyroyal: A Study of the Influence of Geology and Physiology upon the Industry, Commerce, and Life of the People*. Frankfort: Kentucky Geological Survey, 1927.

Schwartz, Michael. *Radical Protest and Social Structure: The Southern Farmers' Alliance and Cotton Tenancy, 1880–1890*. New York: Academic Press, 1976.

Shannon, Jasper B., and Ruth McQuown, comps. *Presidential Politics in Kentucky, 1824–1948: A Compilation of Election Statistics and an Analysis of Political Behavior*. Lexington: Bureau of Government Research, College of Arts and Sciences, University of Kentucky, 1950.

Shaw, Peter. *American Patriots and the Rituals of Revolution*. Cambridge: Harvard University Press, 1981.

Shifflet, Crandall A. *Patronage and Poverty in the Tobacco South: Louisa County, Virginia, 1860–1900*. Knoxville: University of Tennessee Press, 1982.

Shugg, Roger W. *Origins of Class Struggle in Louisiana: A Social History of White Farmers and Laborers During Slavery and After, 1840–1875*. Baton Rouge: Louisiana State University Press, 1939.

Siegel, Frederick F. *The Roots of Southern Distinctiveness: Tobacco and Society in Danville, Virginia, 1780–1865*. Chapel Hill: University of North Carolina Press, 1987.

Simkins, Francis Butler. *Pitchfork Ben Tillman: South Carolinian*. Baton Rouge: Louisiana State University Press, 1944.

Singal, Daniel Joseph. *The War Within: From Victorian to Modernist Thought in the South, 1919–1945*. Chapel Hill: University of North Carolina Press, 1982.

Sklar, Martin J. *The Corporate Reconstruction of American Capitalism, 1890–1916: The Market, the Law and Politics*. Cambridge: Cambridge University Press, 1988.

Smead, Howard. *Blood Justice: The Lynching of Mack Charles Parker*. New York: Oxford University Press, 1986.

Snively, W. D., Jr., and Louanna Furbee. *Satan's Ferryman: A True Tale of the Old Frontier*. New York: Frederick Ungar Publishing Co., 1968.

Spain, Rufus. *At East in Zion: Social History of the Baptists, 1865–1900*. Nashville: Vanderbilt University Press, 1967.

Starling, Edmund W. *Starling of the White House*. New York: Simon and Schuster, 1946.

Steffens, Lincoln. *The Autobiography of Lincoln Steffens*. New York: Harcourt, Brace and Co., 1931.

Stickland, W. P., ed. *Autobiography of Peter Cartwright: The Backwoods Preacher*. Cincinnati: N.d.

Tapp, Hambleton, and James C. Klotter. *Kentucky: Decades of Discord, 1865–1900.* Frankfort: Kentucky Historical Society, 1977.

Taylor, Carl C. *The Farmers' Movement, 1620–1920.* New York: American Book Co., 1953.

Thelen, David P. *Paths of Resistance: Tradition and Dignity in Industrializing Missouri.* New York: Oxford University Press, 1986.

Thompson, E. P. *The Making of the English Working Class.* New York: Random House, 1963.

Thorelli, Hans B. *The Federal Antitrust Policy: Organization of an American Tradition.* Baltimore: Johns Hopkins University Press, 1955.

Thornton, J. Mills, III. *Politics and Power in a Slave Society: Alabama, 1800–1860.* Baton Rouge: Louisiana State University Press, 1978.

Tilley, Nannie May. *The Bright Tobacco Industry, 1860–1929.* Chapel Hill: University of North Carolina Press, 1948.

Trelease, Allen W. *White Terror: The Ku Klux Klan Conspiracy and Southern Reconstruction.* New York: Harper and Row, 1971.

Tufte, Edward R. *Data Analysis for Politics and Policy.* Englewood Cliffs: Prentice-Hall, 1974.

Tuttle, William M., Jr. *Race Riot: Chicago in the Red Summer of 1919.* New York: Atheneum, 1970.

Tyler, Charles W. *The K.K.K.* 1901. Rpt. Freeport, N.Y.: Books for Libraries, 1972.

Vanderwood, Paul J. *Night Riders of Reelfoot Lake.* Memphis: Memphis State University Press, 1969.

Waller, Altina L. *Feud: Hatfields, McCoys, and Social Change in Appalachia, 1860–1900.* Chapel Hill: University of North Carolina Press, 1988.

White, Hayden. *Metahistory: The Historical Imagination in Nineteenth Century Europe.* Baltimore: Johns Hopkins University Press, 1973.

Wiebe, Robert H. *The Search for Order, 1877–1920.* New York: Hill and Wang, 1967.

Wiener, Jonathan M. *Social Origins of the New South: Alabama, 1860–1885.* Baton Rouge: Louisiana State University Press, 1978.

Williams, Marion. *Story of Todd County, Kentucky, 1820–1970.* Nashville: Parthenon Press, 1972.

Williamson, Joel. *The Crucible of Race: Black and White Relations in the American South since Emancipation.* New York: Oxford University Press, 1984.

Wilson, Emma. *Under One Roof.* New York: Funk and Wagnalls, 1955.

Winters, Ralph L. *Historical Sketches: Adams, Robertson County, and Port Royal, Montgomery County, Tennessee, 1779–1968.* Clarksville: Privately printed, 1968.

Woodman, Harold D. *King Cotton and His Retainers: Financing and Marketing the Cotton Crop of the South, 1800–1925.* Lexington: University Press of Kentucky, 1968.

Woodward, C. Vann. *Tom Watson: Agrarian Rebel.* New York: Macmillan, 1938.

———. *Origins of the New South, 1877–1913.* Baton Rouge: Louisiana State University Press, 1951.

———. *Thinking Back: The Perils of Writing History.* Baton Rouge: Louisiana State University Press, 1986.

Wright, Gavin. *The Political Economy of the Cotton South: Households, Markets, and Wealth in the Nineteenth Century.* New York: Norton, 1978.

———. *Old South, New South: Revolutions in the Southern Economy since the Civil War.* New York: Basic Books, 1986.

Wright, George C. *Racial Violence in Kentucky, 1865–1940: Lynchings, Mob Rule, and "Legal Lynchings."* Baton Rouge: Louisiana State University Press, 1990.

Wyatt-Brown, Bertram. *Southern Honor: Ethics and Behavior in the Old South.* New York: Oxford University Press, 1982.

ARTICLES AND UNPUBLISHED WORKS

Abrams, Richard M. "The Failure of Progressivism." In Abrams and L. W. Levin, eds., *The Shaping of Twentieth-Century America.* Boston: Little Brown, 1971.

Appleton, Thomas H., Jr. " 'Like Banquo's Ghost': The Emergence of the Prohibition Issue in Kentucky Politics." Ph.D. dissertation, University of Kentucky, 1981.

Barnett, Albert. "The Marketing of Dark Tobacco in Kentucky and Tennessee." M.A. thesis, George Peabody College for Teachers, 1916.

Barton, Lon Carter. "The Reign of Terror in Graves County." *The Register of the Kentucky Historical Society* 46 (April 1948): 485–95.

Beach, H. L. "The Great Tobacco War." *Saturday Evening Post* (August 3, 1907): 3, 4, 18.

Benedict, Michael Les. "Preserving the Constitution: The Conservative Basis of Radical Reconstruction." *Journal of American History* 61 (June 1974): 65–90.

Bennett, James D. "Some Notes on Christian County, Kentucky, Grange Activities." *Register of the Kentucky Historical Society* 64 (July 1966): 226–34.

Bland, Gaye Keller. "Populism in the First Congressional District of Kentucky, 1892." *Filson Club History Quarterly* 51 (January 1977): 31–43.

———. "Populism in Kentucky." Ph.D. dissertation, University of Kentucky, 1979.

Blanks, W. D. "Corrective Church Discipline in the Presbyterian Churches of the Nineteenth-Century South." *Journal of Presbyterian History* 44 (June 1966): 89–105.

Brown, Richard Maxwell. "The American Vigilante Tradition." In Hugh Davis Graham and Ted Robert Gurr, eds., *Vigilantism in America: Historical and Comparative Perspectives.* New York: Frederick A. Praeger, 1969.

———. "Legal and Behavioral Perspectives on American Vigilantism." *Perspectives in American History* 5 (1971): 95–144.

Burckel, Nicholas C. "From Beckham to McCreary: The Progressive Record of Kentucky Governors." *Register of the Kentucky Historical Society* 76 (October 1978): 285–305.

Bush, Gregory W. "Heroes and the 'Dead Line' against Riots: The Romantic

Nationalist Conception of Crowd Behavior, 1840–1914." *Hayes Historical Journal* 8 (Summer 1989): 34–57.

Campbell, Tracy Alan. "The Politics of Despair: The Tobacco Wars of Kentucky and Tennessee." Ph.D. dissertation, Duke University, 1988.

Chirot, Daniel. "The Growth of the Market and Service Labor Systems in Agriculture." *Journal of Social History* 8 (Winter 1975): 67–76.

Clark, Thomas D. "The Changing Emphasis in the Writing of Southern History." *Filson Club Historical Quarterly* 45 (April 1971): 145–57.

Cohen, William. "Negro Involuntary Servitude in the South, 1865–1940: A Preliminary Analysis." *Journal of Southern History* 42 (February 1976): 31–60.

Copeland, James E. "Where Were the Kentucky Unionists and Secessionists?" *Register of the Kentucky Historical Society* 71 (October 1973): 344–63.

Corwin, Edwin S. "The Anti-Trust Acts and the Constitution." *Virginia Law Review* 43 (February 1932): 355–78.

Craig, Berry F. "Northern Conquerors and Southern Deliverers: The Civil War Comes to the Jackson Purchase." *Register of the Kentucky Historical Society* 75 (January 1975): 17–30.

Crissey, Forrest, and Harrison L. Beach. "The Whipped Man: A Story of the Night Riders in the Tobacco War." *Everybody's Magazine* 20 (April 1909): 548–59.

Crouthamel, James L. "The Springfield Race Riot of 1908." *Journal of Negro History* 45 (1960): 164–81.

Crowe, Charles. "Racial Massacre in Atlanta September 22, 1906." *Journal of Negro History* 54 (1969): 150–73.

Cunningham, Bill. "The Black Patch War." *Rural Kentuckian* 36 (December 1982): 6–9.

Daniel, Pete. "The Tennessee Convict War." *Tennessee Historical Quarterly* 34 (Fall 1975): 273–92.

Darnall, Sherry. "The Night Riders." Undergraduate paper, Murray State University, May 7, 1979.

Diggins, John Patrick. "Republicanism and Progressivism." *American Quarterly* 37 (Fall 1985): 572–98.

Du Bois, W. E. Burghardt. "The Negroes of Farmville, Virginia: A Social Study." *Bulletin of the Department of Labor* (January 1898): 1–38.

Ellis, William E. "Robert Worth Bingham and the Crisis of Cooperative Marketing in the Twenties." *Agricultural History* 56 (January 1982): 99–116.

———. "Robert Worth Bingham and Louisville Progressivism, 1905–1910." *Filson Club History Quarterly* 54 (April 1980): 169–95.

Erwin, Carlos Clifton. "Economic Analysis of the Dark Tobacco Growers Cooperative Association of Western Kentucky and Tennessee." M.S. thesis, University of Kentucky, 1948.

Farnham, Wallace D. " 'The Weakened Spring of Government': A Study in Nineteenth Century American History." *American Historical Review* 68 (April 1963): 662–80.

Fife, George Buchanan. "The So-Called Tobacco Trust." *Century Magazine* (March 1903): 788–94.

Filene, Peter G. "An Obituary for 'The Progressive Movement.'" *American Quarterly* 22 (Spring 1970): 20–34.

Fischer, Claude S. "The Revolution in Rural Telephony, 1900–1920." *Journal of Social History* 21 (Fall 1987): 5–26.

Fort, Charles. "How Sentiment Was Discouraged in Sim." *Tom Watson's Magazine* 3 (January 1906): 297–98.

——. "A Radical Corpuscle." *Tom Watson's Magazine* 4 (March 1906): 73–76.

——. "Those That Are Joined Together." *Tom Watson's Magazine* 4 (April 1906): 228–38.

——. "Ructions." *Tom Watson's Magazine* 4 (May 1906): 363–75.

——. "The Fat Lady Who Climbed Fences." *Tom Watson's Magazine* 5 (August 1906): 228–32.

——. "Mrs. Bonticue and Another Landlord." *Tom Watson's Magazine* 4 (October 1906): 542–54.

Fuller, Wayne E. "The Rural Roots of the Progressive Leaders." *Agriculture History* 42 (January 1968): 1–13.

Galambos, Louis. "The Emerging Organizational Synthesis in Modern American History." *Business History Review* 44 (Autumn 1970): 279–90.

——. "Technology, Political Economy, and Professionalization: Central Themes in the Organizational Synthesis." *Business History Review* 57 (Winter 1983): 471–93.

Gildrie, Richard P. "Lynch Law and the Great Clarksville Fire of 1878: Social Order in a New South Town." *Tennessee Historical Quarterly* 42 (Spring 1983): 58–75.

Gilje, Paul A. "The Baltimore Riots of 1812 and the Breakdown of the Anglo-American Mob Tradition." *Journal of Social History* 13 (Summer 1980): 547–64.

Gorn, Elliot J. "Gouge, Bite, Pull Hair and Scratch: The Social Significance of Fighting in the Southern Backcountry." *American Historical Review* 90 (February 1985): 18–43.

——. "'Good-Bye Boys, I Die a True American': Homicide, Nativism, and Working-Class Culture in Antebellum New York City." *Journal of American History* 74 (September 1987): 388–410.

Grantham, Dewey W. "Black Patch War: The Story of the Kentucky and Tennessee Night Riders, 1905–1909." *South Atlantic Quarterly* 59 (Spring 1960): 215–25.

Greenberg, Kenneth S. "The Nose, the Lie, and the Duel in the Antebellum South." *American Historical Review* 95 (February 1990): 57–74.

Gregory, Rick S. "Desperate Farmers: The Dark Tobacco District Planters' Protective Association of Kentucky and Tennessee, 1904–1914." Ph.D. dissertation, Vanderbilt University, 1989.

——. "Robertson County and the Black Patch War, 1904–1909." *Tennessee Historical Quarterly* 39 (Fall 1980): 341–58.

Guthrie, Charles S. "Tobacco: Cash Crop of the Cumberland Valley." *Kentucky Folklore Record* 14 (April–June 1968): 38–43.

Gutman, Herbert G. "Work, Culture, and Society in Industrializing America." *American Historical Review* 78 (June 1973): 531–88.

Hackney, Sheldon. "Southern Violence." *American Historical Review* 64 (February 1969): 906–25.

Hahn, Steven. "Class and State in Postemancipation Societies: Southern Planters in Comparative Perspective." *American Historical Review* 95 (February 1990): 75–98.

Haines, Stephen M. "Southern Baptist Church Discipline, 1880–1939." *Baptist History and Heritage* 20 (1985): 14–27.

Hall, Suzanne Marshall. "Breaking Trust: The Black Patch Tobacco Culture of Kentucky and Tennessee, 1900–1940." Ph.D. dissertation, Emory University, 1989.

Hall, Tom G. "Agricultural History and the 'Organizational Synthesis': A Review Essay." *Agricultural History* 48 (April 1974): 157–69.

Harris, James Russell. "The Harrodsburg Tankers: Bataan, Prison, and the Bonds of Community." *Register of the Kentucky Historical Society* 86 (Summer 1988): 230–77.

Henderson, William W. " 'The Night Riders' Raid on Hopkinsville." *Filson Club Historical Quarterly* 24 (1950): 346–48.

Henretta, James A. "Families and Farms: *Mentalité* in Pre-Industrial America." *William and Mary Quarterly* 3d Series 35 (January 1978): 3–32.

Holmes, William F. "Whitecapping: Agrarian Violence in Mississippi, 1902–1906." *Journal of Southern History* 35 (May 1969): 165–85.

——. "Whitecapping in Mississippi: Agrarian Violence in the Populist Era." *Mid-America* 55 (April 1973): 134–48.

——. "Moonshining and Collective Violence: Georgia, 1889–1895." *Journal of American History* 67 (December 1980): 589–611.

——. "Whitecapping in Georgia: Carroll and Houston Counties, 1893." *Georgia Historical Quarterly* 64 (Winter 1980): 388–404.

——. "Moonshiners and Whitecaps in Alabama, 1893." *Alabama Review* 34 (January 1981): 31–49.

——. "The Southern Farmers Alliance: The Georgia Experience." *Georgia Historical Quarterly* 72 (Winter 1988): 627–52.

Ireland, Robert M. "Law and Disorder in Nineteenth-Century Kentucky." *Vanderbilt Law Review* 32 (January 1979): 281–99.

James, Sally L. "American Violent Moral Regulation and the White Caps." Senior thesis, College of William and Mary, 1969.

Jonas, Edward A. "The Night Riders: A Trust of Farmers." *Worlds Work* 17 (February 1909): 11213–18.

Lane, Roger. "Crime and the Industrial Revolution: British and American Views." *Journal of Social History* 7 (Spring 1974): 287–303.

Lears, T. J. Jackson. "The Concept of Cultural Hegemony: Problems and Possibilities." *American Historical Review* 90 (June 1985): 567–93.

Link, Arthur S. "The Progressive Movement in the South, 1870–1914." *North Carolina Historical Review* 23 (April 1946): 172–95.

Lyle, Eugene P., Jr. "They That Rode By Night: The Story of Kentucky's Tobacco War." *Hampton's Magazine* 22 (February 1909): 175–87.

——. "The Night Riders: A Trust of Farmers." *Hampton's Magazine* 22 (March 1909): 339–52.

——. "Night Riding—A Reign of Fear." *Hampton's Magazine* 22 (April 1909): 461–74.

McCormick, Richard L. "The Discovery That Business Corrupts Politics: A Reappraisal of the Origins of Progressivism." *American Historical Review* 86 (April 1981): 247–74.

McCulloch-Williams, Martha. "The Tobacco War in Kentucky." *American Review of Reviews* 27 (February 1908): 168–70.

McCurdy, Charles W. "The *Knight* Sugar Decision of 1895 and the Modernization of American Corporation Law, 1869–1903." *Business History Review* 53 (Autumn 1979): 304–42.

McDonnell, Lawrence T. " 'You Are Too Sentimental': Problems and Suggestions for a New Labor History." *Journal of Social History* 17 (Summer 1984): 629–54.

Maier, Pauline. "Popular Uprisings and Civil Authority in Eighteenth-Century America." *William and Mary Quarterly* 3d Series, 27 (January 1970): 3–35.

Montgomery, David. "Workers' Control of Machine Production in the Nineteenth Century." *Labor History* 17 (Fall 1976): 485–509.

——. "Labor and the Republic in Industrial America, 1860–1920." *Le Mouvement Social,* no. 111 (April–June 1980): 201–16.

Muhse, Albert Charles. "The Disintegration of the Tobacco Combination." *Political Science Quarterly* 28 (1913): 249–78.

Nugent, Walter T. K. "Some Parameters of Populism." *Agricultural History* 40 (October 1966): 255–70.

Oestreicher, Richard. "Urban Working-Class Political Behavior and Theories of American Electoral Political Behavior, 1870–1940." *Journal of American History* 74 (March 1988): 1257–86.

Percy, David O. "Agriculture Labor on an Eighteenth-Century Chesapeake Plantation." Paper presented to 45th Conference on Early American History, September 13, 1984.

Prichard, Edward F., Jr. "Popular Political Movements in Kentucky, 1875–1900." Senior thesis, Princeton University, 1935.

Ransom, Roger L., and Richard Sutch. "Debt Peonage in the Cotton South after the Civil War." *Journal of Economic History* 32 (September 1972): 641–69.

Reid, Joseph D. "Sharecropping as an Understandable Market Response: The Post-Bellum South." *Journal of Economic History* 33 (March 1973): 106–30.

——. "The Evaluation and Implications of Southern Tenancy." *Agricultural History* 53 (January 1979): 153–69.

Reinders, Robert. "Militia and Public Order in Nineteenth-Century America." *American Studies* 11 (April 1977): 81–101.

Reynolds, Albin Lee. "War in the Black Patch." *Register of the Kentucky Historical Society* 56 (January 1958): 1–10.

Russell, James Madison. "Business and the Sherman Act, 1890–1914." Ph.D. dissertation, University of Iowa, 1966.

Saker, Victoria Alice. "Benevolent Monopoly: The Legal Transformation of

Agricultural Cooperation, 1890–1943." Ph.D. dissertation, University of California, Berkeley, 1990.

Saloutos, Theodore. "The American Society of Equity in Kentucky: A Recent Attempt at Agrarian Reform." *Journal of Southern History* 5 (August 1939): 347–63.

Scott, Anne Firor. "A Progressive Wind from the South, 1906–1913." *Journal of Southern History* 29 (February 1963): 51–70.

Senechal, Roberta. "The Springfield, Illinois Race Riot of 1908: Class, Racism, and Anti-Black Violence in the Urban North." Paper presented at the 1989 OAH Convention, St. Louis.

Smith, Cortland Victor. "Church Organization as an Agency of Social Control: Church Discipline in North Carolina, 1800–1860." Ph.D. dissertation, University of North Carolina, 1966.

Smith, Leland. "A History of the Tobacco Industry in Kentucky from 1783 to 1860." M.A. thesis, University of Kentucky, 1950.

Stone, Sue Lynn. " 'Blessed Are They That Mourn': Expressions of Grief in South Central Kentucky, 1870–1910." *Register of the Kentucky Historical Society* 85 (Summer 1987): 213–36.

Sweet, William W. "The Churches as Moral Courts of the Frontier." *Church History* 2 (March 1933): 3–21.

Sydnor, Charles S. "The Southerner and the Laws." In George Brown Tindall, ed., *The Pursuit of Southern History: Presidential Addresses of the Southern Historical Association, 1935–1963.* Baton Rouge: Louisiana State University Press, 1964.

Tachau, Mary K. Bonsteel. "Comment: Law and Disorder in Nineteenth-Century Kentucky." *Vanderbilt Law Review* 32 (January 1979): 301–4.

Tevis, Charles V. "A Ku-Klux Klan of To-day: The Red Record of Kentucky's 'Night Riders.' " *Harper's Weekly* 52 (February 8, 1908): 14–16.

Thelen, David P. "Social Tensions and the Origins of Progressivism." *Journal of American History* 56 (September 1969): 323–41.

Thompson, E. P. "Time, Work-Discipline, and Industrial Capitalism." *Past and Present* 38 (December 1967): 56–97.

———. "The Moral Economy of the English Crowd in the Eighteenth Century." *Past and Present* 50 (February 1971): 76–136.

Turner, James. "Understanding the Populists." *Journal of American History* 67 (September 1980): 354–73.

Tyack, David B. "City Schools: Centralization of Control at the Turn of the Century." In Jerry Israel, ed., *Building the Organizational Society: Essays on Associational Activities in Modern America.* New York: Free Press, 1972.

Volz, Harry A., III. "Party, State, and Nation: Kentucky and the Coming of the American Civil War." Ph.D. dissertation, University of Virginia, 1982.

Waldrep, Christopher R. " 'Human Wolves': The Night Riders and Community Consensus: The Killing of Axiom Cooper." *Register of the Kentucky Historical Society* 81 (Autumn 1983): 407–24.

———. "Augustus E. Willson and the Night Riders." *The Filson Club History Quarterly* 58 (April 1984): 237–53.

———. "Tobacco Farmers, the Tobacco 'Trust,' and the Federal Government." *The Journal of Kentucky Studies* 1 (July 1984): 187–201.

———. "The Law, the Night Riders, and Community Consensus: The Prosecution of Dr. David Amoss." *Register of the Kentucky Historical Society* 82 (Summer 1984): 235–56.

———. "Planters and the Planters' Protective Association in Kentucky and Tennessee." *Journal of Southern History* 52 (November 1986): 565–88.

———. "Rank and File Voters and the Coming of the Civil War: Caldwell County, Kentucky, as Test Case." *Civil War History* 35 (March 1989): 59–72.

———. " 'So Much Sin': The Decline of Religious Discipline and the 'Tidal Wave of Crime.' " *Journal of Social History* 23 (Spring 1990): 535–52.

———. "The Reorganization of the Tobacco Industry and Its Impact on Tobacco Growers in Kentucky and Tennessee, 1900–1911." *Mid-America* 73 (January 1991): 71–81.

———. "William Faulkner, Robert Penn Warren, and the Law." *Southern Studies* 2 (Spring 1991): 17–38.

———. "Federalism and Community Justice: Kentucky and Tennessee Night Riders and the Law." *Georgia Journal of Southern Legal History* 1 (Fall/ Winter 1991): 281–320.

———, ed. "A 'Trust Lawyer' Tries to Help Kentucky Farmers: Augustus E. Willson's 1907 Letter to George Cortelyou." *Register of the Kentucky Historical Society* 83 (Autumn 1985): 347–55.

Waller, Altina L. "Community, Class, and Race in the Memphis Riot of 1866." *Journal of Social History* 18 (Winter 1984): 233–46.

West, Anna Imogene Bennett. "The Night Riders." Manuscript lent by Geneva Dycus, 1977.

Willey, Day Allen. "The Night Riders." *Metropolitan Magazine* 28 (July 1908): 355–66.

Wood, Gordon S. "A Note on Mobs in the American Revolution." *William and Mary Quarterly,* 3d series, 23 (October 1966): 635–42.

Wrather, S. E. "Tobacco Marketing Organizations in Western Kentucky and Tennessee with Special Emphasis on Early Organizations." M.A. thesis, University of Kentucky, 1933.

Youngman, Anna. "The Tobacco Pools of Kentucky and Tennessee." *Journal of Political Economy* 18 (January 1910): 34–49.

Index

Christopher Waldrep is Assistant Professor of History at Eastern
Illinois University.

Library of Congress Cataloging-in-Publication Data
Waldrep, Christopher, 1951–
Night riders : defending community in the black patch, 1890–1915 /
Christopher Waldrep.
Includes bibliographical references and index.
ISBN 0-8223-1359-6. — ISBN 0-8223-1393-6 (pbk)
1. Vigilantes—Kentucky—History.   2. Vigilantes—Tennessee—History.
3. Violence—Kentucky—History.   4. Violence—Tennessee—History.
5. Kentucky—Rural conditions.   6. Tennessee—Rural conditions.   I. Title.
F456.W27   1993
976.9—dc20   93-10077 CIP